EXPRESSIVE ARTS

THE ULTIMATE CREATIVE GUIDE TO TRANSFORMING STRESS

JEAN VOICE DART

Contributing Authors: Laura Elizabeth Ballerini : Katie Bruzzone : Brigette Burton
Solarzar Dellaporta : Megan Edge : Terri K. Fitzsimmons : Norman Gordon
Kathy Harmon-Luber : Kate Hawkes : Mari Jack : Sara Jane
Gabrielle Ariella Kaplan-Mayer : Laura Mayer : Dr. Charleen M. Michel
Anna Pereira : Grace Rosen : Bonnie Sheldon : Sensei Timothy Stuetz
Mindy J. Trisko : Ingrid Tyson : Sofanya White

"This book is a breath of fresh, colorful air for anyone carrying the heavy weight of stress—a soul-sparked invitation to heal and reconnect with the joy that lives inside us all. As someone who's spent a lifetime in the media spotlight, I know firsthand the power of creative expression to transform pain into purpose. Through painting, writing, dancing, and more, each author reminds us that creativity isn't just an outlet, it's a lifeline. Raw, honest, and deeply empowering, this book gently guides you back to peace (and joy) one expressive breath at a time."

~**Shari Alyse**, America's Joy Magnet, TV Host "Good Morning Joy," Author of *Love Yourself Happy* and *Joy Unleashed*

*

"We are continuously immersed in an experience of the arts as entertainment. And yet so many people are oblivious to the healing power of the arts. The vulnerable and moving stories in *Expressive Arts* open our minds and hearts to the true nature of the arts, the direct expression of the human heart and soul that catalyzes healing and alignment. Thank you, Jean Voice Dart, and all the contributing authors of this book, for sharing your profound stories of transformation through the arts and tools all of us can use to bring health and happiness to our lives. Congratulations on such a practical and healing gift. I look forward to helping you share it with the world."

~**Sharon Carne**, B.Mus., M.F.A., Founder of Sound Wellness and the Sound Wellness Institute

*

"Art, in all its forms, connects us to our heart and higher consciousness. As a professional artist, hypnotherapist, and life coach myself, I recognize how it can be a vehicle to transcend beyond life's challenges and ascend our spirit! The pages of this book offer many brilliant ways to travel life's path with artful self-expression!"

~**Desiree Holmes Scherini**, BCH, MHt, LBLt, CRMT, Master Hypnotherapist, Life Coach, Artist, and Author of *Journey to Joy— The Written Path*

*

"*Expressive Arts* is a wonderful testament to the healing power of creativity. The shared stories remind us we are never alone in our struggles, and the practical tools offer a compassionate roadmap for emotional restoration. As a writer, counselor, and registered art therapist, I have a deep understanding of the importance of this book. It is more than a guide—it's a sanctuary for anyone seeking to transform stress into meaning through the arts."

~**Jenn Seniuk**, ATR, RCAT, CCC, CT, Registered Art Therapist and Counselor

*

"This book is incredible! I was blown away by the magnitude and integrity of the authors. *Expressive Arts* is a living treasure trove of the transformative power of creative expression. From victim to victor, survivor to thriver, you cannot help but be constantly inspired by these tales of transmuted trauma and stress. Leaving no room for excuses, these expressive art experts invite you into their worlds and show you how easy it is to access your own creative expression as a means of overcoming any challenging life circumstance. It was a joy to read, and I gained many valuable insights into my own creative process. I feel I am far richer because of it. I highly recommend it to anyone looking for a creative way to move from pain to empowerment."

~**Bradford W. Tilden**, M.M., CMT, Author, Composer, Master Vibrational Healer, and Owner of Crystal Music Healing

Expressive Arts
The Ultimate Creative Guide to Transforming Stress
©Copyright 2025 Jean Voice Dart
Published by Brave Healer Productions
Cover Art by Davide De Angelis
Interior design by K.J. Kaschula
Paperback ISBN: 978-1-961493-78-0
eBook ISBN: 978-1-961493-79-7

EXPRESSIVE ARTS

THE ULTIMATE CREATIVE GUIDE TO TRANSFORMING STRESS

JEAN VOICE DART

Contributing Authors: Laura Elizabeth Ballerini : Katie Bruzzone : Brigette Burton
Solarzar Dellaporta : Megan Edge : Terri K. Fitzsimmons : Norman Gordon
Kathy Harmon-Luber : Kate Hawkes : Mari Jack : Sara Jane
Gabrielle Ariella Kaplan-Mayer : Laura Mayer : Dr. Charleen M. Michel
Anna Pereira : Grace Rosen : Bonnie Sheldon : Sensei Timothy Stuetz
Mindy J. Trisko : Ingrid Tyson : Sofanya White

Dedication

To those misdiagnosed, misunderstood, and misinformed while tirelessly searching for relief, I dedicate this book to you, seekers of solace, strength, and healing through the expressive arts.

To the expressive arts teachers, therapists, coaches, trainers, healers, guides, practitioners, musicians, artists, actors, crafters, designers, dancers, writers, filmmakers, performers, and creators—I thank you for bringing stress relief, comfort, hope, and joy to others. Your dedicated service through the arts is a guiding light for those who suffer. This collaborative effort is a tribute to you and your compassionate commitment to the creative and performing arts, making them accessible to everyone.

DISCLAIMER

This book is designed to provide competent, reliable, and educational information regarding health and wellness, stress relief, and other subject matter covered. However, it is sold with the understanding that the authors and publisher specifically disclaim all responsibility for any liability, loss, or risk, personal or otherwise, incurred consequently, directly or indirectly, of the use and application of any of the contents of this publication.

To maintain the anonymity of others, the names and identifying characteristics of some people, places, and organizations described in this book have been changed.

This publication contains content that may be potentially triggering or disturbing. Individuals who are sensitive to certain themes are advised to exercise caution while reading.

The opinions, ideas, and recommendations contained in this publication do not necessarily represent those of the Publisher. The use of any information provided in this book is solely at your own risk.

Our authors represent cultures worldwide, and as such, there may be differences in language and expressions. As a global publisher, we have made the conscious choice not to edit these nuances, so each chapter is authentic and in its author's words.

Know that the experts here have shared their tools, practices, and knowledge with you with a sincere and generous intent to assist you on your journey. Please contact them with any questions you may have about the techniques or information they provided. They will be happy to assist you further and be an ongoing resource for your success!

Contents

Introduction

"You are a spiritual being of divine essence,
a sparkling Light to the world whose ultimate purpose
is to imagine, express, and create pure joy and love."

~Jean Voice Dart

Each evening, my father and mother provided a banquet of creativity and joy, generously served through family games, crafts, art, music, dance, and dramatic play, stretching the imagination and lifting us to an alternate reality.

We sat on the living room floor, playing "Ring on a String." Mom created a large circle from white cotton baker's twine, but before tying the knot to complete it, she removed her wedding ring and put it onto the string. We each grabbed the twine, moving our fisted hands upon the circle, grimacing at the effort, raising our eyebrows with feigned surprise, wiggling our tight-fisted fingers as if to pass a hidden ring from hand to hand to an eager receiver. With everyone acting, no one was certain of the ring's location (except for the ring bearer).

Whose hands had passed it successfully to a confidante?

"It's you, Daddy! You have the ring!"

My sister pointed and shouted at him, releasing her grip on the twine for a moment. Dad opened his empty hands.

"It's not me." He raised his eyebrows, dramatically exaggerating his tone and movements while shaking his head from left to right.

"Oh! You tricked me, Daddy. You're so sneaky." The excitement of three young girls was difficult to contain.

We giggled and wiggled, with palms cupping the baker's twine. Clenched hands slid in opposite directions as we tried to be clever, dramatizing our facial expressions and imitating our parents' playfulness. Those times are precious to me and stay close to my heart.

As we slid our hands along the string, we also moved through the rhythms of our lives, learning to be aware of one another, ourselves, and our combined efforts as a team. We discovered how to manage, release, or remove stress through fun and joyful activities using the power of creative, dramatic play.

THE MAGIC OF CREATIVE FLOW

You are a creative soul, born to make miracles happen. The magic of those evenings was not in the activities we shared but in how they brought us together as a family, respecting our unique qualities, teaching us to embrace our creative power, tapping into the simple joys in life, and dissolving the stress and worry of the day.

Research has shown that engaging in the creative arts has physical, mental, emotional, sociological, and spiritual benefits. It helped me manage chronic pain, heal emotional wounds, repair broken relationships, and open my heart to receiving divine love. Witnessing the magic of creative flow inspired me to become a registered therapist and credentialed teacher in the arts, helping others live a better life. Moreover, it opened my heart to a deeper connection with God. It changed my life, and it can change yours.

The expressive arts magically help us when other treatments fail. They are safe, effective, and practical. Witnessing others heal through the transformative power of the arts sparked the vision for this collaborative book. It features diverse, talented, worldwide creative artists, therapists, practitioners, teachers, and specialists who share their unique healing methods through the creative and performing arts.

THE RIPPLE EFFECT

Stress is an invisible weight everyone carries, often bubbling quietly within us until it reaches a rapid boil. We know it must be released, yet we may not know how to do it safely and effectively. However, within each of us lies a powerful antidote: creative flow.

The world is grappling with overwhelming turmoil—climate change, economic instability, global conflicts, and the pressures of hyper-connected consumers using multiple devices to interact and engage with others. We've abandoned the simple joys in life and created more stress-related illnesses. Simply put, stress is killing people of all ages.

Managing stress has ripple effects on relationships, workplaces, society, and the planet. So, this book is not only about stress—it's about creating a healthy, happy, harmonious world where people thrive and achieve their dreams.

STRESSED OR BLESSED?

Stress is a natural part of being human, so there's no shame in experiencing it. We can accept feelings of stress, such as anxiety, anger, victimization, or regret. However, we can instantly shift from stressed to blessed with a simple change of perception using the expressive arts.

Are you feeling happy or fatigued, lost, and hopeless? Do you wake up each morning energized and excited to begin the day, or do you feel confused, unmotivated to finish projects, or accomplish goals? Are you driven to achieve your hopes and dreams, or have you forgotten your passion and purpose?

Stressed individuals sometimes isolate, procrastinate, have headaches, use recreational drugs or alcohol, have trouble concentrating, and stop engaging in enjoyable activities. Chronic stress might cause others to overeat, stop exercising, have trouble sleeping, clench their fists, grind their teeth, or have a rapid heartbeat. They might be sad, angry, depressed, foggy-headed, hopeless, or unmotivated.

Each chapter in this book provides tools to transform stress, not to remove stress. Nor does it teach us to attain artistic perfection. It's about providing practical methods and techniques to shift from stressed to blessed through creative action, regardless of our chosen modality or skill level.

WHAT YOU CAN RECEIVE FROM THIS BOOK

Our chapter authors share unique creative methods for overcoming multiple life challenges. For example, a teacher or coach might share a specific sound exercise to relieve daily stress. Another might share their experience with post-traumatic stress using a journaling exercise to safely face and embrace a painful memory. Each co-author provides their real-life story, tool, techniques, or a step-by-step process to manage stress through the expressive arts. The expressive arts therapies are one of the safest healing modalities, yet it is always best to consult your trusted health-care practitioner before starting something new.

Expressive Arts: The Ultimate Creative Guide to Transforming Stress is a collaborative celebration of the arts, created by creative arts specialists, therapists, coaches, teachers, authors, performers, and workshop presenters. They share their unique creative techniques for releasing stress and embracing joy, such as chanting, dancing, painting, paper crafting, photography, piano playing, poetry writing, role-playing, mindful movement, creative problem-solving, singing, fashion designing, redecorating, and much more.

YOU ARE A GIFT TO THE WORLD!

You are a brilliant being with unique gifts to share with this world. Are you ready to face and embrace stress and take creative action? If so, I'm excited for you as you succeed. My hope is this book will inspire you to set your creative imagination free and discover limitless possibilities through the arts. I would love to hear from you. Please reach out to me with your insights, questions, or creative revelations. Thank you.

You were born to share a
remarkable gift with the world.
What is it?

For me, the expressive arts are dynamic, unstoppable waves of light and sound—the ultimate universal force, always with me. I become one with the arts, surrendering with each breath to relax in creative flow, a channel for divine love—limitless and free.

Jean Voice Dart

CREATIVELY SOOTHING SORROW

INSTANT GRIEF RELIEF WHEN WORDS AREN'T ENOUGH

Jean Voice Dart, CATP, Expressive Arts Therapist

MY STORY

"If I were you, I wouldn't go in there."

I never imagined a horrific tragedy would be the impetus to shed decades of protective armor.

The taller one unlocked the door and took two steps toward us.

"Stay away from the back bedroom."

It sounded like a line from a 1960s Alfred Hitchcock horror film. His foreboding words triggered old trauma. Fortunately, I had my toolbox.

CREATING THE TOOLBOX

I began collecting grief relief tools at an early age. The creative and expressive arts were there when I needed them: the death of a family member, my parents' divorce, a startling health diagnosis, the loss of a job, physical assault, homelessness, and more.

When Grandpa died, I couldn't process what happened.

My mother moved more quickly than usual, avoiding eye contact and wiping her eyes and nose. She whispered in the other room with Dad, then reached for a tissue and gently patted her eyes.

"What's wrong, Mom? Why is Dad home today?"

"Grandpa died."

"Grandpa is gone?" I cried softly. Later, people knocked at our door, bringing gifts: green bean casserole, meatloaf, cookies, and other goodies.

"Chocolate pie!" my younger sister shrieked in delight.

Mom turned for a moment to halt us from finger-scooping. "No, don't touch."

She prepared the babysitter, then bent down to hug us.

"Why aren't we coming with you?"

"Your dad and I talked it over, and we feel you should stay here. It will be too upsetting for you both."

I was confused and deflated. Later, the sitter told me what a funeral was. I drew pictures of our family, created a little storybook, and dressed in costumes. I was sad, but drawing, craft making, and dramatic play became my first essential expressive arts tools in my toolbox. I felt better.

SOOTHING SOUNDS

Music and movement were two other powerful tools I used for soothing sorrow. I danced to my favorite records, created original songs on the ukulele, and sang, stomped, and clapped in the car while listening to the radio. But the piano was always my safe space.

I sat on the bench for hours, releasing anger, joy, and sorrow when life became challenging. The solid, rhythmic support of piano chords grounded me while I released my feelings through my fingertips, sometimes pounding the keyboard and other times gently dancing upon the keys like tiny fairy feet.

TUNING IN TO THE ZONE

Piano recitals were an entirely different thing. Often, I found myself in the bathroom, feeling dizzy and nauseated. Sometimes I fainted. But I knew I'd be in the zone once I sat on the bench, felt the smooth ivories, and tuned in to the soothing sounds.

After several trips to the restroom, I was ready. I sat upright, wearing my mother's homemade dress, nervously tapping my patent leather shoes while waiting my turn. My palms were sweaty, and my heart felt like it would burst through my chest.

Mrs. McBride furrowed her gray eyebrows when Jenny stumbled over the keys, hitting a sour note. Jenny finished her piece and walked back to her seat.

"You are next after Sarah, Jean," she whispered. "Now, remember, watch your fingerings. Thumb under and third finger over." Mrs. McBride subtly introduced anxiety while maintaining a kind demeanor.

"Yes, I will remember."

As Sarah's fingers gently played *Clair de Lune* by Debussy, I let my imagination soar. An emotional story unraveled before my eyes. The moon reunited loved ones in its light. Heartache and tension dissolved, and I felt wrapped inside a comforting blanket of peace and love. A vision of luminescent moonlight and the sweet, melodious sounds dissolved all stress. I was at home. Old feelings of sorrow, grief, and pain brought tears to my eyes, but they immediately dissolved into acceptance, forgiveness, and knowing all would be well.

I applauded Sarah. The emotion evoked by her performance was a mixture of pain and love. It felt good and brought instant stress and grief relief.

"Next, Jean will perform *Le Coucou (The Cuckoo)*, by Louis Claude Daquin."

I quietly rose from my grey metal folding chair in the church basement, walked over to the piano bench, sat down, and placed my fingers on the keys, ready for my journey. I melted into creative flow. The quick, repetitive finger tapping brought me to my safe space again. I felt no fear or pain. I became energized, releasing all anxiety through the rapid rhythmic patterns, freeing me from tension and empowering me with creative flow. I was in the zone.

POETICALLY NAVIGATING ADOLESCENCE

Adolescence was a tumultuous time. As I grew into young adulthood, life became more challenging. My parents divorced, and I fell into a deep depression. I had trouble managing my vestibular episodes, frequently fainting or feeling dizzy. Doctors had no diagnosis. Mom stared blankly out the window, Dad moved away, and I began writing poems. I didn't want awkward feelings bottled up inside me, and it felt alleviating to release them abstractly through lyric writing, storytelling, and poetry.

I loved my creative writing class. As soon as we entered the room, social status disappeared. We found our tribe. The teacher encouraged us to praise one another: not the football player, stoner, nerd, cheerleader, or prom queen. We applauded the honest expression of feelings, instantly connecting through the transformative power of creative flow. Relationships blossomed, and I gained confidence.

"Nailed it. That's so cool, Jean."

"Thanks. Your poem about bullying was classic, Joe."

Writing has remained my instant grief relief tool for managing pain and sorrow, and my teacher inspired me to become an author, editor, and creative writing coach for others.

IF I WERE YOU, I WOULDN'T GO IN THERE

As an expressive arts therapist and creative arts teacher, I learned to help others release blocked emotions. Yet, my life wasn't all about soft, gentle remedies. Sometimes, the balm I needed was making a loud racket, throwing my hair around, screaming, stomping my feet, or splattering paint on the canvas. And sometimes, I unconsciously shielded myself with heavy armor, blocking the opportunity to bathe in the light.

This past year, my family members experienced shock, grief, guilt, anger, and a whole plethora of emotions when my ex-husband ended his life through multiple violent acts.

Shortly afterward, my son received a phone call from the apartment manager. "We can't legally clean or remove anything without your consent. Do you want to look at the items before we dispose of everything?"

He did. I silently questioned the sanity of this decision.

We quickly arranged for someone to drive my husband, son, and me to the apartment. When we arrived, we found two maintenance workers outside the door.

"If I were you, I wouldn't go in there."

The horrific tragedy that unfolded next would be the impetus to shed decades of protective armor.

The shorter one said, "Stay away from the back bedroom."

I felt the trigger. My teeth clenched and my legs locked.

My inner coach spoke.

Don't let his fear rattle you. You can do this.

The groundskeeper looked at my son, raised his eyebrows, and mumbled with quizzical concern, "Are you gonna be okay? Prepare yourself."

How can anyone prepare for something like this?

Often, well-meaning do-gooders will try to prevent others from experiencing pain. But it isn't helpful for us to put a cork in it. We must feel the feelings to heal.

I accepted the loving concern from this stranger and moved forward. "Thank you. We will be fine. My son will stop by the office before we leave."

I looked around at my surroundings. The senior apartment complex was pleasant and clean, with lovely shade trees. The people were friendly. I was surprised. The last I'd heard, he was living on the streets.

We can do this. Trust is the answer.

I no longer needed to hear the music. I had become the music.

BREAKING THE SHIELDS OF ARMOR

He had left us long ago, moving from place to place, evicted, addicted, and homeless. Now, the three of us stood together in his final earthly home, piecing together a life abruptly terminated.

I must embrace the feelings with compassion and detachment.

I must armor up while opening up—a paradoxical feat, but decades of working with the expressive arts prepared me.

My son reached for the door and courageously entered the home where his father ended his life. It remained untouched since that final day.

As I stepped forward, my senses took in the pungent herbs amidst piles of unfinished projects, schematic designs, and visions of things he imagined accomplishing.

The feeling was surreal. Suspense and tension tugged at the mind. "Please, I can't go in there, Mom."

I sheltered my son. "Okay. Why don't you sort through this storage closet filled with keepsakes? We will check out the bed and desk."

Wam. Bam. I saw it.

We each carried our unique shields to guard our hearts. My protective armor went up as I slowly walked, gazing around the room. Pills. Weapons. Chaos. The disturbing final moment was on display.

The sneaky thing about traumatic grief is that it's cumulative. When a shocking event occurs, it feeds off old trauma memories, like a two-headed snake. Seeing that final scene triggered a post-traumatic stress mess, but I had my toolkit.

A robotic, protective numbness helped us handle necessary business, sorting through the mundane remnants of our lost loved one.

"Bank statements, bills, medical records."

"Okay. Put those over there."

"Don't look over there."

"Okay."

"Photos and keepsakes are over here."

"Got it."

Then I realized the truth.

All my life, the expressive arts weren't just teaching me how to escape my pain by sculpting clay, writing poetry, or tooting a flute. They taught me how to masterfully shift my consciousness and open my heart to Divine love.

Using the creative tools I mastered, I shifted my perspective and focused on the love bonding us. We were a family, and we loved one another.

I spoke to the Divine creative power, the Holy Spirit.

God, please cradle our family with love and show us precious moments to be treasured.

THE LIGHT OF TRUTH, WISDOM, AND LOVE

The musical sound of my son's voice morphed into a joyful melody. "Mom, look. He made these."

Precious moments followed: sifting through his "Inventions" folder, discovering impressive stone carvings, and exploring a collection of beads, wire, and necklaces. I perused the contents of a cedar chest, leafing through photos of treasured memories. It was an opportunity to receive joy during tragedy.

"Ahh, yes," my face widened into a smile, and peace filled my heart. "Happy moments."

I accepted his choices and embraced my own.

REMOVING THE ARMOR

Although I went through the motions, I was still blocked. Old trauma housed itself in my belly and chest and rose into my throat and eyes. My inner child yearned to release old sorrow.

She spoke to me.

Love can't enter when you shield your heart. Remove the heavy armor and set yourself free.

Remove it? Why should I do that? I might die.

Remove the armor and open your heart to limitless love.

Being vulnerable was scary. I trusted my inner guidance, breathed slowly, imagined removing my armor, and asked inwardly to receive Divine love. I tuned in to gentle, energetic sounds and vibrations. My legs and body instinctively moved into the living room.

Where am I going?

I watched my body, letting a higher power guide me. My legs stopped before a comfy stuffed armchair draped with a blanket. I extended my hand, reaching toward a dark brown end table cluttered with papers, a bag of ginger snap candies, and a book.

He must have been reading this.

In an instant, I saw him sitting there, silently reading. My fingers touched the textured book cover. I asked for guidance, flipped the pages randomly, and saw five words jump out at me in the middle of a sentence: "Find time for creative things."

FIND TIME FOR CREATIVE THINGS

A few days after scattering the ashes, life was hectic. Another family member died before the suicide, and we needed to settle the estate. We remodeled our home, leaving every room in disarray, and suddenly I was busy teaching, writing, and coaching. Yet, as the months passed, I felt a beautiful transformation.

Like the blossoming of a rose, the traumatic events healed old wounds, bringing fresh color and transfiguration. Our home soon became a sacred haven, each of the three writers I coached completed their books, and I felt peace and joy I had never encountered. I giggled at the metamorphosis.

"You're so busy, Jean. I'm concerned about you."

"Oh, thank you. Yes, I'm busy, but I feel amazing. It's creative flow."

Was I in denial? Was I stressed?

Walking the family dog provided a happy break. We approached a neighbor.

"Hello. How are you and Tom doing?" I stopped to give her love.

She furrowed her eyebrows and tipped her head. Then tossed her hair while bending to pull weeds. "It's so hard for him. He can't get out and do things like he used to. I must do all his work and mine, too." She reached down to remove a few dandelions near the curb. I listened with an open heart.

When I arrived home, a friend called, crying.

"Jean, I just don't have any energy. Work is overwhelming, and my job is at risk." I asked inwardly for guidance and listened.

A business partner texted me, "I can't meet with you. I'm sorry. My father is in the hospital, and I must fly out tomorrow to see my mother and sister." I reassured her and gave her my love.

An email message arrived from a coworker. "Something has happened, and I need to move earlier than expected. I can't make our deadline. I'm sorry." I comforted him.

What is happening? Is Spirit providing opportunities for me to give love?

Three words immediately appeared on my computer screen:

"Creativity is essential."

CREATIVITY IS ESSENTIAL

Instantly, I understood. Creative action is how I serve life. It's essential to my health and happiness, but because of the remodeling, I wasn't painting, crafting, or writing. I must express my joy and gratitude through conscious creation. If not, the universe provides me with other opportunities.

As I walked through my home, serenaded by the hammering of helpful workers, I felt grateful for the incredible transformation in my life. I entered the craft room, temporarily used as a storage space for our workers. The newly painted room generously offered a variety of creative tools: paint brushes, paint, markers, canvas, wooden plaques, embroidery thread, knitting needles, and a tub of yarn. Looking at them made my heart dance.

This is my happy space.

Suddenly, I turned, hearing my childhood friend calling. It was my faithful companion, the piano.

I'm here for you, dear friend. Share yourself with me, and I will bring you comfort and joy.

Eyes closed, I sat on the padded bench and released my deepest gratitude through the rich sounds of this beautiful instrument, effortlessly discovering new patterns and harmonies. My heart overflowed with immense gratitude for God and my spiritual guides, always with me, whispering words of comfort and wisdom. The armor was gone.

I was home.

The creative and performing arts are a powerful way to receive and give instant grief relief when words aren't enough. Each day, I begin again, experiencing the transformational power of creative flow. It is my conscious prayer and a special way of giving to life. What about you? What brings you joy? What is your way of soothing sorrow when words aren't enough? Now it is your turn. Below, I have shared my tool and the process I use to navigate challenging times. It is my gift of love to you.

THE TOOL

I use this process to soothe sorrow and embrace joy. These steps work for me, and they can work for you.

THE ACTIVITY

The expressive arts can be divided into seven categories with many subcategories. Which category interests you most?

1. Visual Arts

2. Music and Sound

3. Dance and Movement

4. Dramatic Arts

5. Creative Writing

6. Filmmaking or Digital Arts

7. Nature Arts

MATERIALS NEEDED

The materials depend on which activity you choose. Supplies might include paper and pen, paint, scissors, magazines, glue, a camera, musical instruments, knitting needles, yarn, clay, gardening tools, home decorating supplies, etc. Let your imagination soar.

THE PROCESS - INSTANT GRIEF RELIEF

1. Slowly inhale and exhale several times.

2. Close your eyes, surrendering to your creative imagination.

3. Face and embrace unwanted, disturbing feelings.

4. Identify life situations associated with these feelings.

5. Engage in an expressive arts activity while focusing on the disturbing life situation (such as dancing, listening to music, or painting)

6. Release the emotions and feelings associated with this situation through the creative process or activity.

7. Feel all emotions and surrender them through the arts for instant grief relief.

8. Open your heart to a higher perspective while expressing gratitude and love through the expressive arts.

9. Stop the creative activity and gently inhale and exhale love and gratitude several times.

10. When you are ready, open your eyes and write down your new perspective as a positive affirmation (such as "I am limitless," "Life is beautiful," or "Love is here now.")

When you follow the process, the transformational power of the expressive arts shifts your perspective and provides instant grief relief. Are you ready to take the next step? If so, please contact me at the link below to attend a free workshop or private session. Thank you for embracing joy and sharing yourself through the expressive arts. I'm happy to meet with you.

Jean Voice Dart, M.S., CATP, Expressive Arts Therapist, is a best-selling author, certified expressive arts therapy practitioner, credentialed teacher, and certified coach specializing in grief, trauma, and chronic pain. She has witnessed thousands of miraculous transformations with the creative arts, assisting clients with emotional or physical challenges such as generalized anxiety disorder, PTSD, TBI, coma, neuropathy, paraplegia, assault, autism, memory loss, chronic pain, aging, ADHD, speech disorders, stroke, hearing loss, blindness, depression, and more. People working with Jean learn to feel, reveal, and heal by identifying buried emotions and rediscovering abandoned or neglected pathways to healing. Jean assists others in accessing their creative imagination, embracing their unique positive power, and transforming their lives to discover joy. She lives near the ocean with her husband, Matt, and their dog Pumpkin.

HONORS AND AFFILIATIONS

- Kappa Delta Pi Member, Honors Society in Education

- Illinois State University, Dean's List; BS in Music Therapy, MS in Special Education

- Certified Grief and Trauma Coach (CCF)

- Certified Expressive Arts Specialist and Coach (CCF)

- Certified Art Therapy Practitioner (CATP)

- Credentialed Adult Continuing Education Teacher in Music, Art, and Writing (California Commission on Teacher Credentialing)

- Credentialed Teacher K-12, Special Education (Illinois State Board of Education)

- Licensed and Registered Music Therapist (RMT)

- Certified Sound Therapist (CST)

- Certified Master Level Energetic Practitioner and Master Teacher (MEP and CMET)

Connect with Jean:

Contact: https://www.jeanvoicedart.com/contact

Website: https://jeanvoicedart.com

Facebook: https://www.facebook.com/jeanvoicedartauthor

LinkedIn: https://www.linkedin.com/in/jeanvoicedart

Classes: https://tinyurl.com/LearnitLiveJeanVoiceDart

Where is your happy place?

The Expressive Arts: Essential to Our Well-Being

Life devoid of the expressive arts is no life at all; it is merely an existence. It's the spark that ignites us, that leads us to self-discovery, a fulfilling life, and provides us with the tools to overcome life's obstacles.

Terri Fitzsimmons

2

EMERGING FROM THE ASHES

JOURNAL YOUR WAY THROUGH EMOTIONAL TRAUMA

Terri Fitzsimmons, M.S., PPS

MY STORY

November 8, 2018, was the turning point of my life. Who I was before that date is buried in the ashes of the Camp Fire that ravaged Paradise, California. A tragedy befell me, a treacherous fire. With its merciless flames, it wiped out my home and then chased me for hours as I tried to escape its wrath. Behind me was the inferno that was once my home. It was this tragedy that transformed me into who I am today.

It was a beautiful autumn morning: leaves, fiery red, orange, and yellow, fluttering to the ground, the sun streaming through the clouds, promising another warm day. *I'm so blessed,* I mused as I sipped my coffee, appreciating the view from our newly finished deck. Looking up at the blue sky, I noticed a red cloud in the distance. *Hmm. A fire? It's nothing to concern myself with, as it seems too far away.* I finished my coffee and kissed Jim goodbye before I left for work as a substitute teacher.

Two hours later, I escorted my students to the gymnasium. As we got outside, ashes fell upon us, and our clothes were immediately coated with grey powder. The air was thick with smoke, almost choking us. Parents began picking up their children, but when it came time to evacuate, I still had four children in my care. I got onto the bus with them and made the harrowing journey out of town. Cars scrambled to escape, cutting us off at times; propane tanks exploded in the distance. Still, the bus lumbered on.

Five hours later, we arrived at a church in Chico, which was transformed into a rescue center. I stayed with my students until their parents came. My daughter-in-law picked me up, and then Jim and our cat joined us. Later that night, we emerged from Walmart with a plastic bag containing all my belongings, totaling $126.00. Two days later, I heard the fateful words: "Your house is completely gone."

Before that date, I tied my identity to stuff—possessions I owned to impress others. I sought approval and acceptance from others to validate myself. Clothes, jewelry, books, awards, and diplomas covered my walls and cluttered my home. I'd now lost everything I owned, not once but twice.

THE ROAD TO LETTING GO

Years ago, my first husband took off in the middle of the night with a U-Haul containing everything I owned. Over time, I began accumulating stuff to make me feel better about myself.

Then, the Universe intervened once again. When I managed to escape from an abusive relationship a few years later, I could only take what I was wearing.

Of course, my neighbors were on the street. I knew I was going to throw up. Oh God, no! That would be the ultimate humiliation, heaving my dirty laundry in front of these hypocritical people who heard my screams in the middle of the night, who witnessed the police cars, and who did nothing to help me.

So here I was, once again, with nothing. *What is the Universe trying to tell me this time?* Was it because I refused to let go of meaningless stuff I'd lose anyway? Let's face it: I was still me after losing everything. Of course, those who were my friends didn't see it that way. Not having chic clothing became an embarrassment to them! *Ugh, really, Terri! Wearing clothes from a thrift store?*

AFTERMATH

After lashing out at God and screaming at my husband, I became galvanized. I had to take action to get some control back. That fire couldn't take anything more from me. It already robbed me of my identity (at least on paper)—my green card, birth certificate, passport, Social Security card, and all my degrees. I was overwhelmed by the tasks presented to me. The first order of business was to buy a laptop and start getting "me" back. I filed a claim with the insurance agency. Mounds of paperwork ensued, but I wouldn't be deterred by the work I had to do.

The one impediment to this was my fear of going to sleep. When I drifted off, I heard the screaming of people in the streets and the crying of the terrified students on the bus. I felt the ashes falling on me, smelled the acrid smoke, and saw the persistent flames chasing our bus. I finally got counseling and was encouraged to use my writing as a recovery tool. "Your writing is a major part of your therapy," my therapist said. "You are able to confront your fears on paper." Eventually, my journals became the impetus for my first two books about the fire.

I always kept a journal, and I almost wept when I opened the new one after my therapy session. Blank pages faced me. They dared me to share my nightmares, to unleash my anger and grief. I took the plunge and started at the beginning, the day we decided to move to a town ironically called Paradise. Over the next few months, I wrote, and I cried, and then I cried again as I read my words to my therapist. *My house, my belongings, everything that defined me was gone.* My journal became my best friend, my confidant: *I am now in the company of Buddha, the Dalai Lama, and Jesus, I wrote. I had to lose everything to gain everything.*

As I wept over the loss of my material things, I slowly began to realize that what truly mattered was the fact that my husband and I escaped the dreadful fire, along with our cat. When I returned to Paradise a month later, I rounded the corner to the school and closed my eyes tight, not wanting to see my car, like all the others I just saw—unrecognizable charred skeletons. But I was blessed. The school, partially burned, loomed in the background. My angel car sat untouched in the parking lot. My car became my beacon of hope for the future. I didn't lose everything after all!

My therapist wept with me as I read about that monumental day. She leaned over and took my hand. "Your words need to be shared, Terri, " she said gently. "Publish your journals to help other victims." With her encouragement, I published my books about the fire.

THE RELENTLESS FLAMES

The Universe wasn't done with me, though. More challenges came fast and furious. We again had to evacuate our home in Medford, Oregon, as the Almeda fire ripped through Rogue Valley, Oregon. Some survivors from the Paradise fire lost their homes again in that fire. Then I learned I had a massive aneurysm in my brain, ready to burst. And so, I wrote, and I cried, my words echoing my fears and anxiety. My prayers were soon answered: A coiling procedure saved my life.

I AM THE PHOENIX RISING FROM THE ASHES

Jim and I decided to start fresh in Indio, California. Living in a sunny climate was the medicine I needed. My new life coach's words of wisdom turned my life around!

She listened and her eyes focused on me as I rattled off all the horrible things that had befallen me. "All those events didn't happen at once. Let's deal with them one at a time," she said, "and, continue writing in your journals."

When I cried about losing everything, she made me look at all my saved books on my phone. I did not lose everything! I had the teachings of all my spiritual masters and counselors!

LESSONS LEARNED

What lesson did I learn from the fire? Wow! Through my perseverance, I got my identity back. I also helped other victims work through their trauma.

And when I sat on the pity pot, bemoaning the fact that I was alone with Mother when she was dying in Canada and how I managed her affairs amid the Pandemic, my coach gently got me to realize how strong I was, relying on my resilience to get me through those difficult times. "You learned that in times of crises, you can soldier on. You have that inner strength to overcome trauma."

The fire forced me to examine my life and to acknowledge that who I was before November 8, 2018, no longer existed. I emerged from that fire transformed into a thriver.

JOURNAL WRITING: MY TRANSFORMATION

My daily journals morphed into books and lectures. The words flowed onto the blank pages, filling them with my rage, sorrow, loss, and then, magically, gratitude.

This morning, I sit with my cat (I rescued Spooky from an animal shelter) *on my lap as I watch the sun make its way across the darkened sky; I am at peace.*

I found the courage to publish my memoirs, *I've Got Class: From College to the Classroom and Beyond,* and its accompanying workbook for women in transition.

Was the fire a divine intervention telling me to let go? I didn't listen the first two times when I lost everything. So, was this the ultimate warning? I'm inclined to think so. The fire became the defining moment in my life, the impetus to become a better me who relies on her inner strength and belief in a higher power.

I am not, by any means, finished transforming. I'm beginning the 76th chapter of my life and looking forward to filling the blank pages of my journal with joyful adventures! I'm meeting other thrivers in the eighties and nineties, actively engaging in sports and activities. What do they have in common? Their optimistic outlook!

But my primary focus is helping others, one person at a time. I borrowed Ghandi's "Be the change I want to see." Tragedies are no strangers to us, but we can find the strength to overcome them by using the power of the written word to document our transformation.

Journaling is how I transcended victimhood to thriver. It works.

THE TOOL

Now it's your turn to make a change. Find a safe space and a few simple materials to process conflicting emotions such as anger and grief. Journal writing is the perfect tool to enable this. Words are powerful, allowing us to explore and understand our feelings without judgment.

By continuously writing in our journals, we make sense of how trauma affects us. Yes, trauma is a part of our life story, but we have the power to alter our story by reframing the events. We work through the tragedy, feel its pain, and emerge stronger than ever.

MATERIALS AND PREPARATION

Before you use my tool, consider these preparatory steps:

1. Comfortable, safe space.

2. Journaling materials: pen and paper, note-taking app, computer, Smartphone, laptop, or recording device with a microphone.

3. Courage to face yourself.

4. Willingness to change your perception.

5. Choosing to be a thriver.

CHANGING PERCEPTION IS KEY TO SUCCESS

The key is perception. How we view what happens to us determines how we'll heal. If we view our predicament as a tragedy so severe or catastrophic that it affects our entire being, then we'll react accordingly: We'll be so overwhelmed that it's impossible to think about the healing process. We become victims, our language reflecting our beliefs. "Why did this happen to me?" "I have lost everything!" "Life isn't fair!"

I know the initial reaction to any tragedy attracts those feelings. The shock of the occurrence pulls out every angry thread of our being. We blame the universe, God, and whoever we can for what happened to us. But when the anger diffuses, leaving us drained, we rally. We examine our options. We recognize what we're grateful for, even if it's the fact that we survived.

When the realization hit me that I lost my home and, most likely, my car, I had choices to make. I didn't know this at the time, but I had options. I could keep moaning about my loss, perpetuating my victim status, or I could choose to take action to get through the process of grief and loss. The key to thriving is perception.

THRIVER NOT VICTIM

As I interviewed victims about their experiences, many of them chose to remain victims. They repeatedly replayed the events of November 8, 2018. They wrote the story of their experience from the status of a victim. I, however, chose to write my story from the perspective of a thriver. I had a plaque made for my desk. "She did," was all it read. "She did." Two tiny words sum up my life. I don't want to sit in my rocking chair at the end of my life, ruing what I never did.

A JOURNALING PROMPT FOR CHANGING PERSPECTIVE

Facing a blank page is, as we all know, a daunting experience sometimes. Writing prompts are an excellent tool to get your juices flowing. You can find many writing prompts on the internet. This is one of my favorite prompts because it forces me to reflect on my life, and I can examine it in any location, at any time.

1. Imagine your lifetime in this physical world has ended. You're in your spiritual body, approaching the gates of heaven. Before you can pass through the pearly gates, you must fill out a resume with your mission statement describing your life on Earth and the following questions:

   • What did you accomplish to benefit the common good without the motivation of money or self-recognition?
   • What are your values?
   • What legacy are you leaving behind?

2. After writing these answers, take a moment to reflect.

   • Are you pleased with your answers? If not, what do you want to change?
   • What steps must you take to come into alignment with your goals, values, and legacy?
   • What is your first step to take today?
   • Put your steps on your calendar and start experiencing success in leaving your legacy.
   • Celebrate your success each week by treating yourself to something special.
   • Write in your journal daily. Choose a time when you are free of distractions and can write freely. Initially, you may feel self-conscious about putting your feelings on paper, but soon you will discover that your journal will become your best friend, your confidant.

You will soon experience a shift in perspective. Looking back at your past entries will provide a sense of progress and a reminder that challenges are temporary. Journal writing is a mindful practice, keeping you in the present moment. My journal is a constant source of support accessible at any time. I invite you to check out my bio below and reach out if you need help with the next steps. You've got this/ I'm here for you.

Terri Fitzsimmons is a retired educator: she spent over thirty years teaching in the public school system and at colleges and universities. She's a counselor, specializing in women's issues. Currently, she's a reporter for the local newspaper and submits articles to various magazines while working with the Women's Historical Museum. She has written several books, the first two about her experience with the campfire of 2018. *Phoenix Rising from the Ashes* and *Smoldering Embers of Paradise* were the culmination of her journal entries while she was in therapy.

Her love of Sociology inspired her to write two historical fiction books, along with a book on socialization. Her latest books are her memoirs and a workbook for women. *I've Got Class!: From College to the Classroom and Beyond* was written to help women in transition. Each segment of the book is followed by helpful hints and points to ponder. *You've Got Class!* is the accompanying workbook helping women focus on gratitude.

When Terri is not engaged in her writing activities, she is meditating and attending fitness classes. She loves interacting with her neighbors and playing corn hole on her street.

Visit her website to see her printed works and interact with her blog.

Connect with Terri:

Website: https://tkbanner.com

Facebook: https://www.facebook.com/terri.bannerfitzsimmons

Email: author.tkbanner@gmail.com

Expressive arts are powerful for helping us heal our stress responses and embody peace in challenging times. It's as simple as getting curious and asking, "Which artform is my medicine?" When we suspend perfection and just play, we enter the theta zone of flow and deep peace.

What's your medicine?

Kathy Harmon-Luber

3

EMBODY PEACE IN CHALLENGING TIMES

THE HEALING POWER OF SOUND AND CREATIVITY

Kathy Harmon-Luber, Sound Healing, Reiki, Art

"Intention + Breath + Sound + Creative Moodling =
Powerful Stress Relief and Healing"

~Kathy Harmon-Luber

MY STORY

Standing in the kitchen with my hubby, waiting for coffee to brew, debilitating pain seared through my lower back like a bolt of lightning—a 20 on the zero-to-ten pain scale.

Here we go again—another spinal disc rupture, my mind wailed, vividly imagining the shock-absorbing jelly donut between the vertebrae exploding. *Wait, what's happening? I've had these disc ruptures before, yet never so excruciating! Sports injuries, dance injuries, but nothing as agonizing as this.*

Blinded by tears, unable to stand on my own, we shakily hobbled me off to our bedroom to lie down. In that moment—9:10 a.m., December 8, 2016—my entire life drastically changed forever.

It was the fourth disc rupture in two decades, made complicated and inoperable by several hereditary spinal diseases, diagnosed decades ago in my early 20s, converging in a perfect storm.

I'd previously scheduled a routine checkup with my primary care physician that afternoon. However, still writhing in pain, I physically couldn't move an inch. Not that day. Not for months. Not for years. All told, I was bedridden and incapacitated for five years, followed by glacial-paced recovery, which continues to this day.

Today, I have a thriving life again, although it doesn't resemble what it once was. Before the rupture, I lived the life of my dreams: hiking in the mountains we call home, traveling abroad, swimming, dancing, spending time in nature. I was a nonprofit charity executive making the world a better place, an award-winning fine-art photographer, a painter, a professional classical flute musician and teacher, and a board member of community organizations. A wife, daughter, stepmom, sister, friend, neighbor. With this health crisis, for the first few years, my life shrank to small and isolated—in bed 24/7, unable to do much for myself, reliant upon others, microscopic improvement, unbearable pain, and quite depressed. I suffered.

SUFFERING IS A CHOICE—SO IS THRIVING

I was afraid, overwhelmed, stressed, and anxious. As months rolled by, staring at the ceiling through endless, burning tears, I began plummeting down the elevator shaft of despair. Then I heard my Andean shamanism teacher, Puma Freddy Quispe Singona's wisdom echoing: *Nothing happens to you; it's all happening for you.* Everything is a gift, not one I'd put on my wish list, but a gift, nonetheless.

Then the aha moment whispered insistently: *My healing journey is embedded in my life's journey, which is embedded in my soul's journey. Everything happens for a reason, for my soul's journey. In every moment, I have a choice. I can choose to accept what is instead of fighting it. I can choose thriving over suffering. I can choose to ask better questions.*

Duh, I was asking the wrong questions: *Why did this happen to me? Will it always be like this? What if it gets worse? What if I become a burden to my husband?* Yep, all the wrong questions.

ASK THE RIGHT QUESTIONS

I began asking better, bigger questions: *What if I decide to fall in love with my future, no matter what happens? What if there's a better way of doing this?* (Spoiler alert: The answer's always *yes*!) *What can I learn from this experience? What's the opportunity for growth here? How can I create a life of meaning?*

Then the all-important question: *What can I do right now that will help me feel better?* Which I turned into my intention: *I choose peace,* peace from worry, stress, and fear.

I took a few deep, cleansing breaths, practiced my grounding meditation, and *hummed!* I know, it's probably not the first thing to occur to you, but humming poured out of me. Tentatively at first, then more robust and heartfelt. As I got into the humming, I saw swirly colors in my mind's eye. That felt nice!

Call me crazy, but I asked my husband, "Honey, bring my watercolor satchel and let's see if I can prop myself up in bed and paint." With raised eyebrows, he replied, "You want to what?!" But fetch my satchel, he did. With trusty water brush-pen in hand, I began to "moodle" around on the page in a meditative state. As I hummed and painted, in the flow of joyful creativity (which I thought had been stolen from me), I lost track of time. Amazingly, I was distracted from my situation. The relentless pain's edge softened a wee bit. That was huge for me.

I discovered a magic, powerful stress-busting formula that honors sound and creativity as the medicine, and I'm here to share it with you, dear reader.

THE TOOL

You're not meant to live in stressed-out misery.
You're here to live in peace, joy, and abundance.

This is one of the most effective tools to manage stress easily and quickly, to anchor, integrate, and embody peace throughout your day. I spent some of my convalescence time finally becoming certified in sound healing and vibrational medicine. Let me share why this tool works:

- **Intention.** It's well documented that power and manifestation flow where attention goes. Words, spoken or thought, are magic. They change the vibration within and around you and rewire your brain. They can transform your life. Ultimately, it's not only what you do daily that heals you, but the intention set by you. The real alchemy comes when we brew words—intentions, affirmations, or mantras—with *belief.*

- **Breath.** Breath is life. For thousands of years, across many cultures, breathwork has been foundational to healing. Throughout the day, your breathing is somewhat shallow. Yet a deep, conscious breath is an anchor, bringing nourishing oxygen through your blood and cells, which accelerates healing, reduces discomfort, and lowers inflammation and pain. Another benefit is deep relaxation, which works to combat the damaging effects of stress.

- **Sound.** Modern medical research is confirming what indigenous cultures, the ancient Greeks and Egyptians, and traditional ancient holistic practices such as Ayurvedic and Chinese medicine have long known: sound can be deeply healing and restore balance to our bodies and minds.

  UCLA researcher Dr. James Gimzewski discovered that every cell in your body, as it respirates, "sings." (https://bodiscience.com/our-bodies-cells-sing-discover-how-singing-cells-are-the-foundation-of-your-health-and-vitality/) Reported in *Science Magazine* (2004), this is called sonocytology, or more poetically, song of the cell. Every cell sings all the time, except when there's a challenge, like disease. The good news is, "our body's cells can be energized and purified by the very thing they emit: Sound." In other words, when our singing cells become dormant, sound can restore them to perform maximally. As one of my teachers says, every frequency is a nutrient.

Humming stimulates the vagus nerve, the longest nerve, which wanders through the body, controlling digestion, heart rate, immune response, etc. According to sound pioneer Jonathan Goldman, humming is a massage for all the organs. Sonic scientist John Stuart Reid and Rutgers University's Professor Sungchul Ji have proven that 20 minutes of music regenerates old red and white blood cells. Interestingly, sound isn't waves, but spheres! What's more, sound creates exquisite cymatics, sacred geometry patterns which become imprinted on our cells. How cool is that?

As the Brothers Koren say, "Your voice is more than sound—it's a sacred bridge between your inner and outer world, a channel through which you can express the deepest parts of yourself." What's more, it's not possible to hum and have much of an internal dialogue at the same time (try it!). Humming silences monkey mind chatter. I've found it has great healing and relaxation power when we combine it with other forms of creative expression, like the synergy of humming and painting to bring your inner energetic landscape to life. For a deeper dive into sound healing, read my *Yoga Magazine* article at SufferingToThriving.com.

- **Creative Moodling.** Studies demonstrate that art reduces stress. I like to differentiate "moodling" from simply "painting" because it's not about producing a piece of art. It's entirely about the process, the flow of creativity, intuition, listening to your heart, daydreaming, and imagination.

  Why watercolor? Across world cultures, the element of water is associated with emotions. Water can be a powerful ally: When negative thoughts linger, visualize them in water, floating away. You cannot grasp water, it's free, it flows—especially around obstacles. So watercolor is the perfect meditative medium for playing with creative expression, flow, and alchemical exploration.

HARNESSING THE POWER OF SOUND AND CREATIVITY AS MEDICINE

Stress relief is as simple as bringing together your intention, breath, sound, and creative moodling. This practice isn't about creating a work of art. The sum is greater than the parts as we journey through a process that reduces stress. Our only goal is to allow our hum to flow like water, expressing emotions as they move through us moment by moment, surfing feelings as they emerge.

It's an easy, effective, four-step intuitive practice. Read through, make it your own, and just flow.

Supplies:

- A time and place where you'll be safe, uninterrupted, and unplugged for 20 minutes

- A comfortable chair and table

- Watercolor paints, paintbrush, paper, small jar or cup of water

- An open heart

1. **Set a Powerful Intention**

    - Get comfortable in your chair. Take three deep breaths. Now think of your intention. Not sure? Consider: *I am at peace.* Or, *I'm disrupting stress patterns in my life.* Or, *I'm deeply connecting with my compassionate, loving heart.* Or, *my life is easy, effortless, enjoyable.* Or, *I'm guided, guarded, and protected.* You get the idea. Feel into it.
    - Dip your brush in water and write your intention on paper, allowing the watery words to fill the page. As they evaporate, your intention's energy remains.

2. **Ground and Center Through Breathwork and Visualization**

    - Breathe deeply into your belly, permitting it to fully relax and fill with air (don't worry, no one's watching!). Slowly exhale, letting go of anything that no longer serves you: worries, heaviness, anything you're carrying that belongs to someone else. Repeat and feel your body, your sacred temple, relax. A beautiful stress-busting tool I learned from Thich Nhat Hanh is, "I breathe in, I breathe out, I smile." This simple ritual dissolves heaviness and tones your vagus nerve.

- Feel Mother Earth's gravity holding you in love, harmony, and wellbeing, like a hug, and deeply relax your muscles. It might help to imagine you're at a hot spring in nature. As you ease your legs, torso, arms, shoulders, and neck into warm waters, feel tensions melt away. Alternatively, visualize sitting against your favorite tree's trunk and breathing deeply. Your body relaxes as little roots in your belly travel down your legs and into the earth. Pick whichever works for you and enjoy feeling centered and grounded.

- Conscious breath can be healing. When we breathe normally, without intention, we may take in negative energies of the collective. A powerful Andean practice is to consciously breathe in energy from a healing source: the ocean, a tree, animal, star, planet, or from the depths of the Universe. What energy do you need right now? The strength of a mountain? The joy of a hummingbird? The support of Mother Earth? The light of our sun star? Intentionally breathe with your chosen source in mind. Feel the energy shift. Then send your exhale lovingly, gratefully from your heart.

- Now drop into your heart and become aware of the world within. What is the essence of your inner world in this moment? Stress? Peace? Anxiety? Joy? It's all okay. Just breathe. Just be. There's nothing required of you. Observe the essence of you.

- Connect with something bigger. From this peaceful, calm space, can you connect with nature? Feel a sense of oneness with the Universe? Expansiveness? Bliss? (If you're not feeling it yet, that's okay. You're enough, just as you are. Move on to the Sidebar.)

Sidebar: **3 Tips for Meeting Challenging Emotions**

- If you're still experiencing stress, panic, anxiety, or the like, ask your mind to sit on the sidelines. Thank it for always working so hard, but now it can rest while you play in your heart energy. If thoughts and/or worries intrude, put them in a thought room and gently say you'll get back to them in a bit. Back to humming and painting.

- Feeling fear? It may help to visualize yourself inside a luminous crystal where nothing can harm you, you're shielded from negative energies, and only radiant light can enter. Experience this for a couple of minutes. This is a powerful Andean practice that might sound woo-woo, but consider that crystals are very high-frequency superconductors of energy (that's why they're in our cellphones, computers, GPSs, LCDs, and clocks).

- Another way to gently shift challenging emotions is to remember that negative and positive thoughts cannot coexist. Try being grateful and angry at the same time. Or loving and fearful. Not possible, right? So, if you find yourself simmering in negative thoughts, take a breath and pivot to gratitude, visualizing it as a golden-white light in your heart. Expand this light throughout your body. Then, as you think of all the things you're grateful for, imagine this light expanding into your torus, the energy field around your body, then filling your room. How are you feeling now?

3. Giving Voice to Your Heart and Soul

- Keeping your eyes closed, open your heart, breathe deep, and exhale the most comfortable sound which authentically, openheartedly expresses your essence. Unfiltered. Without judgement. You could start with "Sssssssss," "Shhhhhhhh," or "Ahhhhhhhh." Or tone "Ommmmmmmm," "Whaaaaaaa," or "Haaaaaaaa." Continue for a few minutes, feeling increasingly relaxed, until you're ready to move into a hum.
- With curiosity, explore your inner landscape, giving it voice through your hum. Curiosity is the antidote to stress!

What wants to express through me? What does it feel like? Where does it want to go? Allow your hum to wash over you, flowing from your heart. Don't think about musical correctness, prettiness, or what note "should" be next. Simply allow notes to intuitively slide, bend, and dance. Hum to your heart's content, literally.

- Ask, *if my spirit were completely free, what would that sound like?* Have fun with this! Aim for five minutes of humming with complete abandon—and without attachment to melodious outcome.

4. Watercolor Moodling Meditation

Remember that bit about how sound is spherical bubbles? Let's play with that!

- First, mindfully honor the water. Hold your jar in both hands, thank it, and bless it. Graciously accept Mother Earth's gift of water, which beautifully reminds us to step into the flow of life and surf the waves.
- From this space of deep mindfulness, resume humming. Visualize your unique hum creating spherical bubbles of sound all around you.
- Now, generously wet your paintbrush and loosely begin creating playful circles with water onto your page. They can be big or small, flowing with your hum.
- Softly gaze upon your paints as you continue humming, intuitively select the warm (reds, oranges, yellows) or cool (blues, greens, turquoises) color palette. *If I were to color my hum, would I choose warm or cool colors?*
- Silence your mind, feel from your heart which color beckons. *What color am I drawn to? What color makes me feel calmer right now? Where in my body do I feel that color?* Choose that particular color, load it onto your paintbrush, and paint the circumference of the circle(s).
- Mindfully watch the color flow within your circles. If your paints aren't flowing around, add more water with your brush.

- Looking at your chosen palette, which color wants to speak next? Add another color from the same color family. In other words, if you began with a warm color like red, choose another warm color like orange or yellow. (When we mix cool and warm colors, it makes mud. If that's not your intent, avoid it.)
- Continue this process, adding mark-making, like dots, squiggles, and splatters, if you wish.
- Add drops of water to your painting and watch them "bloom"—a sweet metaphor for how **you're** blossoming in your own authentic way. As Magaly Singona reminds me, "We're either blossoming or preparing to blossom." *As I continue humming, what does blossoming sound like?*
- Instead of circles, try painting juicy, wet lines of colors across a new page, one beside the other, tilting the paper a tad so paints flow. With mindful awareness, let yourself get lost in watching colors dance and blend.
- When complete, ask, *How do I feel now?* Remember, this deep stress relief via immersion in the flow of the present moment is always available to you.
- Before you jump back into daily life, express gratitude. Thank yourself for gifting this time for a reset. Thank your precious heart and voice. Thank your mind for suspending judgment and allowing play. Thank Mother Earth for providing art supplies and being your very life support system.
- Importantly, integrate this beautiful energy into your day. Anchor this vibe with your breath to embody peace as you go to work or school, wash dishes, walk your dog, prepare dinner, do fix-it projects, and such. You'll be a beacon of peace, radiating sparkling light in these challenging times.

Variations on the Theme: Watercolor's not your jam? Apply this breathwork and humming protocol to get into flow as you discover your own medicine: crafting projects, baking, yardwork or gardening, dance or gentle movement, walking meditation. Follow your heart to find your medicine.

It doesn't matter whether you believe you have artistic talent or not. You indeed have everything it takes to do expressive art! Follow the thread of inspiration wherever it leads you. Just play. There's no right or wrong way. A perceived "mistake" can reveal a delicious new exploration.

That's the gift of creativity. Your true expression is the medicine. That, my friend, will heal you. Namaste.

Kathy Harmon-Luber is a certified sound therapy and sound healing practitioner, Reiki master, classically trained flutist, award-winning fine art photographer and painter, published and award-winning poet, shamanic practitioner, and inspiring author and wellness guide whose passion is helping people navigate the challenging terrain of the healing journey.

Kathy's best-selling book, *Suffering to Thriving: Your Toolkit for Navigating Your Healing Journey ~ How to Live a More Healthy, Peaceful, Joyful Life,* is full of wisdom gleaned from decades of healing from debilitating health crises. Kathy helps others find their compass and chart a course for navigating illness, injury, and loss—learning how to become more resilient, joyful, and thriving. With insight and enthusiasm, she opens people's eyes to the potential of becoming more physically, emotionally, and spiritually healthy by offering a toolkit of practical, powerful solutions.

She has appeared in *Yoga* Magazine, *Best Holistic Life, Authority,* MindBodyGreen.com, *Elephant Journal, Kindred Spirit, Pretty Woman Hustle, Woman's World,* and has been featured in the Society for Shamanic Practice's Creative Arts feature, and as a guest on numerous highest-ranked podcasts internationally.

Connect with Kathy at sufferingtothriving.com, where you can read articles, listen to podcast interviews, and download a free course, *Healing the Heart Chakra,* by Kathy and Doctor of Functional Medicine Charlyce Davis, MD.

On her YouTube channel, you'll find free "Moments of Peace" sound healing videos.

Visit dancingbetweenworlds.art for expressive paintings and poems inspired by her dreams, and kathyharmonluber.com for her fine art photographs.

Connect with Kathy:

Website: https://sufferingtothriving.com/

Art and Poetry: https://www.dancingbetweenworlds.art/

Fine Art Photography: http://www.kathyharmonluber.com/

Book an appointment:
http://seekersfieldguide.com/guide/kathy-harmon-luber

YouTube: https://www.youtube.com/@kathyharmon-luber

Instagram: https://www.instagram.com/kathyluber/

Facebook: https://www.facebook.com/SufferingToThriving/

LinkedIn: https://www.linkedin.com/in/kathy-harmon-luber-4b38158/

Whether it's a poem, painting, sculpture, choosing what to wear, cooking, singing, or dancing among the trees, artistic expression is life-affirming, healing, and essential to knowing one's very soul. Art is life shared, and crucial for the heart of humanity.

Sofanya White

4

DANCE WITH YOUR HANDS

PAINT YOUR WAY TO PEACE

Sofanya White, Artist

Every human being has talents and gifts. Some of these may seem hidden, but they are very near, just behind fear.

MY STORY

MY ROOM OF LAVENDER WALLS

When I was about ten years old, I had my first experience of escaping a rather harsh reality for a sensitive child. The yelling and hysterics became a screeching, intolerable pain in my very being. I quietly entered my room of lavender walls, where I found a little time of sanctuary. *I hope she stays out of here and leaves me alone!*

I stood on my tiptoes in front of my dresser to look in the mirror and see that I existed, and that I was okay. On this particular day, I chose to try something new. In my frustration, I decided to draw instead of digging my nails into my skin until I bled. Before this, I made simple drawings or copied cartoon figures.

On this day in my room of lavender walls, I sat at a small table behind the window, train tracks outside a chain link fence just beyond our grassy little yard. I had a piece of newsprint paper, a couple of pencils, an eraser, and an old photo of my grandparents, Lifsha and Benzian. I was attracted to the old European look with my ancestors' ancient faces. My first memory in this lifetime was with my grandmother, whom I called Bubbie.

I think I sat for hours drawing, totally immersed and unaware of anything around me. All noises disappeared, and I was in an altered state. I didn't even notice a train go by just outside our backyard, the overbearing roar of airplanes above our house, or most notably, my mom's voice.

Hours later, I stood up to look at my drawing. Oh, what a profound moment! I experienced a sense of pride for the first time in my young life! *I made this!* It was amazing and exciting. At the same time, I feared it wouldn't last. I'd finally found a sense of value, that I could be capable of something good.

My mom came into my room and made a fuss about the portrait of her parents, and that was huge for me. She was so surprised I could do this, and perhaps her daughter had some talent. Mom seemed proud of me—a new feeling, and one I didn't want to lose. "Did you do this? Who showed you how to do this?!"

She was a very intense person and a strong force, so receiving praise at any level was important for this little girl who always tried to be "good."

I held onto this in my very being for years, and even to this day. In the following weeks, I made a few more drawings, but it wasn't long before I decided that although I could draw and copy things fairly well, I didn't have a good imagination. I didn't feel I could come up with spectacular ideas or paint them beautifully. I quit on and off from that point for years, but was able to hold onto one feeling of victory, and a nagging pull to do more.

Can you think of a moment in your childhood when you created or discovered something new about yourself?

DISCOVERING THE STREAM OF CONSCIOUSNESS PAINTING PROCESS

Soon after I gave birth to my first son at 19, I decided to try painting again. At that time, I was under the mistaken impression that to be a good artist, I would have to come up with a spectacular idea and then execute it perfectly as it was in my vision.

It wasn't long before I became frustrated at my imperfections, until one day I decided to continue painting even though I made mistakes. I simply kept painting and didn't quit in despair. I didn't allow the inner judge to halt me. To my surprise, painting became much more interesting than anything I could preconceive or imagine ahead of time.

This experience birthed a new understanding. *Wow, being a creative artist isn't at all what I thought! I feel so much freer with this now!*

This was the beginning of the adventures of Stream of Consciousness art.

In other words, I allowed myself the freedom to discover my painting as I engaged with it, to allow it to unfold moment to moment. Suddenly, I felt I could dance with my hands! I had a new sense of excitement and liberation from limiting ideas.

I could be present to play and discover what was to come. To this day, it takes continued conscious choices to let go and allow this to unfold.

My mantras help! "Trust the process, there are no mistakes in art, dance with your hands, stay open, play like a child."

Yes, easier said than done, but the practice is rewarding.

In the process of all this, I discovered something called synesthesia. It's a natural ability I believe anyone can nurture. It is an amazing confluence of combining more than one sense, like tasting music, seeing the colors of names, or seeing the shapes of sounds. I love to dance with my eyes closed and witness the colors and moving shapes of the music. When dancing, I'm painting inside.

Within the practice of art, one can enhance the senses, intuition, and psychic awareness. In each painting process, observe in yourself where you shift from enthusiasm to critical judgment. You may want to give up, feel like throwing it out or starting over. You may feel stuck or even afraid to make another brush stroke for fear of ruining it. Just keep painting!

Every human being has talents and gifts. Some of these may seem hidden, but they are very near, just behind fear.

Can you come up with reminder words or phrases to help change limiting habits?

MOVING TO THE DOME HOUSE IN BIG SUR, CALIFORNIA, 1995

I moved into my magical dome house in the redwoods in Big Sur on December 24th, 1995. It was my birthday! Mesmerized in a state of ecstatic shock, I often asked, *How did I get here* and *why am I here?* I was bewildered and in awe at the same time. *Do I deserve this? Was I brought here for a purpose?*

I wept in gratitude for days or even weeks, always asking for an answer to, "Why was I led here?"

Everywhere I looked, I gazed into profound beauty, 360 degrees, above and below. The level of consistent joy and even bliss was beyond anything I'd ever known. The direct experience of natural beauty became a mirror, reminding me that not only am I nature, but the beauty I witness and experience on the outside is connected to the beauty within me. It became very clear that this is true for all human beings. One of the profound blessings of being human is our ability to become consciously aware of profound beauty and to express gratitude for it. This sense of thankfulness for life opens the channel for ever more love and joy, and even ecstasy. From this state, a human being becomes heightened to all senses, intuition, and the ability to see and feel pure energy.

I remember years ago reading the book "Celestine Prophecy." I recall the section about observing a plant until you begin to feel and see the light or aura colors emanating from it, filling one with a heightened sense of euphoria. This state of ecstasy lifts one to a new level of perception.

I prayed often in profound gratitude, with rivers of tears. I asked and pleaded fervently. "Please, show me, how can I be of service? What can I do with all this gratitude and joy bursting from inside me? Please guide and show me how I can depict a human being's connection to nature."

I always loved drawing and painting the faces of people and depicting the human form. A person's life experiences show in their faces, particularly the eyes. I no longer felt interested in painting the more realistic style, but was open to another way. What was it?

How do you feel while in nature? Can you get quiet and just listen and feel it?

HOW I DISCOVERED ESSENCE PORTRAITS

I went on with daily life in ecstatic bliss, living and arising into love with trees.

A couple of weeks later, I awakened in the night—sort of half awake, I think. I wasn't certain whether I was in a dream state, somewhere in between, or having a vision. I witnessed colors I'd never seen before, brilliant hues beyond this realm. They moved and swirled, creating patterns of colors, interweaving and undulating in constant motion, forming and renewing.

I saw images emerging, beautiful eyes coming forth out of this mixture of patterns. Soon there were more features, faces, bodies, animals, and full scenarios. It seemed like a surreal time out of time—past, present, and future all at once. The following day, still mesmerized by this vision, I realized my prayer was answered! I will create a flow of unique color patterns specific to the person's portrait!

I painted their image, mainly focusing on rendering their eyes into the patterns, and then just saw what else appeared in the process. From these patterns emerged animal spirits, ancestors, and entire scenarios from the past, present, and future. Sacred and very profound imagery emerged, always a delightful surprise to me and my subjects.

I thought I'd have to take some time to prepare each liquid color and pour them into bottles with droppers. When I made it to the art supply store, there they were, all ready to go! They existed in the perfect little dropper bottles, and the colors were brilliant! I took some home, along with watercolor paper.

It took a while to find the courage to attempt this experiment live with a willing person. That first summer living here, I showed my art in the courtyard of the River Inn in Big Sur. It was there I nabbed my first subject: a local Big Sur man who looked like a wizard with a long, pointy white beard. He was delighted to pose for me! I was a bit timid, but it was important. This began what I later named Essence Portraits.

Almost 30 years and thousands of portraits later, I can say it's been a profound dive into a realm of many surprises, powerful information, high inspiration, and clear guidance for myself and those I've had the privilege of painting. I've painted portraits of individuals, couples, families, pets, and tributes to loved ones who've crossed over. It's also been my pleasure to teach Essence Painting classes in my studio and at other locations.

My mantras have become "Trust the process," "Honor my choices," and "There are no mistakes, only opportunities." In doing so, the self-doubts that often come to mind become ineffective and are replaced with confidence in the process.

I'm always enticed by and eager to witness the imagery unfold through moving patterns of colors. I become enthralled with a childlike, wide-eyed curiosity.

When finished with a portrait, I can refer to the images that appeared and glean information, inspiration, and guidance with an intuitive interpretation.

Essence Portraits are interactive with the person or people I'm depicting, if they are present in my studio. If not, the process works just as well from a photo, and I usually record my guided interpretation to send along with the finished painting.

What makes you feel childlike and blissful? You can consciously create situations that bring you to feel this way.

WAS I LOST, OR WAS I FINDING MY WAY?

For so long, I wondered why I couldn't simply stay with one method, one type of material, a subject, a style. I consistently question, *What is my style? What do I create with my art and why?* I've worked in clay, wood carving, stone carving, mixed media, sculptural paintings, oil paint, acrylic paint, pour painting with house paints, pen and ink, and gouache paint. I've painted realism, surrealism, and everything in between.

Was I lost, or was I finding my way?

Eventually, I began to see that regardless of materials or even style, there is a common thread or purpose that continues to evolve. We are, after all, an ever-moving and changing, evolving spirit. It's a blessing to be that tiny peephole through which Universal Consciousness, combined with individuality, can dance together, creating the most fascinating and meaningful imagery. Through art, one can discover messages, guidance, personal symbols, knowledge, past or future scenarios, spirits, animals, and whole worlds imbued with intrigue and inspiration.

Learning one's symbolism and patterns is enlightening and, I must say, so much fun! Life is the art, after all! You don't have to be a poet to write a poem, you don't have to be a dancer to love to dance, you don't have to be a singer to sing.

As I stand before each new white canvas, I recognize a brand new opportunity, a portal to possibility. *Just go for it, jump in and know the blessings of this new adventure.*

In the painting process, you can observe how you might begin from trepidation to enthusiasm, then encounter your inner judge. You may want to stop, give up, or feel like throwing it out or starting over. You might feel stuck or even afraid to make another brush stroke for fear of ruining it. If you keep going, there will appear a new level, more surprises, and an outcome you couldn't have imagined.

This may require giving up judgment and criticism. You can do it!

Do you allow yourself to change and try new things?

WE ARE NATURE AND NOT SEPARATE FROM IT

Life is a colorful and interesting journey of continual discovery. Art as a means of self-understanding, personal symbolism, imagery, and story brings so much joy and inspiration.

I hope you will give yourself the freedom and the trust to allow an unfolding natural evolution. You can discover that underneath the hurt or emotional scarring, there is a gorgeous, pure spirit longing to be expressed in the world.

Many of my first years of making art brought the deepest healing of core wounds, even though I didn't realize it at the time. My art was a pure visual depiction of my spirit torn apart. There was a visceral beauty to it, and I always had light coming through the cracks. Like a seed or little plant stuck in a seemingly impossible dark space, our human spirit leans toward and will find the light, and continue to grow or even thrive.

We are perfect in our imperfection. Perfect, just like the beautiful chaos of fallen trees in the forest.

Human beings have an innate desire to find purpose, to feel and give love, and to express gratitude for this life.

In finding ways to nurture your creativity, you can recognize and peel away the layers of conditioning that aren't who you truly are. They say you can't wash the clean into a shirt, but you can wash the dirt out. Most of us have been conditioned, socialized in ways that don't feel right. We're taught imposed limitations. With a sense of wonder and openness like the child we once were and still hold within, we can access our gifts and talents playfully.

What lights you up inside? What are you good at? What can you do to heal your emotional wounds? Ask these and other questions, and the answers will come.

It's in our innocent asking, the purity of longing, the trust in a bigger picture, that our nature is revealed. It's natural and obvious once it begins. Of course, your path can change along the way. We continue to discover new talents over a lifetime.

We can learn and grow until the last breath.

My passion is to depict the reality that we are nature and not separate from it, that everything is energy, vibration, frequency, and all things are connected.

I'm so very grateful for the opportunity to share the way creativity brings awareness, healing, and joy.

We always have within us the pure wonder of a child at play!

THE TOOL

DANCE WITH YOUR HANDS!

Gather a few supplies and place them on a table nearby:

- At least three colors of paints, colored pencils, crayons, or watercolors.

- Canvas panel or watercolor paper, and three paint brushes of various sizes: one flat, one rounded, one pointed.

- A paper or plastic plate for dollops of paint.

Say your mantras and ready yourself for an adventure!

1. Prop canvas or paper on an easel or against a wall.

2. Stand or sit in front of your canvas with your eyes closed.

3. Feel the excitement, anticipation.

4. Take at least three deep breaths.

5. Inhale, feel the vibration and energy entering your body, and exhale with big gratitude.

6. Open your eyes; notice the first color that delights you. Choose that one!

7. Squeeze a dollop onto your palette.

8. Using your largest brush, paint the first color onto the canvas!

9. Relax your wrist and shoulder. Make undulating or circular motions, brush and paint in hand.

10. Dance with your hands! Music is helpful; it's like dancing your colors.

11. Do this again with a second brush and then a third, chosen the same way as the first.

12. Try moving from your waist, too. Feel your body engaging in this movement of colors.

13. After a few minutes, stand back from your painting and gaze at it.

14. Do any images, symbols, or messages appear in the color patterns?

Remember to trust the process; there are no mistakes in art. Have fun!

I stand before you in reverence as
You entice, seduce me, nakedly beckon me to take the first step.
With brush and first chosen color, I enter.
A pattern is born.
Secrets revealed in you, the ancestors come through.
I ask, what do you want me to know?

Photo by Donna Shoemaker

Sofanya White is an artist living and creating art on her beautiful property, *The Jewel in the Forest* in Big Sur, California. Her precious dog, StarLilly, is her beloved co-host.

She hosts and facilitates creativity workshops and retreats where participants can enjoy nature and creative expression. Sofanya is also an officiant and often hosts elopements, reunions, and seasonal gatherings. She'd love to give you a tour of the property and answer any questions about your gathering there.

Sofanya owned and operated a successful art gallery in Big Sur from 2002 to 2008, which closed after the 2008 fires. She took her work, gallery, and studio to her magical dome house on her property, where she continues to welcome guests from all over the world.

She works in many mediums with a mission that threads all her creations to a purpose. Sofanya's mission is to depict the reality that we are nature and not separate from it. She loves to show the connectivity between human beings, all nature, and the Universe through art. When a person recognizes their true nature, a great healing will occur, and the world will be a better place.

This desire led Sofanya to Essence Portraits, which came to her in a vision one night after moving to the forest. It was a profound answer to her prayer to be shown how to serve humanity using her talents. Since 1996, she has created thousands of portraits for people all over the planet.

"Art has been my healer and teacher. The creative process can be intense while leading to immense joy and self-love."

~ Sofanya White

Connect with Sofanya:

Websites: https://sofanya.com

https://jewelintheforest.com

Facebook: https://www.facebook.com/Sofanyah/

YouTube: https://www.youtube.com/@Sofanya24

Instagram: https://www.instagram.com/jewelintheforest/

How can you express yourself
creatively today?

Every human is creative, even those who haven't had an opportunity to engage their creative spirit. Expressive arts help each of us to see the world in new ways, discover deeper aspects of our potential, and ignite our imaginations.

Gabrielle Kaplan-Mayer

5

THE WRITE WORDS

HOW TO FIND YOUR SOUL'S VOICE

Gabrielle Kaplan-Mayer, Spiritual Director

"Talking to paper is talking to the divine. Paper is infinitely patient. Each time you scratch on it, you trace part of yourself, and thus part of the world, and thus part of the grammar of the universe."
~ Burghild Nina Holzer

MY STORY

The day I leave the hospital, all I want to do is return to my bedroom: my books, my dolls, my pillows, my bed. At age ten, I know being diagnosed with Type 1 diabetes means my life is forever changed. Over the last five days, I've learned how to pinch my flesh and give myself insulin injections, how to prick my finger with a lancet to test my blood sugar, and how to stay alert for signs that my blood sugar is too low or too high. Either extreme can be deadly.

When Mom and I get home, I run up to my room, drop my duffel bag, and see it on my desk waiting: the blank journal I was given last month as a

Hanukkah present. Caught up in holiday fun before getting sick, I haven't had a chance to open it yet. Alone in my room, feeling so many different emotions as I begin to grasp that my life will never be the same, I grab the journal instinctively.

I open it up. At first, I don't know what to write, what to say. *Who am I supposed to be writing to?*

I pick up a pen, and a voice I didn't know was inside of me pours out onto the page. I write my fears, my hopes, my wishes, my dreams. Things I don't know how to ask the nurses or doctors, or even my parents—questions and ideas about life and death; honest feelings about how overwhelmed and scared I feel about living with this illness; my fantasy that things can go back to the way they were before my pancreas stopped working, when I was just like every other fifth grade girl in my class.

As I write, I feel better, lighter, and less anxious. I read over the words I wrote. *Sometimes I'm realllllllly scared…but then some moments I feel like I know I'll be okay.*

My journal becomes a new kind of home—a place where I can express what I'm not ready to share with anyone else.

As I grow older, I'll return again and again to expressive writing to help me through transitional and challenging times: leaving home for college, my first romantic relationships and breakups, my son's autism diagnosis when he was three, my journey healing through breast cancer.

Expressive writing becomes the way I pray and connect to the deepest part of myself—what I think of as my soul.

WRITING AND HEALING

I'd never been given a journal before that year; looking back, it feels like a beautiful synchronicity that the journal was there just when I needed it most. Writing helped me cope with the stress of such a significant life change. I kept writing because I always felt better and more hopeful after I wrote.

I faced another serious illness at age 37 when I was diagnosed with breast cancer. I was fortunate to not only have the support of my loving husband but also an amazing group of friends who cheered me on and helped with meals after my surgery. My children were only six and three years old, and like many parents of young children, life was busy with work and family responsibilities. It was hard to make any time for self-care.

I didn't write much during the years when my children were young. But facing cancer helped me to see the importance of taking care of myself, not only physically but also emotionally and spiritually. I wanted to be well for myself and for my family. Going through treatment stirred up so many intense feelings, and I knew it was essential for my healing to be able to express them. I set aside a few times a week to close my bedroom door, open my journal, and just pour everything out, much as I did back when I first opened that blank journal so many years ago.

When I wake up in the morning before anyone else in the house, I lie in bed and listen—to my husband's snoring, the sounds of the house, birds outside my window. Soon I hear my children, ready, awake, and running to my room. I feel waves of gratitude for my life, to be here, with all of its beauty and challenges.

Writing became a way of listening and getting reacquainted with my soul. The tender, vulnerable part of myself needed my attention. I'm certain now that the time I spent writing supported my resilience and desire to heal.

Over the last twenty years, over 2,000 studies have demonstrated what I discovered: that expressive writing has both emotional and physical benefits, including improved mood, lower stress-related physical symptoms, and even fewer doctor visits.

Expressive writing is available to you whether you're going through a difficult time, need emotional support, or are seeking greater spiritual connection in your life. It doesn't cost you any money to write, and it can be done anytime, anywhere. There are so many moments when I grab the back of a receipt, an unopened envelope, or even a napkin in a restaurant to write out my worries, capture an imagining or idea, or simply express my gratitude in words.

WRITING AND SPIRITUAL SEEKING

I think I've always been a spiritual seeker—someone who notices the beauty of the natural world and senses a connection to a life force greater than myself.

In the years following my breast cancer treatment, I began to think of my writing time as a form of prayer. I wrote about gratitude for my life— for the big things like my husband, children, and beloved dog, and for small things I often took for granted: the amazing cup of coffee I drank that morning, or the sweet conversation with an older woman while we waited in the grocery line. *This afternoon when I was walking Odin, I noticed it was still light out around 5 pm. I felt my energy shift. A few blocks away, I saw a forsythia bush starting to bloom, a few yellow flowers. Spring is coming–my favorite season–and I'm here to experience it again.*

Looking back recently at a journal from when I went through chemo, I found a funny appreciation I wrote about someone from work who always sent me annoying emails. It said, *I'm grateful to be alive today to receive this ridiculous email!* If I hadn't paused to reflect through writing, I might have stayed annoyed. Instead, that moment became one of gratitude.

As cancer forced me to face my mortality, writing throughout treatment helped me emerge to live even more fully than before. I began to see my writing practice not only as a way to release stress, but to listen to what my soul yearned for.

My journal was always a home, but now it's a kind of sanctuary where I can explore all my deepest questions and concerns about life. In my journal, there's room for my dreams and desires to speak. It's the place where I can process both positive and negative life experiences and find meaning in all I've lived.

TAKING IT OFF THE PAGE

The goal of any spiritual practice—whether it's prayer, meditation, chanting, affirmations, or any other practice—is to help us cultivate inner peace and connect with something greater than ourselves.

Through practice, we can increase our spiritual awareness and begin to sense deep soul connections to others and to the world around us.

When I make time for expressive writing, I feel more grounded and nourished in my life. I'm in closer touch with my dreams, imagination, and creativity when I open my journal. Through this practice, I've become a fuller, more content version of myself.

This transformation inspired me to start teaching expressive writing, to lead online and in-person expressive writing circles, and to train as a spiritual director so I can work with people in listening to their soul's voice. I work with people from all backgrounds and faith traditions—those who are spiritual seekers and those who are agnostic, seasoned writers and folks who don't think of themselves as "creative." Some folks in my circles have not written anything since English class 20, 30, or 50 years ago, and many come in with bad memories of the teacher's red pen correcting grammar and spelling mistakes. This practice is about inviting reflection and curiosity— no one will be checking for grammar mistakes! If anything, I encourage breaking rules. It's magical to watch as people release those experiences and discover the joy of writing for connection. And sometimes, the joy of writing extends into realms of both personal and professional life. One of my recent workshop participants shared this message with me:

Hey–just wanted to drop you a quick note. Not only is this writing practice helping me get in touch with my inner life…it's also helping me at work! I used to take so much to pen communications and now my words flow. I feel unstuck like I never have.

I'm so delighted to share the simple, accessible tools I've developed to help people find their soul's voice. I'm excited for the wonderful discoveries ahead for you!

THE TOOL

TEN WRITING PRACTICES TO FIND YOUR SOUL'S VOICE

Whether you've been journaling for years or are new to putting pen to paper, these ten practices will help you use expressive writing to discover ways to unlock your creative potential, release stress, notice the beauty and wonder around you, build compassion for both yourself and others, and listen to the yearnings stirring in your soul.

1. **Make time to write.** Carving out space to write can be the hardest part of the practice for many people. On Monday evenings, I go to a nourishing yin yoga class at my neighborhood studio. My teacher begins by saying, "Getting to the mat is the hardest part." It's true! As I finish my workday, I walk my dog, get dinner ready, and often think, *I can't make it to yoga tonight.* But once I'm there, I let go and let the practice take over. Be gentle with yourself and start slowly; a writing practice could begin with a once-a-week session for seven to ten minutes. Some of my students like to write at the end of the work week as a reflection time.

2. **Choose your preferred medium.** You may love writing by hand in a journal, typing on a keyboard, or writing on your phone's memo app. There's no one right process; embrace whatever feels right for you.

3. **Set space in your calendar.** Add your writing time into your calendar so it becomes a practice, a date you're keeping with your inner voice. Show up for yourself. It can be five, ten, or 15 minutes a few times a week. Start with a commitment you can keep. Increase time as you feel ready.

4. **Begin with gratitude.** Gratitude connects us to something greater than ourselves and helps us appreciate the gifts in our lives. Coming to the page, I start by making a list of things I feel grateful for at that moment. Writing out my gratitude warms up my creative muscles, opens my heart, and helps create a writing flow.

5. **Ask yourself a question.** A blank page can be intimidating for all of us. Questions invite us to be reflective and listen. Here are a few of my favorite questions to nurture your soul's voice:

   - When do I feel most energized?
   - What do I want to let go of today?
   - What do I hope to learn today?
   - What's giving me hope right now?
   - Who or what is a blessing in my life?
   - What's inspiring my sense of wonder or awe?
   - When do I feel a sense of belonging?
   - What does it feel like to follow intuition?

6. **Notice how the time of day impacts your writing energy.** Some folks love to write first thing in the morning. Others take time out of their afternoon or feel most energized by writing in the evening. Notice your energy flow and patterns. Experiment with writing at different times and pay attention to how the time of day impacts your process.

7. **Generate a list.** You don't need to write in complete sentences. Making lists is another great way to get your writing practice started. List beautiful things you've noticed over the week, like all your favorite people, or songs that make you cry. Look over your lists and pick one thing you want to write about more.

8. **Choose a value or emotion to explore.** I love to pick a quality and write about it several times a week to get deep and intimate with that topic. I might choose honesty, compassion, joy, respect, or other values that are important to me, or emotions I want to explore. After I write about it, I'll play with the opposite of that emotion or value, exploring its shadow side.

9. **Have fun.** Writing as a spiritual practice doesn't need to feel heavy or be serious! I think of humor as a spiritual quality; it helps me notice how absurd and often silly our human lives can be. Your soul's voice may be really funny! Don't edit the jokes, joy, or laughter that emerge. Encourage playfulness by adding doodles

or stickers to your writing. Try using different colored pens or markers—whatever brings lightness to your spirit.

10. **Make time to reflect.** You may want to begin your writing practice by looking over what you wrote in previous sittings. Notice: What has shifted in you since you last wrote? You might want to underline or highlight words, phrases, or images that stand out. This way, you offer yourself a kind of medicine. You become your own teacher.

Be gentle, kind, and compassionate with yourself as you begin this process. It may take time to find your soul's voice. I know it's there, waiting for you. May your journal become a nourishing home, and may your writing time become a sanctuary.

Gabrielle Kaplan-Mayer is an author, educator, and spiritual director whose work focuses on creativity, disability, and spirituality. She's working on a memoir about the power of intuition, healing from illness, and ongoing conversations with her ancestors.

Gabrielle writes a weekly newsletter with creative prompts, leads online expressive writing circles, and works one-to-one with clients who are seeking greater creative and spiritual connections. She and her family live in the Philadelphia area (Go Birds!), where she loves to explore the city's art, culture, and food scenes and find new nature trails to walk with her Saluki, Odin.

Connect with Gabrielle:

Website: https://gabriellekaplanmayer.com/

Substack: https://gabrielleariellakaplanmayer.substack.com/

Instagram: https://www.instagram.com/gabkaplanmayer/

LinkedIn: https://www.linkedin.com/in/gabrielle-kaplan-mayer-94827b39/

Our world is filled with labels and the expectations of others. Expressive arts allow us to share our inner life, to express as we choose to express, to show that labels don't define us. Our expressive art is a mirror of our inner life, shown to the world.

Solarzar Dellaporta

6

A MAGICAL JOURNEY OF BECOMING

STRESS REDUCTION GUIDED MEDITATION

Solarzar Dellaporta, Magical Ambassador

"A journey of a thousand miles begins with a single step."
~Chinese proverb attributed to Lao Tzu

MY STORY

I was the little bastard.

Family and geography are the early definers of our identity. Then we spend our lives finding out who we really are.

I'm originally from New York. The second child of two first-generation Italian American parents.

My parents married during World War II. My father was a tank commander in the 2nd Armored Division under General Patton. He met my mother during a leave. They dated, they danced, they fell in love, they married in 1943, then he departed for North Africa.

BECOMING AN OBSERVER

It was ten years before they had children. First was my sister. A year later, I was born.

My birth was clouded by the shadow undercurrent that I was not my father's son.

Until I was twelve years old, my father called me "the little bastard."

If that wasn't enough, I was born with a heart murmur. "Mrs. Dellaporta, it would be best to limit his physical activity to see if he can outgrow the heart murmur," shared the family doctor.

So, the little bastard spent more time inside than his sister and friends. I read, and read, and read. Reading exercised my mind in a world of information, knowledge, mystery, and magic.

I became and still am an observer. When I was younger, it was out of shyness, now it's out of habit.

As an observer, I learned by watching and studying. I also became a mimic. I found I could get attention by mimicking TV actors or lip-syncing records while acting out the song.

Performing became a way to get attention, express myself, and get grudging acceptance from my father. It seemed I didn't exist to him.

When I got my library card, I found the library had books on magic, and I became a devotee to learning the mystic arts.

I bought my first magic set at Marion's Stationery for five dollars. Mr. Marion always let me look through his abandoned box of tricks and gags.

One day, he asked me if I knew Clayton Rawson. I said, "I read his books!" His magic books for children are still considered classics for learning and performing magic.

"Well, he lives over on North Barry right around the corner."

I ran home as fast as I could, pulled out the phone directory, found his address, and excitedly wrote him a note about my interest in magic, that I read his books, and that Mr. Marion told me he lived locally. I asked if it would be possible to meet him.

MY MAGICAL YEARS WITH CLAYTON RAWSON

The next Saturday, I was looking at the comic books in Marion's Stationery when Clayton Rawson came walking in holding my letter. He asked Mr. Marion about me, and Mr. Marion pointed and said, "That's him right there."

Clayton Rawson said, "So you read my books, huh? Do you live nearby?"

"Just down on Hillside," I said.

"Well, come by my house next Saturday, there is a Boy Scout troop trying to learn magic as one of their merit badges. Bring some things to perform, let's see what you've got."

Once he left, I thanked Mr. Marion and walked on the clouds back to my house, waiting for next Saturday.

I went, I performed, and Clayton was impressed. While the Boy Scouts ultimately drifted away, I became a regular fixture at his house. He shared magic and let me borrow books from his library. In return, I trimmed the hedges, cleaned the gardens, and cut the lawn.

Clayton was my first mentor. He became a fixture in my life until his passing when I was sixteen.

During my Clayton Rawson years, I attended St. Vito's Catholic School through eighth grade. I was an honor student and received a Cardinal Spellman High School scholarship in Bronx, New York.

At the age of 16, my father and I disagreed about a haircut. I got a square back; he wanted it shaved up the sides.

Our disagreement became an argument; the argument became a fight that travelled from the dining room to the kitchen to the living room.

During a snowstorm on a cold, wet, east-coast, February winter night,

I was put out of the house with an overcoat, a few things thrown into a carry bag, and 16 cents.

Two weeks later, Clayton Rawson died. He was a mentor and father figure who encouraged me; his passing seemed appropriate in my new circumstances. It was as if the Universe said, "A new chapter begins; you have to find your own way."

I mourned.

CONCRETE CLASSROOMS—LEARNING FROM THE STREETS

For over two years, I lived on the streets and kept myself alive. I worked at an offset printing plant, did odd jobs, painted houses, did pick-up labor, and even did street performances.

During one period when I hadn't eaten in two days, I decided to try panhandling.

There was a small bus station on the corner of Fordham Road and the Grand Concourse in the Bronx. Usually, there were two or three buses at a time.

I thought I might be successful based on the number of passengers coming and going.

I was working at not being successful when this old fellow shuffled up to me and said, "Here, kid, let me show you how to do this."

He told me how to approach people, catch their eye, and appeal to them emotionally.

"Talk from your heart…let them see you're hungry because you are."

He let me try an approach, then called me back, gave me more tips, and sent me back out.

Soon, I began to make money. "Come here kid," he said.

He reached into his pocket—a deep pocket that went down below his knees—pulled out a handful of coins, gave them to me, and said, "Here, kid. Now go get something to eat."

My homeless guide mentored me, and then he fed me. I never even learned his name.

He had been crumpled, dropped, and ground under foot by life, but he knew he had value. He had wisdom to share. He was my second mentor.

WRITING MY LIFE STORY WITH MRS. MODELL

Two years later, my father and I reconciled. I returned home, but I was restless. I returned to high school. I was offered the opportunity to meet with a published author.

Mrs. Miriam Modell, an author of short stories, suspense, and pulp fiction, who wrote primarily under the pen name Evelyn Piper, took in six students interested in writing.

Each week, I shared my writings with her. Mrs. Modell became my third mentor.

She enjoyed my 'adventures' from the street, my journal, my ideas, my poetry, and my thoughts

But I was still restless. I realized I needed to move on from high school. I looked at the college catalogs in the Vice Principal's office, realizing I didn't know how to afford college. I thought of the G.I. Bill earned through military service.

There were five service catalog binders. I looked in the Army binder; there were no mail-back cards asking for more information. Next, I checked the Navy binder, the Coast Guard binder, and the Air Force binder, but there were no mail-back cards. Finally, I checked the Marine Corps binder—there was one mail-back card. I tore it out, filled it out, and sent it in.

FINDING MYSELF IN THE MARINES

I took my Armed Forces entrance exam in New York City within two weeks. Following my exam, I completed my physical. I was accepted for enlistment into the U.S. Marine Corps.

Within six months, I completed my high school GED and shipped to Marine Corps Recruit Depot, Parris Island, South Carolina, for a two-year enlistment. I honestly didn't know if I could handle it. I was afraid that with all my bravado, I would fail.

Two years turned into twenty-one years. After five and a half years, I was a Staff Sergeant; in just over seven, I was selected from the top one percent of my field and appointed a Warrant Officer. I spent my last 12 years in the Marine Corps as an Officer.

My time in the Marine Corps allowed me to explore different elements of who I was. Like magic, it was another form of performance, trying things out to see what fit.

While in the Marine Corps, I continued writing to Mrs. Modell. She wrote back how proud she was that I never let the Marine Corps take away the spirit of the tall, lean, fit, young man with the ponytail she kept in her mind. "P.S.," one of her letters said, "You've become a writer. I don't know if you knew that!"

In 1993 and 1994, I experienced a particularly challenging time in my Marine Corps assignment, so I wrote to Mrs. Modell to bring her up to speed on my life and share my concerns. As was often the case, Mrs. Modell didn't respond immediately. She maintained a healthy correspondence with many people and rotated responses so that she was never overwhelmed.

I retired from the Marine Corps in July 1994. That August, I received a letter from her son. He was a professor at Carnegie Mellon University in Pittsburgh, Pennsylvania.

He had seen my letter to his mother. She had lived with him for many years and liked to take daily walks. On July 1, 1992, she died in

Presbyterian University Hospital from a pulmonary embolism after being struck by a bus on her walk. She was 86.

I mourned.

LIFE-CHANGING LESSONS FROM MY MENTORS

These three mentors imprinted the foundational lessons on everything that followed in my life.

Clayton Rawson taught me the reality of magic, how to present myself to the world; my homeless mentor taught me how to be resilient, that we never lose our value, there is always a solution; and Mrs. Modell taught me to see my inner strength and believe in my worth.

When I was a Sergeant in the Marine Corps, my Captain encouraged me to apply for a commissioning program. I shared all the 'reasons' why I should not do it. He turned to me and said, "You're right, if you don't apply, you don't have to hear them say 'No.'"

That simple phrase brought me back to my mentors. I could believe it was possible, be resilient no matter the answer, and believe in my worth.

I was no longer the little bastard.

That was when I began my self-healing journey, and the tool I share is what I've learned and developed along the way.

THE TOOL

A. H. Almaas, the founder of the Diamond Approach to spiritual psychology, tells us: "To contact the deeper truth of who we are, we must engage in some activity or practice that questions what we assume to be true about ourselves."

When it comes to stress, our choices and belief systems are the anchors that keep us moored to our stress.

But our belief systems are not permanent. As we take in new information or adopt a new practice, our belief systems shift to accommodate the information.

Brendan Burchard shares, "First, it is an intention. Then, a behavior. Then, a habit. Then a practice. Then, second nature. Then it is simply who you are."

TOOLS FOR PRACTICING GRATITUDE

A gratitude practice you can do is the one I use every evening when I get in bed, and every morning before I get out of bed. "Thank you for everything, I have no complaints whatsoever."

It's simple and direct. In the evening, it reframes my thoughts from the day as I settle into sleep. In the morning, it frames my thoughts as I approach the new day.

I accept where I am, who I am, and what I have.

Even with a gratitude practice, negative, judgmental, or critical thoughts can still find a place in my mind during the day. Those thoughts often trigger or increase an existing stress response.

TIPS FOR TRANSFORMING STRESS

Stress is driven by our mindset. An effective way to resolve the tension and anxiety created by stress is through a practice of mindfulness.

Jon Kabat-Zinn, the developer and founder of mindfulness-based stress reduction (MBSR), has brought mindfulness into the mainstream of medicine, health care, and science as an effective way to heal and transform stress.

"Mindfulness is the awareness that arises through paying attention, on purpose, in the present moment, and non-judgmentally." – Jon Kabat-Zinn

This means intentionally focusing your attention on what's happening now, openly, and without trying to resist or change your experience.

To break the sense of stress, you have to take an action, an action that says I am not immobile, I can control this element.

THE RELAXATION RESPONSE

In his book, *The Relaxation Response,* Dr. Herbert Benson, from Harvard Medical School, shared his extensively researched process called "the Relaxation Response." His technique was recommended to treat the effects of stress, anxiety, depression, and high blood pressure.

His technique and those like it are tools to put us in the present and to help manage our body's autonomic response to stress. The autonomic response is the part of our nervous system that controls involuntary bodily functions like heart rate, breathing, and digestion. When we are triggered by stress, our heart rate increases, our breathing becomes shallower, and our stomach produces more acid, leading to difficulty digesting food.

THE STRESS REDUCTION GUIDED MEDITATION

I use a combination of his technique with a guided meditation and Theta music to do a daily stress reduction exercise.

The *Stress Reduction Guided Meditation* can be downloaded here: https://www.magic4life.com/hypnosis, along with the "10 Ways to Relieve Stress" guide.

Choose a regular time each day when you will listen to the Stress Reduction Guided Meditation. Listen to it for 22 consecutive days. Twenty-two is the Master Alchemist. The Alchemists of old believed they could transmute base metals into something more precious, which could then be used for elixirs and cures.

The number 22 imbues the ability to manifest ideas into reality. By following a 22-day regimen of guided meditation and stress reduction practice, you will develop a new approach to managing stress. Additionally, you will build a new stress reduction muscle in your autonomic system.

Don't seek immediate results. Within a week, you will develop a consciousness about your response to stress that was not there before.

This consciousness will begin to become your new normal. Be patient.

You've spent years building up the habits and practices automatically triggered when encountering a stressful experience.

Your daily practice will reinforce your stress reduction response through mindful meditation.

GENTLENESS AND KINDNESS

One last element to incorporate is to always check in to see if you are being kind and gentle.

These are gifts you give to yourself first, then extend to others. When you react, always consider whether you were being kind to yourself. Were you being kind to others? How can you respond with more kindness in the future?

Gentleness is another gift you extend to yourself as you work through this new practice. We may be spiritual beings in a human form, but we are still in a human form with human reactions. Be both Kind and Gentle with yourself as you explore your new practice.

In Max Ehrmann's poem "Desiderata," he shares, "Beyond a wholesome discipline, be gentle with yourself. You are a child of the universe, no less than the trees and the stars; you have a right to be here."

My recommended daily practice is:

1. Express Gratitude – as many times during the day as you choose.

2. Listen to the Stress Reduction Guided Meditation, which is an excellent tool to guide you into sleep at night.

3. Review the "10 Ways to Relieve Stress" for ideas on immediate release in a stressful situation.

4. Be kind and gentle with yourself.

By learning to de-stress, you will gain more enjoyment from your life.

You have a right to be here. Blessings always.

Solarzar Dellaporta has lived many lives in one.

He is a subject matter expert in the areas of Leadership, Communication, Customer Service, and Presentation Skills.

He's also a master trainer, award-winning speaker, and entertainer bringing value, relevance, and magic to every presentation.

A high school dropout-turned-Principal of a publicly traded company, Solarzar's diverse background includes two years of homelessness as a young teen; a 21-year career in the U.S. Marine Corps, both enlisted and officer; a career as a subject matter expert, consultant, and trainer for the Department of Defense (DoD).

Solarzar is an award-winning Distinguished Toastmaster (DTM), the creator of Magic-4-Life, a certified stage hypnotist, an ordained minister with a degree in metaphysics, and a master Mentalist experienced in palmistry, numerology, Tarot, astrology, and handwriting analysis. He's a member of the Society of American Magicians (SAM), the International Brotherhood of Magicians (IBM), and an alumnus of the Jeff McBride "Master Class of Magic," the only Magical Arts training school of its kind in the world.

He shares a wealth of real-world experience in his powerful, life-changing presentations.

Connect with Solarzar:

Website: https://www.magic4life.com/

LinkedIn: https://www.linkedin.com/in/solarzar/

Facebook: https://www.facebook.com/Magic4Life.solarzar

Leadership Magic: The Journey from Trickster to Sage:
https://tinyurl.com/Leadership-Magic

Rapid Manifestation Training Course:
https://www.magic4life.com/rapid-manifestation

You, Too, Can Read Minds: https://www.magic4life.com/read-minds

The Stress Reduction Guided Meditation:
https://www.magic4life.com/hypnosis

10 Ways to Relieve Stress guide: https://www.magic4life.com/hypnosis

What are you becoming?

The expressive arts are just that—a means by which you express your emotions and feelings and then let them go, clearing the way for a healthily expressive life.

Kate Hawkes

7

PERSONAL MAGIC

CREATING AND OWNING YOUR UNIQUE LIFE

Kate Hawkes, M.F.A.

Sometimes we arrive at who we are incrementally, through a series of little events rather than one seismic shift. I'm one of those people, and I didn't see the story until I sat down to tell it.

MY STORY

"I can't write a chapter for this book! My life's been pretty ordinary. I haven't had a life-changing experience or trauma."

Being asked to write a personal story about my connection to the expressive arts and wellness gave me an opportunity to piece together my collection of experiences.

I saw that the drip, drip of short stories—some were more like haikus—contributed to who I am today, and the work I do with people to grow their empowerment.

"You're so brave," people tell me. "It's not bravery if you're not scared," I usually answer.

What is it about my story that made me bold and more prone to seeing the vicissitudes of life as adventures rather than overwhelming problems? All my life, I've facilitated others to find their power and confidence—as a theatre professor, arts and wellness creator, and a parent. I've never asked myself what facilitated *my* development.

LIFE LESSONS FROM HORSES AND MY FATHER

"Your horse bucks?"

When I arrived in America, I was surprised by how many people had horses that bucked them off. In my world, people fell off because of something they did—or didn't do. A horse that really bucked was in the rodeo, not the backyard.

"More mistakes are made by not looking than not knowing." My father's mantra to his daughters growing up on a cattle and horse property in Australia. The onus was on us to observe, ask questions if needed, make a decision, and take action.

His other life lesson was personal responsibility in all things. Having dogs, horses, birds, guinea pigs, and numerous other living beings, we had a lot of practice. One day, my sister and I raced our horses in opposite directions with a strip of scrub between us. The horses couldn't see each other but could hear hooves pounding in the deep sand. I wasn't listening or using any common sense, so when the team on the other side of the scrub turned, my horse turned. I didn't. It wasn't a soft landing!

No one was hurt. The horse went home, and I followed on foot. My father asked for the story—we were all great storytellers. Afterward, he commented, "So you fell off because you made a poor choice?"

I learned early that, generally speaking, if there is a mishap between a human and another animal, then, as the species highest on the chain, we have the greater responsibility for the outcome.

To fulfill the My Story part of this chapter, I made a list of my life's little earthquakes. It surprised me. I recommend making your list one day!

ACTIONS THAT SHAPED ME

1. Leaning into my horse's soft, hot neck—Christmas in Australia, aged ten. Tears and confusion; the vague awareness that we were all playing the "happy family" game.

2. "I bought my ticket, quit my job, and re-homed my horses. I'm going to America." That's how I found the courage to tell my mother I was off to America with a handsome Yankee. I made sure all the objections were covered.

3. Whoa! Bringing a real, live being into the world. I started my journey into unearthing and articulating the baggage we carry. A Tarot reader told me, "The person you're bringing into the world is an old soul. You'd better do your work so that you'll be there when she needs you."

4. That work paid off when I lost a bitter custody battle, then supported my daughter through the years when we both had to answer to her father, despite her repeated requests to live with me. "Don't you hate him?" She was on her bedroom floor, wielding a pair of scissors, removing his face from photos.

   For a moment, I wanted to scream, "Of course!" But looking at her desperate face, my heart flooded with memories of those first years, of the gift of this child. "How can I hate the person who gave me you?" I meant it. Her long, skinny legs curled up, trying to fit into my lap on the floor, and we talked about loving the person while abhorring the behavior. Later, we taped his face back into the photos.

5. "Mum, are you going to die?" My ten-year-old saw a Disney program about Annette Funicello (one of the original Mouseketeers), who had multiple sclerosis. My diagnosis was recent. I assured her I wouldn't, and then learned about stress—how it's unique to each

individual. I learned about mine. I ran more, kept my horses, upped the theatre work, and I quit cleaning and cooking!

6. You can buy the farm or sell it. The time came to sell it to meet our unfolding story's needs. After rehoming horses (again), sorting books, packing up years of kid stuff for the future, renting a house in town, and heading into the last year of high school, we were finally together. But oh! There was so much to learn, process, and forgive. Reality is not always in tune with dreams.

7. Running in an Oregon morning beach mist, preparing for a marathon, I stopped and faced the sea. Beckoned by the endless forever waves, called by gulls circling above me, I was drenched in longing. I needed the desert; I had discovered Sedona, Arizona. I realized it was time to leave the little apartment where I found myself after the graduated teenager happily left our large, rented home. What did it matter that I only knew two people and didn't have a job? I was free; with freedom comes uncertainty, and with uncertainty comes opportunity. I stayed for 17 years.

8. "You're the only one of us who doesn't have a school-age child, doesn't have a job, and doesn't have a house," my sister in Australia pointed out in her practical way. "You might be in the wrong hemisphere, but you're the only one who can be there." My father was diagnosed with a nasty late-stage cancer. He and his wife, on their working horse and cattle farm, needed help.

   The next three months were extraordinary and well supported by the spiritual work I did in Sedona. Later, I spent four months deep in the outback, working jobs from bartender to small-town council gardener. I also wrote the article for *Hektoen International* that became the basis of the book *Personal Magic*.

9. "A few of us went out for a drink after the show." I was eager to share the joy of the friendships I made in my new theatre community with my new husband. "You'd like them! When you come and see it, come with us."

"Was that guy there?" I missed his anxiety.

"You mean the actor who makes us laugh? Of course."

His face changed, and the latent fears he carried rose to the surface. They struggled with his love and in the end, smothered it. I became someone who never used a male pronoun. We went round and round, trying to arrive at a place where his demons would rest. "Please let someone help you."

"You can. You do that sort of thing."

"I can't be your wife, lover, friend, and therapist."

In desperation and grief, I left one day while he was at work. A team of friends turned up, helped me pack up my things, and we drove away.

"The old, open Kate is back," a long-time friend observed over coffee a few months after that. "You disappeared inside yourself over the last year."

Months later, he and I walked by the creek, forgave each other, and as a symbol of completion, exchanged the rings made specially for our wedding eighteen months prior in the desert. Our love was recast as friendship, ties released. It's so big, even on my thumb. He had strong, large hands that worked clay and built boats.

There is, of course, more, but today at 68, I've packed a house into a well-organized storage unit and am setting off on the next adventure into the unknown—and writing the chapter for a book I never thought I would. Every move has been a choice, some informed by unexpected events and some by an awareness that it was time to make a change.

AND HERE I AM

The stories of my personal life shaped the main threads of my work, each with its key challenge and gift. My long relationship with horses is its own story. Suffice it to say, they have kept me honest, grounded, and accountable.

I experience stress when I'm not in control, when the winds of life are blowing me away from myself. I catch it, look stress in the face, and say, "Hey! I'm in charge here." I take a breath, step out of the emotional dervish, claim my space, and with it, find myself again.

Much of my life and work have been in live theatre as an actress, director, producer, and writer. My challenge is to maintain passion while holding the vision with discipline and endless belief. The gifts are those shimmering moments of connection between collaborating artists and the audience. The earthiness of work combines with the flight of art, and stories come to life.

As an educator, the journey began with little kids, when I was an assistant teacher at the two-room country schoolhouse I had attended myself! After many years, from Australia to the USA, I ended up as a long-time adjunct professor in the theatre department of a liberal arts college.

You will learn to tolerate ambiguity.

I included that in the list of goals in all my curricula. Offering acting, directing annually, and devising ways to make theatre history alive and active took place within the purpose of a liberal arts education. I interpreted that as learning to learn, being responsible for your outcome, and expanding the edges of what you think you can do.

Later, the job included offering acting classes to nursing students. I created a course in arts and wellness, focusing on self-care, inspired and informed by my work in the field and my Performing Wellness program.

THE MOMENT OF TRUTH

"Professor Hawkes?" Leaning back in his chair, paper in hand, the student regarded his not-so-great grade. "Aren't you concerned about your bell curve?"

"Bell curve?"

"Yes, you don't give enough As."

"Everyone has an A on day one. Your job is to keep it. And I don't give a darn about my bell curve."

"But won't you lose your job if the students don't do well?"

I looked at this strong, capable young person with every opportunity behind him and more to come, and felt sad for him. *If doing well is dependent on someone else's need for a job, then where's your power?*

"That would be my problem," I told him, "Not yours. Your responsibility is to the work you do for yourself."

There was a point when I renamed what I did. I don't teach; I facilitate others' processes in their learning. I take no responsibility for the students' outcomes, their failures, or successes. I'm responsible for all that I do, not what the students or clients do or don't do.

As a theatre director, I can't go on stage for the actors. As a writer, I can't control what a production does with the words. As someone who supports others on their journey to personal empowerment, I follow the same premise. I will give you every opportunity to learn the skills to swim, but I can't swim for you.

These threads led me to create two foundational processes:

1. **Performing Wellness:** Articulate and release the trauma story.

2. **Personal Magic:** The gift of your unique self, uncovered and fed by the skills of personal responsibility and joy.

They overlap, stand alone, or inform and expand each other.

PERFORMING WELLNESS

"This writing project allowed me to step out of the role of 'patient' into the creative role of 'writer.' [After months of not being able to walk, etc.] [A]fter just a few weeks of writing, I was walking further distances, my balance was better, and I was getting out more."
~ Performing Wellness writer

Performing Wellness™ is a text-based writing process for a small group of individuals with a shared illness or trauma they're ready to explore and share. The three to four-month process culminates in a public theatre performance by professional performers. Guided imagery, art, and music support and facilitate the writer's growth and play. Each writer finds their form, using the group's games and exercises as tools.

Grounded in the belief that every person is an artist and has a story to tell, and that the process of artistic discovery and expression facilitates wellness, Performing Wellness operates on the principle of artistic collaboration, rather than the therapeutic relationship, and is readily adapted to different groups and lengths of time, from two-hour workshops to a full four months.

"I watched my story on stage through the actor and realized while it was still my story, I wasn't there anymore, it didn't define me."

~ Writer feedback

PERSONAL MAGIC

I wrote the *Personal Magic* book after the Performing Wellness programs were well-developed to understand how that worked so well, and after studying shamanism.

"It was magical."

We use the word "magic" to describe something inexplicable that happens and makes us feel happy, full of wonder, and joyful. There's a transformation of experience out of the day-to-day reality. Magic happens when you relax into the moment of discovery. It's simply being in the awareness of "now." You're operating at a spiritual level. A creative experience can be magical.

Magic isn't so much about *changing what is* as it is about *adjusting* how we perceive, understand, and experience life. The brainwave patterns associated with both creativity and meditative states are similar. And in those states, we achieve distance from the emotional impact of life, because we're experiencing our story in the present, the now. We're not concerned with what happened before or might happen in the future.

Essentially, emotional and psychological healing is a matter of transmuting the negative into the positive. You face the illness, fear, grief, rage, or whatever the negative emotional experience, squarely and without anxiety or anticipation, just in awareness. And then take steps to reshape it into something else.

All of us, to some degree, live with stress, anxiety, painful secrets, and self-doubt. We can apply preventative measures by accessing our Personal Magic—the skills and confidence—before trauma, so we are better prepared for the earthquakes, big or small.

Personal Magic, the book, is a series of activities designed to lead you to your magic while building a toolkit of preparedness for whatever comes your way.

Chapter titles include:

- Awareness of Self

- Joy Through Discipline – Empowerment Through Responsibility

- The Hero in Your Story

- Stepping Into Your Personal Magic

- Positive Being

- Your Personal Magic Out In The World

- Resilience and the Future

Weathered by life and shaped by our experiences, as long as we're alive, we're evolving. It's inherently uncertain and, as such, can be stressful. By embracing that journey, becoming a responsible, empowered person, we manage that stress.

As I wrote at the beginning, what is it that makes me more prone to seeing the vicissitudes of life as adventures rather than overwhelming problems? I think it's being able to transmute uncertainty, loss, and fear, and their byproduct of stress, into gifts.

You can too. Embrace your unique self, tell the stories—for your own understanding and to share with others. Give the old story away so you can create the new one.

THE TOOL

You will need a blank sheet of paper and some colored pencils or, better yet, crayons.

SELF AS ART WORK *(FROM PERFORMING WELLNESS*™*)*

Imagine you're a painting on the wall or a 3D sculpture. Focus on your inner landscape, not your physical outside. It may be emotional, spiritual, or something else. Describe it on paper as if you were telling someone on the phone about this painting or piece of art.

Step 1. Write for about ten to 15 minutes.

Start with: I just got this new piece of art.

End with: And I am going to put it…(say where; e.g., the garden, living room, whatever).

Step 2. Now, look back over what you have written and notice the following:

How many times have you…

- Used colors in your description?

- Texture (sharp, prickly, soft, etc.)?

- Shapes (square, round)?

- Images or metaphors (like a river, volcano)?

Step 3. Go back and add to the description, just as it comes to you when you're reading, with each of these areas in mind. Add them into the writing, or simply make a list underneath the body of writing.

Step 4. Now, using your colors and art collage tools, create this visually. Resist the urge to be too real; let it come out fast and messy. Find color, shape, and movement rather than precision. Put it right over the words on the page, design a frame-like edge around the words, or literally cut out the words, place them on another piece of paper, and decorate that as the frame.

Step 5. Finally, where will you place this beautiful piece of art depicting a unique being?

As you go about your life, with the challenges and new chapters, hold that image of your powerful self. Let them carry the stress load, and make a gift out of the story. Stress is a byproduct and can itself create a new product. I'd be honored to guide you in uncovering and creating your story.

Kate Hawkes, M.F.A., Graduate Diploma of Educational Counseling, B.A., is originally from Australia and has lived in the USA for 39 years. A freelance theatre professional for over 45 years, she is an actress, director, producer, playwright, and long-time educator.

Kate taught theatre at a liberal arts college for 18 years, founded an arts in healthcare company focusing on storytelling and performance, and was Artistic Associate at a professional theatre company in Oregon. As Founder and Producing Artistic Director of Red Earth Theatre in Sedona, Arizona, she produced a wide range of theatrical endeavors, as well as storytelling projects with veterans.

For much of that time, Kate was also a grant writer, serving the needs of the organizations with which she worked. She was a consultant with The Society for Arts in Healthcare, guiding nonprofit organizations in development and funding strategies, including grant writing.

She developed Performing Wellness™ and in 2011 self-published *Personal Magic: Conscious Empowerment through Creativity & Spirit* (available as an e-book at many outlets, including Barnes & Noble). An article on the topic was published in the *Hektoen International – A Journal of Medical Humanities* (2009).

A produced playwright, Kate's other writing (mostly poetry) can be found on Substack, and she's been published in *US 1 Worksheets volume 68; Dream Quest; ArtsAscent, The Stray Branch*, and the Winter 2024 LISP *Anthology.*

Kate's mission is to connect the performing arts, mental health, and community across a broad spectrum. Now more than ever, people cry out for support to cope with uncertainty, loss, and depression. Arts organizations have a role to play in addressing the mental health crisis.

Balancing intellectual and creative pursuits, Kate is also a horsewoman, trail runner, and hot springs devotee—the more primitive, the better!

Connect with Kate:

Website: https://wellnesswithkate.com/

Facebook: https://www.facebook.com/HawkesWellness

LinkedIn: https://www.linkedin.com/in/katehawkes4wellnesswithkate/

YouTube: https://www.youtube.com/@wellnesswithkate7025

Substack: https://katewellnesswithkatecom.substack.com/

Expressive arts are not performance—they are transformational journeys. Through spontaneous creative expression, the body, mind, and soul become storytellers. Emotions long held in silence are activated and released. In this sacred unfolding, we access wisdom beyond words and create space for clarity, joy, and deep self-healing.

Dr. Charleen M. Michel

8

SOUL NOTES

AN EXPRESSIVE DANCE TO LIBERATION AND EMPOWERMENT

Charleen M. Michel, Ph.D., Alchemyst

When Dance and Music Move the Soul

It begins with rhythm—a pulse you don't notice.
Music plays, your body responds.

It's unexpected—familiar yet new.

Hips sway.
Arms float.
Happy feet find the earth beneath you.
Remind you who you are.

No one's watching.
No one's judging.
No choreography.
Only presence.

You permit yourself.
Your body moves.

Grounds at the root.
A shimmy stirs the sacral.
Fire ignites the core.
The heart opens wide.
Truth hums in the throat.
Vision sharpens.
The crown lifts to light.

You're dancing to express.
You're dancing to remember.
To return to your soul.
To remember how it feels to be free.

MY STORY

WHISPERS FROM THE PAST

Have you ever felt your voice wither?

Not because you had nothing to say, but because the rules were louder than your truth, or the fear of consequences held you back?

I was a petite girl in a patriarchal family, raised to be a good girl.

Respectful. Obedient. Studious.

They said:
"Speak only when spoken to."
"Girls should be seen and not heard."
"No dancing. No shouting. No questions."

What if my heart aches to dance with delight?

What if I have a question?

What if stillness isn't my nature?

I wasn't just any girl—I was the eldest.

Expected to be perfect, to lead by example.
To behave, guide, and make others feel safe.

I tried to stay quiet.
Swallowed my curiosity and pride.
Most of the time, I stayed calm, composed, and collected.
Most of the time.

"Just do as you're told and everything will be fine."

I froze. My hands balled into fists at my sides.

I wasn't mad, but something deep inside refused to stay silent.

"Says who?" I said, standing as tall as I could—not that it made much difference. I wasn't big, but I wasn't backing down either.

The words hung in the air like a dare.
Not loud, but the kind that knew.

Inside, something deeper stirred.
A longing.

I want a place where I can speak, dance, and be.

A place where I can feel instead of follow, my voice is welcome, movement is free, and rising is an act of devotion—devotion to myself.

SACRED SECRETS IN THE GARDEN

My grandfather's garden was my first secret place.
A sanctuary nestled among rose bushes and petunias, with a white swing where I could dream and enjoy ice cream.

Barefoot, with the grass tingling between my toes, I danced.
Dewdrops kissed my soles.
The wind played with my hair.
The earth embraced me with open arms.

Among the blooms, I planted seeds, nurtured flowers, and let joy ripple through my body.

I'm alive.

It's the only place I could dance.
At home, dancing was forbidden.

"Sacrilegious," they said. "What would the neighbors think?"

Heaven forbid.

But in Grandpa's Garden, no one questioned it.
I danced—it was our secret.
And in that place, I blossomed.

I feel the Earth pulsing beneath me.

I see the sky sparkling above.

I want to be free — to be ME!

SOUL EXPRESSION THROUGH MUSIC

At home, I discovered another kind of sanctuary: the piano.
I was seven when my fingers first touched the ivory keys.
The vibrations ran through me, stirring something deep.
Energy flowed from my fingertips to my toes.

It wasn't just music.
They were feelings.
Beethoven's *Moonlight Sonata* became my beacon of strength.
Its haunting melody whispered of longing, beauty, and mystery.
It whirled and swirled through my core.

My soul's dancing—even if no one can see.

But as time passed, life got louder.

Responsibilities and success took over.

My grandfather passed, and my sacred place to dance was lost.

The music faded.
My voice grew quiet.
My body carried the weight of everything I couldn't say.

I'll slip into the quiet corners of my soul, waiting for the right moment to rise again.

FROM SILENCE TO SOUL CALLING

After nearly 50 years, something stirred within me, no longer ignorable. A deep knowing rose from the shadows, persistent, and clear.

The barefoot girl who once danced through gardens, who poured her heart into the Moonlight Sonata, reappeared.

And with her, a yearning—
to express,
to move,
to be free.

Then came another loss.
When my parents passed, grief shattered something deep inside me.
In the silence that followed, I understood:
Words dissolved into emptiness.
Only the soul spoke where language couldn't reach.

I started researching.
I read about spiritual practices, the chakras, and ancient wisdom traditions.
Little by little, something deeper called to me.

Again and again, I found myself returning to the chakras—invisible, spinning energy centers along the spine, each one governing and supporting a vital aspect of my being.

Their colors, their energy, their ancient knowing—it all pulled at something deep inside me. Feeling their spin was like stepping into an invisible dance.

And still, I craved more.
Something to gather the scattered pieces of me
and bring them back into rhythm.

That's when I found Chakradance™.

Ahh, a sacred answer to my cravings.

Dance—the thing once forbidden—called me back.

I'm ready to return and become ME!

CHAKRADANCE: A SACRED DANCE UNFOLDING

The moment I stepped into a Chakradance space, it became my sanctuary.
This wasn't a class—it was a sacred reunion.

No choreography, performance, or judgment.

As the music pulsed through the room, something within me awakened.
The frequencies were tuned to my soul's language, activating ancient knowledge buried deep in my body.

With each beat, I softened.
My breath deepened.

I surrender.

My body didn't ask for instructions.

I remember.

It moved with an inner wisdom guided by my soul's rhythm.

Chakradance wove together everything I loved—movement, music, meditation—infused with the sacred teachings of the chakras and Jungian archetypes.

Each session became a living ritual: my breath became rhythm, my body the compass, and movement the medicine.

As I danced, emotions long held in silence rose.
Stillness, trembling, tears—then laughter, joy, release.
Memories surfaced from deep within my bones.
I let them go—layer by layer, breath by breath.

I'm not dancing just to be seen.

I'm dancing to awaken.

I'm reminiscing about the woman I was before the world told me to be someone else.

With every step, I reconnect to my life force.

I gathered the lost pieces of my soul.

I feel grounded, more open, more radiant.

This is my path.

My sacred return.

I want to dance the path back to my soul.

REDISCOVERING MY SOUL THROUGH CHAKRADANCE

The room is dim. My feet bare, my eyes softly closed.

A calm voice welcomes me into the sacred space, guiding me inward. The music begins.

As the first sounds vibrate through the room, I feel a stirring at the base of my spine. The root chakra dance begins. The music's deep, primal, and pulsing, like the earth's heartbeat.

I move slowly, hesitantly at first, then begin to stomp my feet. With every stomp, I feel more grounded.

Then, unexpectedly, tears come—not from sadness but from remembering the inner child who needs to feel safe. And as the rhythm carries me, I land fully in my body, rooted and supported.

I'm home.

Then the music shifts—soft, fluid, like waves splashing on the shore. I feel its pull just below my navel as my sacral chakra awakens. My hips move, slow and sensual, circling with ease.

Emotion rises—deep and unfiltered. It moves through me. No holding back. No shame. Just flow.

Pleasure and memory swirl together as I smile through my tears.

It's so good to feel joy and passion.

Suddenly, the beat quickens—the realm of the solar plexus chakra.

My belly's on fire.

My spine's lengthening, my breath deepens.

I'm moving with purpose, each step filled with fire and determination.

I'm expanding, not shrinking—claiming space once surrendered.

I'm fierce, alive, and in control of my rhythm.

I don't have to ask permission.

The power's mine.

The music softens as it enters the center of my chest at the heart chakra. I place my hands over my heart. My arms extend outward to embrace the whole room, then inward, to hug myself.

Tears flow again—this time tender, open.

I feel the protective walls crumbling as old pains surface, mingling with a deep sense of love. Not just for others but for myself.

I'm open to giving and receiving love.

As the melody changes, I feel vibrations in my throat. My throat chakra comes alive. I touch my neck instinctively, my lips part, and a hum rises from deep within.

The hum becomes a sound, then a song. I dance and sing simultaneously—something I've never done before.

It's safe to express.

My voice isn't loud, but it's mine.

I remember all the times I held back.

Never again.

My truth deserves to be heard.

The next rhythm feels different—spacious, subtle. It vibrates between my eyebrows. My body slows, drawn inward toward the third eye chakra.

I place my fingertips on my forehead. Images surface—memories, colors, and symbols. Thinking stops.

I see through my inner vision.

I feel a renewed clarity I thought was lost.

I already have the answers.

I've always known.

Then, the final sound: ethereal. My crown chakra opens like a lotus blossoming at the top of my head.

Movement ceases. Breath and presence are enough—whole, complete.

I stand there, still and light, gently woven into everything around me.

A soft, sacred connection—weightless, yet deeply rooted.

I'm the dancer, the dance, and the light in the music.

And when the last notes fade, I feel something's changed. Not because I learned something new, but because I remembered something ancient.

My body knows the way.

The rhythm of my soul brings me home.

CHAKRADANCE AS A HEALING MODALITY: MY BODY BECAME MY TEMPLE

What began as a dance became a sacred space to listen to my body's wisdom.

There were no steps to follow, only breathwork, music, and spontaneous movement.

And in that space, things stirred: memories, emotions, and truths I'd buried away for years.

With each movement, I reclaimed my voice.

Not the one shaped by roles or expectations, but the true voice of my soul.

I spoke clearly, trusted my instincts, and stood taller in my truth.

I stopped dancing for approval and began dancing for freedom. Not just as a woman, but as a sovereign becoming.

I'm becoming a queen.

And in that reclamation, something else awakened—
a desire to guide others into this sacred space.

I became a Chakradance Facilitator to share with others the same path that helped me remember who I am.

FROM DANCE TO REFLECTION: YOUR SOUL INVITATION

Chakradance awakened something profound in me—a rhythm for my soul.

But the journey didn't end there.
After dancing, I was called inward once more.
To sit in stillness. To listen deeply. To write and create images.

As I reflected on what unfolded, something new emerged.

I crafted a journal to share with others: *The Soul Notes Journal Experience.*

It's designed to awaken your inner voice, reconnect you with your body's wisdom, and guide you along a sacred path of self-discovery and transformation, just as it did for me.

Each chakra invites you to move beyond thought—to engage with feeling, energy, memory, and truth.

This is a space where your soul can flow through creative expression and sacred inquiry. It's about setting your truth free—on the page and in your life.

Are you ready to begin?

THE TOOL

THE SOUL NOTES JOURNAL EXPERIENCE

A SACRED DANCE OF EMBODIED WISDOM AND AWARENESS

Within you lives a map etched in rhythm, breath, sensation, and memory.

Each chakra energy center is a portal into your body's wisdom.
A gateway to expression.
A path to liberation.

As you move through each chakra, you'll meet different aspects of yourself—your:

- Protector

- Dreamer

- Inner fire

- Longing for love

- Unspoken truths

- Deep insight

- Connection to your soul

Your inner voices unfold through energy, movement, and emotion.

This isn't a performance.

It's a remembering—
a sacred dance back to wholeness.

How to Begin:

- Create a sacred space and light a candle.

- Begin with one chakra each day; add more if you like.

- Start at the root and rise to the crown.

- Use the music suggested (found on Apple Music) or choose your own that resonates with the chakra's energy.

- Close your eyes. Begin to move.

- Let your body express the story.

- After the dance, open your journal and reflect on the prompts.

- Use words or images to express your feelings.

- Let your Soul Notes be uncensored and authentic.

- Note: A formatted copy of The Soul Notes Journal Experience awaits you at https://www.wisdomunleashed.ch/expressive-arts.

1. Root Chakra – The Dance of Grounding

Movement Invitation: Stomp your feet. Let the ground hold you as you shake out what's no longer needed and reclaim your belonging.

Music Recommendation: "Rise Up" – Andra Day
Grounded, soulful, and empowering, this music calls you to rise, root, and remember your strength.

Reflective Prompts:

- When have I felt deeply held and protected, like the earth embracing me?
- How do I respond when fear, anxiety, or powerlessness arise in my body?

- What helps me feel rooted, steady, and safe?

2. Sacral Chakra – The Dance of Desire

Movement Invitation: Let your hips lead. Circle, flow, undulate. Express the pleasure, pain, and beauty that live in your lower belly.

Music Recommendation: "Wicked Game" – Chris Isaak

With its slow, smoldering rhythm and haunting melody, this song evokes sensual longing and emotional depth, perfect for moving with fluidity, vulnerability, and desire.

Reflective Prompts:

- How does it feel to be fully alive in my sensuality, creativity, and joy?
- Where have I dimmed my desires or ignored what pleases me?
- How can I let myself move in ways that feel free, expressive, and emotionally honest?

3. Solar Plexus Chakra – The Dance of Power

Movement Invitation: Fire up your center. Punch, twist, spin. Let your body declare its right to occupy space.

Music Recommendation: "Stronger" – Kelly Clarkson
Bold, beat-driven, and unapologetic—a song to move with confidence and fire.

Reflective Prompts:

- How does it feel to move from a place of strength, clarity, and inner fire?
- When have I over-given, overworked, or lost sight of my worth in the name of duty?
- What part of me is ready to rise, lead, and shine—without shrinking back?

4. Heart Chakra – The Dance of Devotion

Movement Invitation: Lead with your heart. Expand your chest, open your arms wide. Dance with softness, surrender, and grace.

Music Recommendation: "Love's Divine" – Seal
Soulful and expansive, this track invites emotional openness and heart-centered movement.

Reflective Prompts:

- How does love feel in my body when it's honest, open, and free?
- Where might I still carry old heartbreak or emotional walls?
- What does it mean to love myself unconditionally, and how can I move from that space?

5. Throat Chakra – The Dance of Expression

Movement Invitation: Move your arms like waves of sound. Let your body sing. Add sound to your movement—hum, sing, chant.

Music Recommendation: "Freedom" – Beyoncé
A powerful, truth-telling song to unleash your voice and express unapologetically.

Reflective Prompts:

- What truth is ready to move through me, whether in sound, gesture, or words?
- How have I silenced or softened my voice to make others comfortable?
- How would it feel to move with fearless authenticity and speak with embodied truth?

6. Third Eye Chakra – The Dance of Vision

Movement Invitation: Slow, fluid movement. Eyes closed. Let your hands draw images in the air. Dance your dreams.

Music Recommendation: "Dreams" – Fleetwood Mac

Hypnotic and intuitive—perfect for opening the realm of emotion and inner vision, guiding you to see beyond what is spoken.

Reflective Prompts:

- What inner vision whispers to me?
- Where am I invited to trust what I sense, not just what I see?
- How does my body feel when I move from intuition, not intellect?

7. Crown Chakra – The Dance of Lightness

Movement Invitation: Barely move. Just breathe. Let the spine float, the hands lift, the crown open. Become light.

Music Recommendation: "Weightless" – Marconi Union
Borderless, expansive, and meditative—ideal to dissolve boundaries, evoke stillness, and connect to the divine.

Reflective Prompts:

- When do I feel most connected to something greater than myself?
- Where am I still trying to control or figure everything out?
- How would it feel to surrender to grace and move in divine flow?

Bringing It All Together: The Embodied Path

Close your eyes and take a deep breath.
Place your hands on your heart.

Reflect on what stirred within you.

- What patterns emerged?
- What's one loving commitment you can make to honor your full expression?

You Are the Instrument. Your Body Knows the Way.

Chakradance is a sacred dance of remembering.
Each step is a reclamation.

Each breath is a truth.
Each movement is a key to your liberation.

Let your soul guide the rhythm of your becoming.
Your body's your compass.
Your dance is your medicine.
And your freedom is already within you.

Are You Ready to Dance Your Soul Awake?

If something stirred as you moved through these pages,
If your body whispered yes,
If your soul longs for more,

Then you are being called.

You've tasted the power of dancing alone.
Now, it's time to experience the next level.

I invite you to join me for a deeper journey,
where sacred rhythm, chakra-resonant music, guided visualizations, and creative expression awaken the wisdom within you.

This is more than an intuitive movement;
It's a return to your rhythm, your voice, your truth, and your soul.

Whether you're new to energy practices or already walking your spiritual path, a guided Chakradance journey can open portals to deeper healing, greater clarity, and authentic self-expression.

Schedule a free discovery call to continue your sacred journey here: https://calendly.com/charleen-michel

Charleen M. Michel, Ph.D., is a spiritual mentor, transformational guide, and expert in embodied healing through the power of Chakradance™. She helps visionary women leaders overcome stress, reconnect with their inner wisdom, and reclaim their confidence, voice, and vitality so they can live with purpose, authenticity, and joy.

With decades of global experience as a Human Resources Business Partner and Leadership Coach, Charleen seamlessly integrates intellectual clarity with the deep, energetic wisdom of the chakras. Her work blends modern leadership insight with ancient healing traditions, offering a unique and powerful path to personal liberation and soul alignment.

A certified Chakradance facilitator, Reiki and Violet Flame Practitioner, and Chopra Vedic Educator (Ayurveda, Meditation, and Yoga), she guides her clients through intuitive, movement-based practices that harmonize the energy body, release old patterns, and awaken the divine feminine within.

Charleen is a two-time Amazon #1 Bestselling Author and a recipient of the prestigious Book Excellence Award. A passionate writer and visionary creator, she designs transformational spiritual journeys that awaken the soul and inspire lasting change.

Originally from New England, Charleen followed her adventurous heart to Switzerland in 1986, where she continues to weave the sacred into everyday life. When she's not holding space for deep transformation, you'll find her tending her garden, perfecting her golf swing, or creating soulful spaces filled with beauty and intention.

Charleen has danced her way to freedom, confidence, power, and sacred self-expression—and now she invites you to join her on your sacred dance through Chakradance.

Come move in a way that stirs your soul...and transforms your life.

Embark on your journey to empowerment, freedom, and liberation now.

Connect with Charleen:

Website: https://www.wisdomunleashed.ch

LinkTree: https://linktr.ee/charleenmichel

Chakradance™ is the registered trademark of Chakradance Pty Ltd.

We can release stress and embrace joy through sound and movement.

Expressive Arts provide a portal for self-expression, vulnerability, and self-honoring. It's the space for you to embrace your sensibilities and sensitivities. Exhale as you engage in the creative process. The medium, just like the experience, is your heart's choice. Expression matters. It's an invaluable experience in truth-telling and soul-sharing.

Laura Mayer

9

THE ART OF CALMING YOUR HEART

A HANDS-ON RESOLUTION FOR NEXT LEVEL ALIGNMENT

Laura Mayer, M.A., OTR, Epigenetic Healer

MY STORY

"There's nothing we can do for you."

The doctor's words pierce through the silence of my hospital room like shattering glass.

Four Weeks Before

It's 6:00 a.m., and I hear that machine approaching my bed. It wakes me every morning between 5:00 and 6:00 a.m. I want to scream, "Can't you come back later?" Instead, I politely say, "Good morning."

Knowing I will never fall back to sleep, I'm restless. *Now, what am I going to do?* The sun isn't even up yet.

I'm so tired of being here. It's already been four weeks of hospital confinement, endless waiting, and still no answers. I want to go home to be with my boyfriend, hang out with friends, return to school, and be *normal* again.

Each day blends into the next, marked only by more diagnostic tests and uncertainty. How many more tests until someone finally tells me what's wrong? I'm exhausted—not physically, but emotionally. *Just fix me already.*

To add to my anxiety, I'm in a room with three elderly women, all diagnosed with brain tumors. If that's not humbling, I don't know what is.

What if I have cancer? Why would they put me in a room with three brain cancer patients?

Thank God, my bed is closest to the window, tucked into the L of an L-shaped room. I can close my hospital curtain and hide. The last thing I want to do is stare at two lifeless cancer patients lying like mummies in their beds. *I'm too young to handle it.* "Would you please crank my bed up?" the only patient in the room who can talk asks me. "Of course!" *It's good to have something to do.*

What an oxymoron—the fifteen-year-old girl who's in the hospital because the muscles in her hands are wasting away is asked to crank up the bed of an elderly woman with a brain tumor.

There is only one place I want to be—at the pay phone at the end of the hall. Every night, I don my hospital robe and walk down the hall to talk with my boyfriend.

Michael's voice calms me. "You'll be okay," he tells me. "The doctors will figure it out."

"I love you so much, Michael." I hang up and rush back to bed, crawl under the covers, and pray I fall asleep.

THE HEALING THREAD

My nana visits every day. One day, she walks in holding something. "What's that, Nana?" I ask.

"I have a needlepoint for you."

What if I can't do this? Until now, my hands only knew how to hold a paintbrush. I learned to oil paint as a kid. This is different. It's slow and methodical, just pulling a thread through the canvas over and over again. I'm losing muscle strength in my hands, and needlepoint seems tedious. Quiet and simple—exactly what I need.

If it helps fill up my time, why not?

I sit for hours every day, gently working the golden healing thread through the mesh of the needlepoint canvas. I'm not aware that I'm learning how to calm my anxious, terrified heart. The needlepoint instinctively becomes more than a pastime—it becomes a lifeline. It's the only thing I can do while sitting in my hospital bed, where I feel any semblance of control in my life.

My nana was right. *Keep your hands busy. It's therapy.* This has become my mantra—something to get me through these arduous weeks.

As I stitch, I wonder.

I wish the doctors would tell me what's going on. Don't they know I can handle the truth? What I can't handle is not knowing!

One day, I muster up enough courage to ask Dr. Horowitz, "Do you know what my diagnosis is?"

"I'm sorry, Laura, we're still trying to figure that out. You're a very unusual case!"

I felt like a beggar desperately seeking the truth.

The days feel endless. At night, I hug my Snoopy stuffed animal—the one Michael gave me—and quietly cry myself to sleep. I'm caught between fairy tales and the terrifying feeling that my life is over.

The neurological tests are constant and brutal. So many needles, so much pain. *Be brave, Laura. You're not a child; deal with it!*

During one of my EMGs, Dr. Horowitz tenderly asks, "Are you okay?"

I want him to see how brave I am. I reply, "I'm fine." Of course, I'm lying. No fifteen-year-old is fine when they're sticking needles in your spine.

Then the day comes.

A MATTER OF FACT

I don't hear the doctor's footsteps—only the murmuring of voices. When the team of doctors turns the corner, I instinctively put my needlepoint down.

The chief neurologist stands directly in front of me. The residents gather around him.

"There's nothing we can do for you," he says without hesitation. "You will lose one millimeter of muscle strength a month until it hits your respiratory muscles, and you won't be able to breathe."

Just like that. No softness. No pause. Just a matter-of-fact death sentence.

Then he adds, "Good luck with your needlework," and turns to leave. The residents follow. You could hear a pin drop.

I feel nothing. Did my soul leave my body?

I pick up my needlepoint and resume stitching, never missing a beat. Keeping my hands busy, the needle with the golden thread calms my heart and tethers me to something bigger than fear. It tethers me to me.

I remember feeling this same way when my dad brought home an oil-by-number paint kit for me when I was eleven years old. Handing it to me, he said, "You might enjoy painting one of these. It will give you something to do!" I recall eagerly running down to our finished basement, excited to be alone with my paints. No noises. No distractions.

I sat for hours at my easel with ease and anticipation as I followed the numbers, watching the colors take form. Creating something out of nothing felt magical. *I love being in my bubble.*

Realizing how meaningful art was for me, my parents soon enrolled me in private oil painting classes. Every Saturday morning, I'd walk into class, feeling healthy and happy, even lightheaded, as I inhaled the smell of oil paints, turpentine, and linseed oil.

Was I carving a necessary niche for myself where art is my go-to to free my heart?

After coming home from the hospital, I received another blow. The doctors tell me I'm no longer allowed to participate in physical activities. No gym class. No cheerleading. No bike riding.

At fifteen, the loss feels unbearable. I'm still trying to wrap my head around my new incurable disease, if that's even possible. *You're taking my body—now you're taking my time with my friends?* The disease is taking more than muscle; it's robbing me of being a normal teenager.

MY SANCTUARY

Instead of any physical activity, the art room in high school becomes my go-to. There, I'm not broken. Whether I'm painting, sculpting clay, or carving out of wood, I feel whole and happy. I spend every free moment I have in between classes. Even when my hands start to hurt and my fine motor skills begin to falter, the art room is my sanctuary. I'm not just creating—I'm reclaiming control, calming my heart, and soothing the ache inside me.

The disease looms like a dark shadow. I never know when or how it will progress. The one thing I know is that no one will ever take away my soul's passion for art. It becomes my declaration of independence, where I remember I'm not just my disease. It's my job to find a creative outlet so I don't feel like damaged merchandise.

By the time I apply to college, my hands are deteriorating, and my energy is unreliable. The dreams I hold—of being a nurse—are slipping out of reach. I know I want to help others. I just don't know how, until occupational therapy finds me.

As I learn about occupational therapy—about the confluence of science, creativity, functionality, and healing—I feel my whole body saying yes. The profession speaks loudly to me. I can help others find purpose in the face of limitations through my passion for science and art. *This is perfect. This is where I belong.*

Walking down the streets of Greenwich Village toward NYU for my admissions interview, I'm alive with anticipation. Wearing my fisherman knit sweater, which I bought in Italy, my homemade denim skirt, tights, and clogs, I project the quintessential vibe of a 1970s teenager looking like she has it all. I'm smiling from ear to ear. Inside, I'm nervous but determined.

Tony, the occupational therapist performing the interview, greets me with a smile as I enter the department, giddy with excitement. *He seems kind.* Although my heart is pounding, I feel a sense of inner calm. It's as if I knew I belonged here. This is my profession. Everything is way too perfect.

Oh, please accept me.

CHOICES

Tony begins. "What percentage of OT is science, and what percentage is art?" Without skipping a beat, I answer: "Sixty-forty."

"And you?" he asks.

"Sixty-forty," I say again. *That's an impressive question, since I love both science and art.*

Then comes the dreaded question—the one my father warned me about.

"What's going on with your hands?"

I pause. I hear my father's voice inside my head. *They won't accept you if you tell them the truth.* I tell Tony the truth without apology.

Tony replies, "You can make it an asset or a liability. It's your choice." Ten days later, I received my acceptance letter.

Occupational therapy isn't just a career—it becomes another lifeline. It allows me to embody a truth I have carried since childhood: Life is about finding meaning, purpose, and a way forward, even in the face of limitation. Despite the challenges, I thrive. I adapt even though the disease doesn't stop. Each loss is another betrayal. But I keep going. My favorite song from the 70s, "I Will Survive" by Gloria Gaynor, reminds me of what Tony said: You can make it an asset or a limitation.

For 35 years, I have helped others find purpose through OT. When I'm home, I sit for hours on my couch or at the dining room table doing my thing. I never feel despair, disappointment, or even physical pain. I'm back in my meditative bubble. It's as if my body and soul knew all along these were my healing moments. Whatever creation I'm designing—my signature needlepoints or quilting—my creative hands lead me psychologically to joy and calmness. My hands, though weakened, are my constant source of truth. They continue to be my north star.

The disease. It keeps progressing. Relentless.

After eighteen surgeries, I say goodbye to my beloved profession and most of my artistic pursuits. The disease won, and I'm broken. *Why am I still alive?* Not sure I have the strength to continue, I fall into a state of despair. I can't keep my chin up anymore. *What do I do now?* There is so little life left in my hands and me. I can no longer needlepoint. Needlepoint is *the thing* I count on to settle my heart. *Thank you, God, for not taking my quilting away, too.*

HEART-HANDS HEALING

After a dark period, I open my heart widely to alternative healing and non-medical practices. I find myself diving deeply into my emotional traumas. I believe that if I can heal my heart, my hands will heal, too.

Not only do I heal my heart and hands beyond anything imaginable, but I also receive the gift of deep intuition that emerges. My creative hands are morphing into healing hands, not just for me but for others. *Oh my, I'm witnessing my heart and hands heal.*

Fifteen years later, I pick up a paintbrush to paint a 36 x 40 canvas. Within moments, I find myself again in that meditative state. *Oh, my goodness, I can't believe what's happening.* Here I am, 40-plus years later, with a paintbrush in my hand: my passion for painting from an intuitive, energetic place opens a whole new dimension in my life. *I am home.*

Empowered and renewed, I start traveling to Florence, Italy, to take formal art classes for the first time since college. I feel like a kid again, anxious to learn and challenge myself. Strolling along the cobblestone streets on my way to class, I'm bursting with anticipation. It's been so long since I sat in art class. I hope I know what I'm doing.

I climb the steep steps typical of Florence and open the door to smiling faces. And here I am, amongst so many talented students. *What am I doing here? I can't do what they're doing.*

Terror sets in. I struggle with reality—my hands aren't like theirs. My heart aches. But my sweet, sensitive Italian instructor, Stefano, meets me with a gentle grace. He helps me do what I can't. He knows this is more than art. Indeed, this is a therapeutic journey.

"Stop saying you can't. Say you can," I murmur to myself.

Some days, the tears come quietly. My hands hurt. My spirit aches. *Why does it always have to be this hard?* Even when my hand can barely hold the brush, I trust that it will guide my truth.

On my fourth trip to Florence, something shifts. I want answers and resolutions to old traumas still embedded deep within. A longing fills my soul to go deeper. With hands and heart ready, I breathe into the moment and ask, *What am I feeling right now? What truth am I seeking? What needs resolution?*

My body tingles as I settle into a calm place. I pick up my brush.

My hand is holding the brush as my brushstrokes take on a personality all their own, creating, flowing, and exploring. I feel an inner chill surging through me. I'm flush with heightened awareness as my brush brings aha moments of clarity and resolve. *Breathe, Laura. Feel the energy pulsate through you.*

Gazing around the room, I notice a woman using clay. *I want this!* I haven't played with clay since high school. *My soul aches for my hands to feel the warmth and sensuousness of clay.* A mixture of grief, loss, and excitement consumes me as my eyes tear up.

My face lights up the whole room. I know immediately that I'll sculpt my fragile, misshapen hands. Excited, I sink into this profound healing. I begin, building my hand with clay. As I add one piece of clay after another, I whisper to myself, "I am giving my hand muscle." I'm not shaping clay—I'm reshaping my story. Piece by piece, I call myself back.

THE TOOL

The golden thread that began in a hospital bed has woven its way through my entire life—through every loss, every creation, every tear, every aha moment. I've learned that healing is about feeling, not fixing. It's our place to meet ourselves in the truth of the moment. It's about finding comfort, resolution, and being at one with ourselves, in perfect alignment.

HeART Energetic Expression is a tool to uncover what part of your story wants to be revealed and healed, a story that will organically unfold on the canvas. It is this story that will bring you calmness, more alignment, and profound resolutions. Take this tender moment and become the creator of your healing. You will feel magical sensations in your body as your energy dances in and around you.

WELCOME TO YOUR GOLDEN THREAD

It's not about being artistic or even knowing what you're doing. Just show up with honesty, willingness, and an open heart. Let your hands lead the way. Trust the energy that comes through. Your hands-on experience is the golden thread that will guide you to resolution and the next level of alignment.

Are you ready to begin?

Take a moment to choose your medium and set up your area.

The perfect medium is the one that resonates the most, since this is all about flow. Examples include markers, crayons, clay, or any kind of paint.

- Find a room in your home where you can walk freely. Next, slowly walk around the room until you feel an energetic pull that automatically stops you. You have entered the Knowing Field, a sacred space that feels calm and energetically aligned.

- Feel your heart open widely to this energetic process.

- Close your eyes and take a few deep breaths. Place your left hand over your heart and your right hand on your belly.

- Ask yourself, "What's keeping me from feeling calm? Why do I feel this way? What do I need to let go of?" Feel into whatever pops up and *lovingly* walk over to the area you set up.

- Pick up your tool and start expressing your energetic knowing. *Feel into the fluidity* and desire of wanting answers to your questions. Let go of any outcome. Your intuition (gut) is your guide.

- When you feel complete with your activity, sit with what you've created.

- Ask yourself: "What do I see in my art? How do I feel? Did I receive the answers to my questions?"

- Breathe. Place your hand over your heart. Give yourself a big hug and say, "Thanks for showing up, for listening, for opening up."

You've got this.

If you enjoyed the HeART Energetic tool, I'd be thrilled to give you an intuitive hit with your creative, expressive art! Visit my website listed below, send me your thoughts or questions, and I'll joyfully reply. It will be fun to connect the dots. And of course, enjoy the process.

Laura Mayer, M.A., OTR, founder of *Opening Doorways Healing Practice,* bridges her clinical expertise with intuitive knowing. With over three decades of experience as a licensed occupational therapist in adult psychiatry and pediatrics, her work reflects a rare fusion of science and soul. She is an epigenetic healer, author, OT consultant, and Paint-Intuit.

Laura's profound healing journey led her deep into the realms of intuition and mysticism, where she explored alternative modalities and embodied wisdom. She now helps others open the doors to transformation by flawlessly weaving medical training with healing intuition, creative expression, and spiritual guidance.

Her specialty now lies in epigenetic healing—supporting individuals in releasing inherited emotional wounds and energetic imprints that no longer serve them. Laura's soul purpose is in offering her clients a holographic healing experience, where she receives guidance directly from Source and translates the information with a mystical depth and compassionate presence for integration and resolution.

As the creator of The CoreRestore Healing Method and HeART Energetic Expression, her transformational process bridges truth, healing, and creative expression. While her work is primarily focused on individual sessions, she also offers HeART Energetic Expression workshops for those seeking to unlock their deepest healing potential through the language of art, energy, and heart-centered presence.

Laura is the author of *Unlocking the Invisible Child* and a contributing co-author of the bestselling *Adventures in Manifesting* and *Healing from Within* series. Her upcoming second book, *Why Do I Feel This Way?,* continues to share her golden thread of transformation and truth.

When she's not in Europe, Laura is hanging with her puppy Jules or painting the next intuitive hit that comes through. She loves to walk, dance, and engage in deep esoteric conversation.

Connect with Laura:

Website: Laurajmayer.com

Instagram: https://www.instagram.com/paint_intuit

Facebook: https://www.facebook.com/laura.mayer.52035

Email: laura@laurajmayer.com

You are the creator of your world—
step into it boldly.
Limitless possibilities are waiting.

Creativity is freedom—freedom to express who you are, to be who you are. Empowering you to do things your way and not follow the crowd. As we open to the flow of creativity through us, colour and joy come back into our lives.

Sara Jane

10

BRINGING COLOR BACK INTO YOUR VOICE AND LIFE

CREATIVITY FLOWS WHERE HEALING ENERGY GOES

Sara Jane

MY STORY

Have you heard the song "Fade to Grey" by Visage? Well, that is what my life did from a very young age.

The color drained from my life; I became almost cripplingly shy and a people pleaser just to fit in.

A thought came to me whilst I was writing this chapter: *What did I do to myself?*

I created a self-imposed prison, devoid of light, color, experiences, growth, and love. A place of safety to protect a broken heart, a place of existence but not living.

WE HAVE HER NOW

A little backstory: I spent three months in the hospital, including my first birthday, following an accident. My parents weren't allowed to stay with me; in fact, when my mother arrived in the ambulance with me, the nurses took me from her. "We have her now; you can go home."

Not only was my mother devastated, but I felt abandoned and rejected at a time I needed them most.

Due to hospital regulations and circumstances, I saw my parents once a week for an hour. When they came to see me, Mummy picked me up and cuddled me. "I love you," she said, comforting me as best she could—but they still left without me.

What did I do wrong?

By the time I was allowed home, the mental and emotional trauma were deeply ingrained. It was compounded by the birth of my sister Gillian, who died when she was nine weeks old—another rejection for me and trauma for my parents.

Bless you, my little one. Every negative word, look, action caused you to retreat further into your prison, solidifying the walls around you. Feeding your monkey mind, which went into fear overdrive to "protect" you.

MY LIFEQUAKE

I have so few memories of my first 30-plus years. What I can say is my happiest times were taking our dogs down to the beach for long walks along the shore, listening to the waves as they rolled or crashed onto the beach, and then climbing the 100-plus steps to the cliff tops.

It was a time of escapism and daydreaming, leaving the real world behind and enjoying being in nature.

As I've come to realize, I was almost permanently depressed, anxious, worried, and fearful; those walks were probably my only respite.

Fast forward 35 years to my "lifequake," which occurred in the form of a broken jaw, causing me six months of pain and sleepless nights.

Now I understand the gift this was. It weakened my prison walls, and the following months and years supported me to push through brick by brick, slowly tumbling them down, freeing me to live my life.

At the time, I studied accountancy; it was the first thing to go. I slowly stopped people pleasing and broke up my marriage. Finally, the company I worked for got taken over; we could move or take redundancy.

On a visit to the doctor following the breakup of my marriage, I asked, "Can I be referred to a psychotherapist, as I wish to understand why I've been this way?"

They sent me to a psychiatrist who proceeded to put me on Prozac; after all, I must be depressed. She also offered that I could take a break in a local institution, but that wasn't an option for me.

It couldn't have been further from the truth. By then, hope replaced depression—hope for a future that would be so much better than the life I left behind.

Endings are new beginnings. This was the gift the Universe gave me.

A PURPOSEFUL LIFE

At work, I was part of the team that helped facilitate the transition from the old company to the new. I accepted a six-month secondment and moved to Bournemouth, Dorset, where I now live.

There I met a lady who introduced me to her group of friends—oh, the fun we've all had over the years.

During that time, I became a member of the UK Wolf Conservation Trust. I read about a trip to Romania to track wolves and lynx in the Carpathian Mountains with the Carpathian Large Carnivore Project.

The old me would've been afraid to consider participating in anything like this, but my confidence was building. I applied and was accepted.

I'm scared and excited all at the same time, a brand-new experience, in a different country with people I don't know.

Not only did I go, but I was also asked to write up the project diary, and three of my photographs were included in it, even though a professional photographer was with us.

I've always enjoyed taking photographs, especially of nature, including wolves, pumas, snow leopards, clouded leopards, black panthers, an underwater shot of dolphins, waterfalls with orbs, and so much more.

I took redundancy just after buying my little house and walked into a new job six days later.

A realization seeped into my consciousness: I was growing. Color and purpose came back into my life, and something—not just me—changed.

One day whilst sitting on the stairs at home, making a fuss of one of my cats, I thought, *What can I learn for me?*

I can't massage myself, so what can I do to support me?

What I didn't realize at the time was that I asked the Universe, and it responded by showing me there was a holistic fayre locally that weekend.

A CREATIVE CHANNEL

On the first stand just inside the door was a lady, Angie, sharing about an angel day and a practice called metamorphic technique.

I've always believed in angels. We got talking and she told me about Reiki, saying, "When you do your level one Reiki, the first person you treat is yourself."

At the angel day, I met the organizer, Elaine, who was also Angie's Reiki master.

A couple of months later, I did my Reiki one. That's when the color blossomed in my life, my voice became stronger, and the stress of what other people thought of me slipped even further away.

Elaine introduced me to sound in the form of toning—the use of the voice but not singing. It resonated with me from the start.

She also introduced a group of us to Karen, and we joined her Lords of Melchizedek energy workshops.

On the first day, as I left home, I remember thinking, *Why am I doing an energy workshop? I don't see things or hear things.* But I'd signed up and paid for it, so I went.

I didn't look back and followed on with all ten of the workshops Karen channeled from the Lords of Melchizedek. We all found ourselves working with the Pleiadeans.

Karen taught Elaine and me quantum touch. She knew us well enough by then. "You can use the toning with it."

Did I ever offer quantum touch sessions, or was I always working with sound? This is a question I've asked myself on many occasions.

My intention was always to only do my level one Reiki, but after nine months, I said to Elaine, "I'd like to do my Reiki two." I did, and I knew as I completed it that I'd go on to Reiki master and teach.

Creativity comes in many forms, and I found myself teaching little workshops about angels, chakras, and sharing channeled meditations.

On one occasion after a workshop, I thought, *There are books and oracle cards for angels, dolphins, mermaids, and crystals, which can give a sense of why they may appear in meditations or dreams, but what about mythical beings?*

I spent time researching on the internet looking for books and information, but couldn't find anything.

One day whilst driving, I thought about it. *How am I going to find the information?* The words appeared in my head: "You are doing it."

It wasn't a voice; it was a strong sense of knowing, and only the second time it happened to me in this way.

Back at home, I sourced a couple of books on myths, legends, and folklore. Once they arrived, I sat with pen and paper, picked a mythical being, read about them, and waited to see what happened.

I'm channeling messages from the mythical realm.

I went from living on my wits as a people pleaser to learning to say no to others and yes to myself; from turning the news off and not reading newspapers to learning Reiki and metamorphic technique, embracing sound energy, and accepting that I'm a channel. I also speak light language.

Another upgrade of my creativity is channeling poems, and this one came to me for this book.

Living Art
By Sara Jane

Living is art
Life is the canvas
Experiences are the paint

How you color your canvas is your choice
Color it with happiness
Paint it with joy
Splash it with laughter
Sketch it with love

Outline it with experiences
Shape it with travel
Fill it with connections

Fill your senses with nature
Let your eyes see the cacophony of color
The beauty of flowers
The majesty of trees
The blue of the seas
The light of the sun, the moon and the stars

Open your ears to the music of the wind
The songs of the birds
The buzzing of insects
The symphony of waterfalls and waves
The rustling of leaves

Feel the caress of the breeze
The warmth of the sun
The kiss of the rain as it falls on your skin

Open your heart
Free your mind
Music, color, poetry, and more
Are all there for you to find

As I released the need to please others, I took better care of myself, and my stress levels decreased drastically.

Worrying about what others thought of me became a thing of the past. I even had the confidence at a mind, body, spirit event I attended with Elaine and a couple of her other Reiki and metamorphic technique students to say, "We need to do some sound for this room and the event."

The room's energies weren't good and the event wasn't doing well. I knew we had to bring the full energy of our toning into the room.

I had no fear, no concerns—something only a few short years before, I couldn't have done.

The four of us stood in a circle on our stand, closed our eyes, and started to tone. We felt the energies shift and lighten; the remaining time was happier for all.

The toning vibration grew through me, initially working on a physical, muscular, and skeletal level, moving inwards to people's body systems and organs, clearing muscular tension, headaches, migraines, and more. It supported the clearing of blockages in the intestinal tract and released water retention.

Then, there was the day I felt someone's bones move under my hands—no pressure applied.

It didn't stop there; I've found it can work at a deep, cellular memory level, supporting people to reconnect with their inner child to heal the hurt, pain, and trauma of their early years.

One thing I learnt is that I channel the sound; it isn't me. I always ask to work with the highest energies who wish to work with me, and I invite in the client's angels, guides, and guardians.

As I've just said, I channel the sound as I channel the Reiki energy. That's when it came to me: I bring Vocal Reiki.

I've opened my life to experiences, and there have been many of them: abseiling off a local water tower, zip-wires, flying a helicopter, doing a wing walk, climbing the highest peaks in England, Wales, and Scotland, and more sedately throwing a pot in a private pottery lesson, making two pots and a dish, which I now happily use at home.

These and more, plus the beautiful gift of the energy techniques, have supported me to expand from the shy, scared little girl and young adult I once was to the person I am today.

Creativity has also bloomed. Over the past few years, I've knitted three blankets, created out of triangles I crocheted together, lined with a fleece blanket and crocheted edging, multicolored and loved by my mother and sisters (200 hours of work to create each, and no pattern to follow).

I enjoy coloring in adult coloring books. Activities like this help me switch off at the end of the day, to unwind, destress, and get a better night's sleep. I always open the Reiki channel as I go to sleep, for myself and all those on my healing list.

If someone had told me I'd write poetry and books, learn energy healing techniques, give talks sharing sound energy, messages from dragons and mythical beings, speaking light language, well, I'd have told them they were crazy.

Yet here I'm doing all of that and more, and it's all due to working with and supporting my inner child to heal from the trauma of my early years.

As she has healed and feels loved, I've stepped from my insecurities and opened to new experiences, physical, emotional, and mental, I found myself growing into the gifts I feel I'm here to bring.

Creativity has no beginning and no ending; it's limitless and can be used, in its own unique way, in every aspect of life.

Bring a little art, creativity, energy, music, poetry, and more into your life every day and experience the changes that occur within you.

I walk every day. I'm lucky to have a small woodland local to me, which has supported my connection with my intuition and younger selves. Bringing me insights and understandings of some of the things that happened to me.

On one occasion, when I invited my inner child to join me, the meditation I share with you below flowed through our walk together.

THE TOOL

Open to your inner child, let him or her teach you how to play again, laugh, and have fun. As a child, you most likely drew and painted, danced, and sang your own songs. Creativity was rife within you, and for too many, was stifled because of those who didn't deem it good enough.

INNER CHILD WALKING MEDITATION

A walking meditation to connect with and have some quality me-time with your inner child, supporting them to feel seen, heard, and loved, freeing their suppressed creativity.

You can do this by finding a quiet space to sit, meditating, and going to a place that brings back happy memories from your childhood, inviting your younger self in.

Or, if you feel comfortable doing this outside whilst walking in nature, you can take yourself into woodlands, a park, by a river or stream, to the seashore, somewhere that your younger self would enjoy.

As you are walking or sitting, invite your inner child to join you. You could start by just putting your hand out so they can take it.

Let them choose what they would like to do—kick up the leaves, jump in a puddle, climb a tree, paddle in the sea, build a sandcastle—there are so many choices. Or they may just like to talk. Listen with your heart, help them feel heard.

As they relax and feel safe in your company, they will feel free to play, laugh, and have fun with you, awakening the creative energy that's already inside you, empowering the joy of creativity for and from your child within.

Enjoy this time with them and know you can do this as often as you choose. Let your child teach you the freedom and innocence of the beautiful being you are.

GIFTS FOR YOU

To support you further in connecting with your younger self and your creativity, I am sharing three gifts with you. The link is at the foot of my bio, called "claim your gifts."

They are a guided meditation, "play and the inner child," especially supporting those of you who prefer guided meditations.

There is a second meditation to bring back the vibrancy of color into your life, "a rainbow meditation ~ a gift from the universe," recharging and re-energizing your chakras, your main energy centers.

Finally, I have included a "light language message," especially for readers of this book. This is a message that will be understood by your heart and soul, helping to activate your creativity, supporting you along your chosen artistic path, whatever that may be for you.

In today's beautiful world, more and more of us choose not to follow the crowd. We do our own thing, our own way. I'm definitely one of those.

Many are being diagnosed as neurodiverse, wired differently, meaning they don't see things as normal people do, don't understand things the same way, and struggle with what many consider simple. They can't make head or tail of these things, but they see things in ways others can't.

Opening to our differences, exploring our strengths rather than our weaknesses, gives us access to so much more creativity and wisdom.

If you feel that you're different, honor those differences and accept yourself for who you are. I do, and yes, I'm different.

Maybe that is why I can do the things I do and can't do the things I struggle with.

Sara Jane is the founder of Gift of Healing TV, a live weekly program sharing interviews with many different practitioners, supporting health and wellbeing on all levels.

They also share meditations, exercises, and conversations to support your healing journey. All the recordings are on the catch-up pages of the website, creating a wonderful free resource.

In 2005, Sara took the leap to self-employment as a Complementary Health Therapist, learning Reiki, Indian Head Massage, Metamorphic Technique, Thai Foot Massage, Ear Candling, and Quantum Touch, she is also the creator of Vocal Reiki, as described in the chapter above.

Sara is a teacher, holding workshops and courses in person and online, and is an international speaker and author, including a #1 international bestseller.

Prior to 2005, Sara worked in retail to area manager level, office management for two toy companies, managed public houses with her first husband, went into insurance, and worked with children with learning difficulties and behavioral problems.

Sara has discovered she's a channel for dragons and many other mythical beings, sharing monthly messages from them and a monthly message in light language.

A fun fact: Sara was a trainee handler with the wolves at the UK Wolf Conservation Trust.

Connect with Sara:

Claim your gifts here: https://vocalreiki.eo.page/expressive-arts-gifts

Websites: https://vocalreiki.com/

https://www.giftofhealingtv.com/

https://ourmagicalfriends.com/

Facebook: https://www.facebook.com/SaraJane.SpiritOfFreedom

LinkedIn: https://www.linkedin.com/in/sara-jane-94b9a117/

YouTube: https://www.youtube.com/@GiftOfHealingTV

https://www.youtube.com/@SaraJane-Vocal-Reiki

https://www.youtube.com/@OurMythicalFriends

Amazon:
https://www.amazon.co.uk/stores/author/B005MZHU42/allbooks

The expression arts have been the thread that binds my life together. Growing up in a creative family, art was intrinsic to many aspects of my life. From sewing to woodworking and culinary skills, creativity was everywhere. Instinctively, art college became my calling and graphic design my passion.

Laura Elizabeth Ballerini

"

THE FALL

SHIFT PERSPECTIVE AND RISE ABOVE LIFE'S CHALLENGES

Laura Elizabeth Ballerini, CGD

MY STORY

I never asked for a sign before this moment, or after it.

Looking into the cloudless summer sky, I whispered, "Dear God, please give me a sign I'm on the right path."

Somehow, it seemed like I was testing fate—manipulating God to show me the future. But I needed validation for my huge project swaddled in an envelope in the backseat.

Within the hour, a sign was presented to me.

I confidently walked to meet my Goddaughter for her birthday, along with her mom, my long-time friend. We were meeting at our favourite coffee shop located in an urban village. The early morning hour evaded the usual hustle and bustle of this inner-city mecca, known for its unique shops, live music, and cultural events. As my quiet stroll began, the sun sprinkled warm kisses on my face, but a cool breeze whisked them away unmercifully.

Is this a subtle sign?

Rather arrogantly, I focused on how nicely my wedge sandals complemented my outfit, believing I looked chic and elegant. The upper suede portion matched my blue blouse and navy capris, scattered with white polka dots. A dark blue sweater with pearl buttons slung off my shoulders, the sleeves fashionably tied in front.

Suddenly, the uneven pavement interrupted my proud runway walk.

Trying to mould my high heels to the bumpy path, my shoes and my body betrayed me. I teetered awkwardly back and forth, attempting to balance on my cork soles, but couldn't correct my doomed destination. I clumsily fell onto the pavement, landing face-first on the sidewalk. The upper left part of my body took the brunt of my tumble. My instinct was to get up quickly and carry on my java journey. But the impact of the fall forced me to lie there for a moment and catch my breath. I tried desperately to gather any ounce of pride I had left in the cracks of the concrete.

Initially, when I headed to my engagement, I recalled a man walked behind me, and a young waitress busily prepared the sidewalk patio. She gave me a quick glance of approval.

Now, sprawled on the sidewalk, I heard a male gasp from behind me, coupled with the squeal of rubber tennis shoes screeching to a halt—inevitably trying to avoid a pileup. While the man and the waitress undoubtedly saw me plummet to the ground, neither of them came to help me. They most likely sensed the embarrassment oozing from my fashionably dressed carcass, collapsed before them. I didn't look up, thinking I could become invisible. Making eye contact would make the situation real. Maybe I can just slither away.

I finally pulled myself up, grateful my dark sunglasses hid my humiliation. Rather than continuing to the café, I quickly headed back to the car. I couldn't open the door swiftly enough. As I slid into the driver's seat, emotions came fast and furious—hysterical, uncontrollable sobbing.

After an excessive number of teardrops poured down my face, my meticulously applied mascara moved like a mudslide into the blush on my cheeks. A murky pool gathered there and slid down my chin to the pristine pearl buttons of my sweater. I was a mess. I would be sore and bruised. But my ego took the biggest hit of all.

As my hysteria transitioned into a slightly less frenzied state, I instinctively grabbed my phone. I shakily texted the birthday girl to inform her of my fall, forcing myself to sound as casual as possible. "Sorry, my love. I won't be able to meet you guys after all." My party of two was disappointed, but we promised to reschedule later.

Missing the birthday celebration was one thing, but I had more on my plate that demanded attention. My huge, personal project sat patiently in the backseat—the manuscript of my new book, *The Green Velvet Chair,* waiting to be delivered for review. While many of my beta readers received a digital copy of this document, my dear friend from grade school preferred a hard copy to read and mark up with her trusty red pen. At the time of her request, I was delighted to comply, but now I had to drop off this package discreetly so she wouldn't see me. I set some tight deadlines for myself, and today was a non-negotiable delivery date.

So, I collected myself as much as possible, applied spit to clean my makeup-smeared face, and focused on my drive to her house.

Upon arrival, I silently exited the car, gently grabbed the envelope from the back seat, and softly closed the door. Moving with covert precision to the front door mailbox, I quietly strained to place the large package into the small box, but to no avail. I had to fold and squish the lovingly designed cover and inside pages into the confined steel container. The paper ripped as I obstinately pushed it inside. My beta reader was now getting a shredded copy of my heartfelt manuscript.

Why did I ask for a sign? Was my dramatic fall and bruised ego a sign?

IGNORING THE SIGN

As time went on, I stubbornly continued with the beta testing of my book. For weeks, concrete feedback and glowing praise flowed back to me.

The stories were well received, and my beta audience was delighted. I went on to produce my book, mindful of the dreaded widows and orphans at the end of each paragraph. My editor and proofreaders were acutely aware of correcting typos, grammatical, and formatting issues with dizzying expertise. Finally, we were ready to publish!

My book was uploaded to online stores. I promoted launch day for weeks with a daily countdown on my social channels. My book proudly reached #21 on a major book publishing website—a huge feat. Congratulations seemed to be in order, but more urgent matters derailed me. Another "sign" came to haunt me.

Three months earlier, and well after my fall, I found a lump in my left breast. I initially thought it was nothing. But I diligently visited my doctor, and went through a battery of tests, many of which put a crimp in my publishing schedule. The diagnosis arrived right smack dab in the middle of the birthing of my book, and it was impossible to ignore this sign.

Cancer.

Was my fateful fall last summer a foreshadowing of this disease? Was this the sign God was presenting to me? The "sign" wasn't about my book after all; it was about my breast.

My life was about to change. Swiftness—not for my book launch, but for surgery—upended my carefully planned schedule. After my initial online success, *The Green Velvet Chair* was orphaned.

WITH LOSS CAME MORE LOSS

A drastic shift in perspective was about to transpire. Looking back, much of my cancer journey centered around loss. Outwardly, it was hair loss. At first, strands gently released, but after weeks of chemo treatment, clumps quickly exited my follicles. I feared that I would end up looking like a monster, with patches of bare scalp next door to clusters of long, brittle hair.

Before the monster appeared, my daughters and I went to a local wig shop that supported people like me. Unfortunately, the showroom was busy, and we had to wait. My anxiety rose as I stared at the foam heads covered in a variety of styles, colours, and lengths of cranial prosthesis. When my turn came, I ordered a hat of hair made of long, beautiful Asian and Indian locks. The order was processed, and the stylist prepped me for my hairpiece. Sitting in the salon chair, the mirror reflected my daughters perched quietly behind me—balanced uneasily on the edge of their seats. As the electric razor mowed my head in rows, like a thatched lawn, I could see their brave smiles cloaked with anxiety. Undue compliments came from the back row as my hair fell to the shop floor.

"Mom, your eyes look so much bigger," my oldest said.

My younger daughter echoed, "Yes, and you have a beautifully shaped head."

This was the day my mothering efforts paid off. All those sleepless nights of rocking and cradling my crying infants were realized. My prize sat on the hard bench behind me. These precious babies grew up into remarkable human beings. As they achieve incredible career success, my crowning glory was seeing the tender, compassionate women they became. While my physical identity changed that day, my soul was forever etched with gratitude for these precious girls.

Writing became my healing implement as I moved forward. As this story will attest, I relentlessly share the trauma of my hair loss. I think it was because I'm a visual person, and my bald head literally exposed the insecurities I hid for years. More makeup, longer tendrils, and bigger earrings always masked the self-doubt that plagued me. I could conceal the many changes going on inside me—but the outside? Damn, it exposed my rawness. Oddly enough, this is when I discovered my quietly fierce, inner badass.

Survival forced me to turn my vulnerability into my strength. Although cancer guided me with grace and honesty, it was time to move on. After my initial book was orphaned, I recently released the second edition of *The Green Velvet Chair: Sometimes Inspiration Comes from the Most Unlikely Places,* filled with more stories.

I worked hard to find my voice and adapt to this brave new world. But sad memories forced their way back in, and created shifts in perspective. I started to understand, and accept loss differently.

AN OLD MEMORY BROUGHT CLARITY

After my breast cancer surgery, various treatments followed. As an overachiever, I always strived for top marks, but in this case, my unusually high recurrence score taunted me. Chemo came with a vengeance.

Oddly enough, I wasn't too frightened of getting sick, but as mentioned earlier, I was terrified about losing my hair. You see, as a shy, quiet introvert, I hid behind my hair my entire life—except for the time my mom marched me to the hairdresser as a little girl, for the dreaded pixie cut. She was frustrated with my long, tangled mane that became too unruly for her to brush. I remember running behind Mom as we hiked through the tall grass in the field, en route to the coiffeur at the local strip mall.

To be clear, my mom was a kind, gentle woman whom I loved dearly. She was my hero. But, as a busy mom of four, my hair was always a challenge for her to style in a timely manner.

It was Saturday morning, and the shop was full. In her haste, Mom didn't make an appointment, so we had to wait impatiently for the next available stylist. Eventually, I was greeted by a pleasant, young woman—probably an apprentice—who regretfully guided me to a chair. She had no scissors; they were all in use. So, she proceeded to use a styling razor. She pulled and tugged at my snarled knot of hair. She started trimming from the bottom, hoping a set of scissors would soon become available. I remember the rough jerking of my mousey strands as she proceeded to cut the twisted locks with what felt like a very dull straight edge. It hurt, and she kept apologizing.

Oh, my gosh, how much longer was this going to take? I continued to brace myself on the salon chair. We were both uncomfortable, but time was of the essence. Hoping for a quick end to this torture was our main goal.

Perhaps it was this pixie cut that instilled a sense of protectionism for my hair. What was once precious to me was hacked off my head like an impetuous enemy. Each strand was painfully removed until I was presented with severely cropped tufts. I cried.

This painful salon chair memory presented itself as I tried to make sense of my current obsession with my hair loss.

MOVING AHEAD

As I grew up, I managed to look after my own hair. My tousled crown gave me shelter and confidence. It was thick, long, and lush. It was my shining star. Complete strangers would stop me to comment on my hair. My husband would shake his head and laugh. "Wow, that hair of yours sure gets lots of attention. No wonder you take such good care of it."

It was my pride and joy. But more importantly, it was my shield against the world—it protected me and kept me safe. It was my soft armor.

But my armor was under attack with aggressive chemotherapy, and it was in a battle it wasn't going to win. Soon, it surrendered to the powerful treatments on a Sunday afternoon in May.

This was the day I planted my flowers so I could watch them grow as the cancer-fighting toxins flowed through my veins. The soft, colourful petals would give me purpose. I would feed them through the warm months ahead, and bask in their beauty. But as I planted them, a soft breeze was catching strands of my freshly poisoned locks and taking them away.

Serendipitously, some of the tresses landed in the flowers I planted. They became entwined within the plants. It was actually quite mesmerizing. There was a dance, a waltz, if you will, with my hair and the draughts of air. A slow rhythm—a gust of air came and took my hair into its arms, lovingly placing it within the flora. This is when something in me shifted.

I could have cried and felt sorrow for this loss of hair. But it was different from the hacking of my tresses as a child. It was gentle and purposeful. There seemed to be a give and take to the movement of the wind and the hair, almost like a gentle goodbye.

It's going to be okay, I thought.

On this perfect day, I could feel, see, and hear the arrival of spring. The warm sun was shining, the children were playing in the nearby park, and the birds were singing.

What a great day to be alive, I thought.

Almost immediately, an overtly optimistic thought popped into my head. With deep compassion, I hoped the birds would come by, capture my hair in their talons, and use my much-loved locks to line their nests for their babies. That gave me such relief, comfort, and hope. My soft armor became someone else's warm, cozy sheath.

That was the moment I became a perspective shifter.

"Now it's your turn…"

THE TOOL

BECOME A PERSPECTIVE SHIFTER

SHIFT PERSPECTIVE AND RISE ABOVE LIFE'S CHALLENGES

My three-step process will guide you to shift perspective, but it's not easy. It takes dedication, practice, and inner work.

1. **FEEL** *with a compassionate heart*

   When life throws you a curveball, the reality is that most of us tend to go to the dark side first—the ugly, negative side. To simply toss your anger and frustration aside isn't that easy. But this is where we must start. While we tend to focus on the worst-case scenario, it's important to realign yourself to the other side. What's the lesson here? What's the message? What's the positive side to this equation? As an extreme example, let's say you've been told you have cancer. This was real for me. I chose to shift my perspective to this: "Well, it's a wake-up call. I need to make some necessary changes in my life through diet, exercise, and state of mind."

   Focus on flipping the switch in your head and heart. This shift will create a calmness and tenderness moving forward—starting with an open, honest heart.

2. **SEE** *with eyes wide open*

   While we all get distracted with the visual noise of the world, look beyond the "eye candy." Look inside and outside yourself.

Sometimes it's as simple as acknowledging the squirrels dancing in the trees or watching the shadows become longer as the sun sets in the sky. Look inside yourself, too. Maybe start a doodle diary. Draw your dreams, your thoughts, and your aspirations.

While this step asks you to see with eyes wide open, that can be taken metaphorically. The irony is that sometimes when you close your eyes, you see things more clearly. Seek the beauty around you, and you'll find it within as well.

3. **LISTEN** *to your inner voice*

Pay attention to the words within you. Negative thoughts swirling in our heads make us feel insecure and inferior. Just silently scream, "Stop!" This is a powerful technique. Think of words that bring you peace and joy.

Also, listen to your soul. That quiet, soft message that persists inside is meaningful. It's trying to tell you something. You need to listen. While it can be easily dismissed, it's part of the power that helps shift perspective. Additionally, when you're surrounded by people, listen to what isn't being said. Being sensitive to this dialogue frequently exposes the underlying essence—but you have to really listen and hear what is being said or not said. Frequently, the message is in the silence.

In my experience, we need to merge these three steps together to shift perspective. Simply practicing one of them isn't enough. We need to feel, see, and listen in order to shift. It takes practice and a conscious effort. This shift may come more easily to some of us than others. I have found it makes me more in tune with my world, more empathetic to others, and has sharpened my critical thinking skills. In our complex, sometimes volatile world, the ability to shift perspective is more important than it's ever been.

We all face our own set of challenges in life. Rise above them with a conscious shift in perspective. Feel with a compassionate heart; see with your eyes wide open; and listen to the silence. It will guide you and shift your perspective so you'll never have to ask for a sign again. It's right there in front of you.

Laura Elizabeth Ballerini is an accomplished designer running a thriving communications firm for over 25 years. She started her creative journey in the Advertising Department of *The Calgary Herald* during the heyday of newspapers. Ballerini has a degree in Visual Communications from The Alberta University of the Arts and is a recipient of numerous awards. While she's a quiet and introverted creative, Laura recently found her inner badass and radiates her "quietly fierce" disposition in her work and personal life.

As the author of ***The Green Velvet Chair: Sometimes Inspiration Comes from the Most Unlikely Places,*** Laura gathered a collection of heartfelt stories depicting how art and design influence us and spur creativity in our everyday lives. The essays are viewed through her unique creative lens. Many capture a piercing parallel between creativity and business.

Running her own design boutique over many decades has enabled Laura to work with a variety of clients from many industries. She deliberately chose to ensure her client base was diverse and sees this as her strength. Laura comes to the table with fresh eyes and approaches every project with unique interest and expertise.

Ballerini lives in Calgary, Alberta, with her husband, children, and a pretentious cat named Gooey.

Be creatively fierce.

Embrace universal experiences meant to spark awareness and awaken us to the rich fields of creativity all around us.

Connect with Laura:

Websites: https://badass-ballerini.com/

https://blubrown.com/

Book Resource: https://badass-ballerini.com/download-ShiftPerspective

LinkedIn: https://www.linkedin.com/in/lauraballerini/

Instagram: https://www.instagram.com/badassballerini

The most important thing to me about expressive arts is using your artwork, literature, music, etc., to express your identity, personal experiences, and to share your thoughts about any issues in our society that you feel aren't getting the attention they need.

Mari Jack

12

RUNNING WITH CREATIVITY

EXERCISING YOUR WAY TO WRITE WITH PASSION

Mari Jack, Romance Novelist and Musician

MY STORY

How did I come to be a novelist with no previous professional writing experience?

I had more background in playing the flute than anything to do with literature. How do I now have published contemporary romance novels under my name when I was a terrible essay writer at school, often getting less-than-good marks in that area of study? How have I now got so many supporters as a writer and flute player when throughout my life, people shook their fingers at me every time I made a choice of my own?

Mariana has failed all her practice essays so far this year. If she doesn't improve, she won't pass English at all, one school report read.

Yeah, well, if you think that discouraged me from writing, you're wrong!

Let me introduce myself: My real name is Mariana Jackson, but my books are published under the name Mari Jack, and I live in New Zealand.

I'm a concert band musician and a contemporary romance writer.

I'm neurodiverse; I have the condition formerly known as Asperger's Syndrome. I'm glad that name seems to be dying out, as apparently, it has Nazi connections—according to an article published in the journal *Molecular Autism* in April 2018, Dr. Hans Asperger, whom the condition is named after, joined organisations affiliated with the Nazi party, legitimised policies including forced sterilisations, and cooperated with child euthanasia projects.

I also hate being labelled an Aspie. I've heard other neurodiverse people label themselves that, and quite frankly, I've never understood why anyone would want to call themselves such a name. To me, it sounds like internalised ableism, and if no one from a racial minority, LGBTQ+ community, or any other marginalised group would use a slur on themselves, no neurodiverse person should, either.

LABELS AND LIES

Growing up as a neurodiverse person, I heard the word "no" more than "yes." Whenever I wanted to try something new without anyone else pushing me into it, I was always told, "No." People thought I was incapable of making choices about my own life. They believed I was too shy to learn a musical instrument and tried to squash me into a box where I wouldn't fit. You know what I mean when I say they tried to put me in a box; they attempted to perpetuate every ableist stereotype on me.

"I don't think you're capable of working with people. You don't have any empathy." Lie.

"You can't handle constructive criticism." Another lie.

"You're too shy to play the flute in front of an audience." Also a lie.

Then, when someone was talking about me to someone else, "Mari is very timid. She's scared of talking to people." Total BS!

Worst of all, every time people tried to make my personal choices for me, they tried to play the hero: "We're only trying to help you." That is one of the most toxic phrases I've ever heard. Helping someone doesn't involve interfering with their freedom of choice, and taking away a neurodiverse person's rights under the guise of helping them should never be tolerated anywhere.

If they weren't shaking their fingers at me, they used my passion for playing the flute to turn me into inspiration porn, trying to make it look like a huge miracle that I could play an instrument *despite my neurodiversity.* "I think it's amazing that you're learning the flute! How about you play a special tune just for me?" one teacher from my school days asked me. Of course, I refused.

As for my writing career, well, I didn't always want to be a writer. At primary (elementary) school, I enjoyed creative writing. I loved to write mysteries and ghost stories at the time, but the low marks I got for essays in high school put me off writing in general.

My romance writing career began as an adult during a particularly bad year. I worked jobs in the horticulture and fruit industry that didn't feel right for me. I only worked those jobs because other people, particularly those in employment recruitment agencies, thought they were most suitable for me.

But they weren't. Not only did I find the tasks I had to do in those jobs stressful to the point they wrecked my physical and mental health, but the supervisors also had unrealistic expectations for me. They expected me to work at a faster pace than I was naturally capable of and used unnecessary aggression on me over the smallest slip-ups. Then, when I tried to report their behaviour to the appropriate authorities, I was met with the following responses:

"Don't you think you're being too harsh?"

"You're just being bitter."

"You can stop being so negative!"

These statements display the very stereotypes society keeps putting on neurodiverse people: lack of empathy, inability to put oneself in others' shoes, etc. This shows utter hypocrisy on these people's part.

If they weren't accusing me of taking things the wrong way, they defended the perpetrator, saying things like, "It was just a misunderstanding," and, "They're just ignorant, they don't understand neurodiversity." I'm sick of hearing excuses like that; not only does it add to victims' distress, it gives perpetrators the message that as long as they *don't understand* their victims, they can get away with bullying, discrimination, and acts of hate. It therefore fuels perpetrators to choose to be ignorant about neurodiversity.

WRITING THROUGH LOSS

Also, that year, I lost two people close to me only months apart. One was a bandmate, and the other was my grandmother. When I lost my bandmate, a trumpet player, to brain cancer at the much-too-young age of 47, I had very supportive friends, but some people made the insensitive assumption that I didn't know the bandmate well enough to grieve for her. Then, just as I was getting over that loss, my grandmother passed away from pancreatic cancer. We all knew that was going to happen; she'd been sick for months. But her death still hit me like a ton of bricks.

It wasn't all bad, though; that year, I discovered my love of contemporary romance stories when I picked up a few Mills & Boon and Bella Andre books for the first time. I found I particularly loved exploring the sexual side of romance (add winking emoji here) as well as the simple falling-in-love part and dark character pasts. I began to toy with the idea of writing my own stories again—this time romance books—but wasn't sure exactly what kind of characters or storylines to write.

Then, at a band barbecue after my grandmother's death, I talked with a fellow flute player about our experiences with flirtatious male conductors, and that gave me the idea to write romance stories about female musicians falling in love with their conductors. That was the healing I needed from my two losses.

Writing has also given me a chance to speak out about social justice issues, especially disability rights, without people trying to talk over me. As a neurodiverse person, I feel these issues are being cruelly tossed aside in our society. To say it's extremely shocking how many people I've come across on social media who deny social injustice even exists is an understatement. These people are downright insensitive and clearly incapable of putting themselves in other people's shoes or feeling empathy, just like the people who accused me of being "harsh," "bitter," or "negative."

For example, a comment I wrote on Facebook got a reply along these lines:

Why are you writing about "injustice?" It's all just liars whining about how other people treat them like crap. How about you show me some examples of the so-called injustice you perceive?

Seriously? How would you feel if you were subjected to injustices and other people denied your experiences? In fact, have you even experienced injustice at all in your life?

AMPLIFYING DEMOCRACY

We need to raise our voices louder when we hear about incidents of hate crime, unnecessary police brutality, or anything like that. I believe that adding my voice to other writers who've written books about injustice will amplify the voices of democracy.

And writing steamy romances was a way to make sure no one would view me as a child in an adult's body ever again. For many of you who are neurodiverse, you will know how it feels to be treated like a child well into your adulthood—people speaking to you like you're five years old, pointing out the obvious to you, giving you age-inappropriate gifts, etc. These things have happened to me. I know some neurodiverse people retain childlike interests and behaviour into adulthood, but not all of them do. Since I went public about writing adult romance stories, people now treat me like a proper adult.

I wrote a neurodiverse opera singer in some of my romance books. This character, instead of being a stereotypical "psychopath" villain, pitiable, or inspiration porn, is a strong, feisty disability rights activist who stands up for others, writes blogs speaking out against ableism, and never allows anyone to treat her like a "singing miracle" or exploit her in any way. She has a very dark past, facing more than just ableist discrimination throughout her life, but that's the fuel for her to stand her ground and keep fighting for what she believes in. She's the main female character in my book *Dawn Rising;* she travels to Los Angeles to take the leading role in an opera show and falls in love with the leading tenor, who struggles with dyslexia himself.

In addition to my musician romances, I'm working on a trilogy about tango dancers falling in love. I became fascinated with tango, both Argentine and ballroom, after watching *Dancing with the Stars* and online videos about tango, as well as reading books about it. I also gave Argentine tango a try when I went to classes at my local tango club and attended milongas there. Both kinds of tango are seductive and passionate dances, and I thought they'd be great topics for spicy romance stories.

As for the future, I'm planning to write a YA novel—with romantic elements, of course. It will be about a group of high school students who form a social justice group at their school, along with one of their teachers, after a student's former friends suddenly turn against her when she gets diagnosed with a disability.

DOING IT MY WAY

As unique as these story ideas sound, my writing didn't come without tough hurdles. Agents and publishers rejected my work because I don't follow trends in the romance market (for example, hockey romances or cowboy romances popular at certain times). I find it difficult to follow trends or know who wants what kind of books and when, so I prefer to write my own kind of stories whenever I want to. I feel much more comfortable doing my own thing, rather than writing what others tell me to write about. Not only that, if I follow trends, I feel my books will be too similar to those of other romance writers when I want my work to stand out among everyone else's.

Like, why would I want to be like everyone else when I can be myself and do things my way?

That's why I'm self-published, and I use whichever editors and cover designers I choose for my books. I still have to work to editors' deadlines as with traditional publishers and submit my manuscripts to them by certain dates, but I can manage my schedule easily when I've got my other commitments, like musical ones, sorted out.

Some people still try to discourage me from writing to this day. "You might think your books are wonderful, but other people might not," one person said to me recently.

"Yeah, well, that's not going to stop me!" I fired back, making it clear that if they have a problem with me writing, it's their problem.

They think they're using water to put out my fire, but instead, they're using petrol (gasoline to my US and Canadian readers). The more someone tells me not to write or play the flute, the more I'll want to keep doing it. Despite that, I still get frequent bouts of impostor syndrome as a result of other people's attitudes towards me. My natural rebellion is much stronger. I think every one of us has natural rebellion within ourselves. Don't be afraid to use it whenever you feel society's constraints.

GO FOR IT!

Writing kept me grounded when I struggled to cope with what life threw at me. Don't give up what you love because someone else tells you to, or society in general thinks it's not suitable for people like you. It's especially cruel and insensitive to tell someone to give up something that's a huge part of their life. You never know; it might be part of their training for their dream job, or they could be going through a lot in life, and this particular activity might be the only thing keeping them afloat.

It's also unacceptable to tell someone to give up their dream job just because you failed to achieve yours. Some people used their own failure to achieve their life goals as an excuse to do this to me, and I fought back. Being unhappy with your own life doesn't give you the right to make me unhappy, too. Now, here I am in the world of romance writing and music, keeping the fire of rebellion burning as long as I can.

For those of you who are considering writing as a potential career, go for it. You never know where your writing might lead you; your books, newspaper columns, etc., might help vulnerable or marginalised people in our society find their own voices and speak up. You could help them feel listened to and less alone in the world.

In between writing sessions, it helps to do other activities to get inspiration and make your literary flow active. Especially physical activities, like running or gardening, which can make up for the lack of exercise in writing, can really trigger some strong ideas for writing. It's good to get exercise when your job involves sitting at a computer for much of the time.

THE TOOL

I have more than one tool I use to help manage my anxiety around my creativity: playing my flute, listening to music, and reading.

One tool I will explain here is meditative running in between writing sessions. Not only does it burn physical energy when my job involves a lot of sitting at a computer, but running also drains negative emotional energy, pushes away my impostor syndrome, and gets the creative flow going.

Here's how I use meditative running:

1. As I begin running, I focus on the distance of my planned route. How much time do I have to run it? Will I be able to release all my emotional energy and activate the creative flow in that time?

2. When I'm running, I let my momentum carry me forward, slowing down or stopping only to get through a gate or tie my shoelaces if they've come undone. I also drink in the scenery around me, making the most of my peaceful surroundings, even if dogs are barking incessantly or someone is having a noisy party nearby.

3. I also allow my mind to focus on whatever writing duties I have at the time. When I run, the creative part of my mind is at its most active, and I make a mental note to retain any new ideas for stories I come up with during that time.

4. After finishing my running session, I feel gratitude for how I released my stress, burned my energy, and fuelled my creative flow.

Gratitude also helps reduce my levels of exhaustion and tiredness after I've finished running.

5. While my creative flow is active, I begin my next writing session. I let the creative flow pour out into the book I'm currently working on.

The idea of running regularly may seem stressful to some people, and it may feel like a chore when you start to do it. However, according to *WebMD's* fitness and exercise webpage, when you run, your body releases hormones called endorphins and serotonin, which play a part in improving your mood. This webpage adds that studies show running can improve your memory and ability to learn, which are important to my writing, as I have to remember storylines when writing a book series. Also, I sometimes have to research topics I want to write about, like police procedures, so I can get them as accurate as possible in my books.

After you finish running, your body releases endocannabinoid hormones. These hormones flood your bloodstream and move into your brain, providing feelings of reduced stress. This can be extremely beneficial for people in creative industries, and all of the above is definitely true for me. As I've mentioned in my step-by-step process for meditative running, my creative flow seems to be most active when I'm exercising, and it reduces my level of exhaustion when I've finished running.

Other websites, as well as WebMD, state that activities that are good for your physical health are also good for your mental health. When your physical health is at its best, your mental health and emotional wellbeing have a greater chance of being in their top condition as well. I'd recommend a daily running session to anyone in any kind of creative industry who wants to increase their levels of physical exercise. When doing a fitness regime, the release of hormones through your system can make all sorts of creative ideas come to you that you wouldn't normally think of when not physically active.

Resource: WebMD Editors, "WebMD Health & Fitness Guide: The Basics of Exercise," WebMD, accessed July 9, 2025, https://www.webmd.com/fitness-exercise/guide-chapter-fitness-overview.

Mari Jack is a flute player with many years of experience in bands and orchestras. Her musical life combined with her love of contemporary romance stories inspired her to write musician romances. She has now published the *Allegretto Band* series (six books) and its spin-off series, *American Opera* (two books). Discovering a love of tango inspired her to create the *Tango Club Trilogy*.

Mari lives in Hawke's Bay, New Zealand. When not writing or playing her flute, she enjoys reading, running, and fawning over Art Deco fashions. She is also passionate about social justice, especially disability rights, and refuses to let anyone silence her over human rights issues—after all, it shouldn't be so hard to accept those who are different from you, and understand that bigotry is the problem, not people who are a certain gender, ethnic minority, disabled, or whatever. While no one chooses to be a member of those groups, hating people from those groups is a choice, and she knows what needs to be fixed here.

In addition to all this, Mari loves chocolate, pizza, pasta, and sushi, along with shopping, listening to jazz music, and watching TV crime shows at home.

Connect with Mari:

Website: http://www.mari-jack.com/

Facebook:
https://www.facebook.com/people/Mari-Jack/100083516284368/

Twitter/X: https://x.com/MariJackBooks

Instagram: https://www.instagram.com/marijack216/?hl=en

Goodreads:
https://www.goodreads.com/author/show/22490267.Mari_Jack

It's a great day to follow your dreams.
What are they?

The expressive arts allow one to connect to the potential we have deep within ourselves. They are a free and tangible way to let go of the stuff holding us back!

Mindy J. Trisko

13

FASHION YOUR MOOD

LET YOUR HEART BE YOUR PERSONAL STYLIST

Mindy J. Trisko, M. A.

"Change your skirt, change your life."

~ Mindy Trisko

MY STORY

And there I was, eight years old, laughing, spinning, and dancing around under the bright summer sun in a breezy, soft, playful dress that changed my life forever.

It was a hot Chicago summer after my third-grade year, and I couldn't wait to spend lazy days playing in the sprinkler, at the pool, or with my hilarious, freckled best friend Erin, whom I could always count on for rolling-on-the-floor belly laughs. My only thoughts were, *What time can I go to the pool today?* And, *please, Mom, can my best friend Erin come, too?*

To my great disappointment, my mom had a different agenda: We had to go to a family friend's birthday party. *Nooooooo!* Insert major pity party scene here.

MAJOR MOOD CHANGER

I stomped up the stairs—my noisy protest something all little girls innately know how to do—sat on the edge of my Laura Ashley pink rose-printed duvet, and gazed sullenly into my closet. *What on Earth am I going to wear to this yucky, no-good, boring party that I have to go to?*

Morosely, I stood in front of my little brown closet, absentmindedly thumbing through some dresses, when my hands stopped on this playful black-and-white printed dress. The top half of the dress was a black ribbed tank top sewn to a three-tiered, ruffled white cotton poplin skirt with a tiny black eyelash print all over it. *I love this dress!*

It was just the right combination of a breezy, uplifting tone while being comfortable enough for active, swirling, playful me. Yet it was also likely fancy enough to appease my mom's party dress standards. I felt instantly happy!

I raced back down the stairs to show Mom my dress choice, hoping and praying for her approval. *She said yes! I can wear the dress!* The party wasn't for three more hours, but I wanted to make sure the dress still fit.

I tossed it on, and my previous sour mood completely vanished. Life can be that simple for an eight-year-old: a cute dress, and voila! A big smile sprouts out of a previously dejected face. I wore that dress throughout the summer. Party or no party, I made my own fun any time I had that summer jewel on my body.

Fast forward to high school me, happily sewing and sketching garments in my free time. I fell in love with clothing and its magical power to transform my darkest moods. I sat in third period, contemplating my future after high school, when my sewing teacher asked me, "Did you know you can design and make clothes for a career?" *Huh? Seriously?*

I gladly took her advice. After high school, I earned a B.A. in Apparel Design and worked in New York City for major fashion designers such as Calvin Klein, Betsey Johnson, and Badgley Mischka. I traveled all over India to study natural fiber dyeing methods, owned a tailoring business, taught fashion design for over a decade, and am now a sustainable brand owner myself.

Little did eight-year-old me know how that one black-and-white printed dress would change my life forever.

Over the years, I've had a zillion transformational moments with clothing. I vividly recall how the blue sequined dress I wore to my senior prom made me feel like a celebrity. And what about those way-too-expensive, dark wash skinny jeans that had me feeling sexy and strutting around Soho, New York City, like I was Mick Jagger? My latest favorite mood transformation is an oversized neon orange hooded sweatshirt with slits at the side seams, which gives me a major sense of empowerment and boldness.

WEAR YOUR PRESCRIPTION

Like me, I'm sure you've also experienced how colors, textures, and shapes affect your mood. Science also validated that. And when you're aware of how these factors are influencing you, you can more consciously design the tone and mood of your day.

As someone who made it her life's career to study and express herself through fashion, I can teach you how to use your wardrobe to help you get into the mood and vibe you want to be in each day.

Who do you want to become? What do you need? Is today a day you need more energy, a pick-me-up? More confidence for a meeting or a date? Do you want to take the edge off and chill out? Look no further than your closet. The clothes hanging in your closet right now can do just that!

Why take a pill when you can wear your prescription?

Too good to be true? Get this: Our levels of self-assuredness and composure can rise based on how we dress. Over 96% of participants in a Northwestern University study felt their emotions changed based on how they dressed. ("Enclothed Cognition," 2012).

I always gravitate towards my oversized, cozy, knitted sweaters when I feel sluggish or a bit wiped out. *This feels like a big hug!* They always help to lift my mood with zero negative side effects.

In a *Vogue* magazine article, "Confidence Dressing: How Clothing Affects the Mind," several prominent women noted how what they wore made a difference in how they thought, and how it helped them handle different situations. These situations included business meetings with investors, fundraising, and job interviews (Bernard, 2012).

What you wear, and how you wear it, isn't only seen by others but by your psyche, and your psyche responds accordingly. It affects the way you feel and carry yourself.

When I need to feel empowered, I put on a crisply ironed white blouse. I pop the color, step into some cute heels and my favorite pair of jeans, and there's practically nothing I can't do!

> "Clothes can transform your mood. You wear a certain outfit, and you feel invincible."
>
> ~ Meryl Streep

> "When you wear something that makes you feel beautiful, it radiates out from you like sunshine."
>
> ~ Helen Mirren

> "I don't dress to impress myself. I dress to empower myself."
>
> ~ Serena Williams

So let's get you in your best mood via fashion—scientifically—starting today!

YOUR WARDROBE IS YOUR LABORATORY

Think of your wardrobe as your laboratory. Let's experiment with how clothes can help you feel better, depending on the mood and goals you want to set for each day. For example, when I feel tired, I sometimes reach for my old grey hoodie. *Hmmm. Does this grey sweatshirt put me in a better mood? Not really!* But if I pay closer attention, I reach for the floral blouse instead to lift my energy levels. *I feel like it's summer in Paris in this top!*

Let's experience the emotion of joy for a moment. I first felt clothing transform my emotions into joy with that playful black-and-white dress from when I was little.

What are your garments of joy?

Maybe it's that crazy-colored, hand-knit sweater your aunt made for you, or a special item you purchased on a romantic vacation in the Greek Isles. Or maybe it's that new top in your absolute favorite shade of blue!

One of my most special garments that makes me feel lighter and happier is a light blue dress I got on a special vacation with my partner.

I remember it was a gorgeous, crisp, sunny summer day in one of my favorite cities, Vancouver, British Columbia. Our bellies were full from a yummy lunch eaten while overlooking the bay. My partner and I leisurely strolled hand-in-hand through downtown. I spotted a sweet-looking dress in a window. "Look at that dress! Can we stop quickly?" *Please, please, please.*

We walked inside, and I grabbed the dress, along with a few other items to try on. As I slipped on the dress, it was yet another transformational moment for me. I pulled it over my head and felt a soft wave of calm and peace land on my shoulders, almost as if it was massaging them. *I love this dress. I feel so at ease in it.*

I stepped out of the dressing room and showed my partner. "Wow, you look beautiful!" he said. Beyond the fact that the soft blue dress felt soft on my skin, the memory of buying that dress with my partner, and the trip overall, always makes me smile with joy when I wear it.

Whatever these garments of joy are for you, I promise you the rest of your garments also have a mood-enhancing quality.

What can you do if you'd like to experience different moods? Maybe you're like me and have days where you do nothing but run errands. You might need a feeling of more energy, a get-things-done attitude. *Where is that bright blue jumper and those summery yellow tennis shoes that help spring me into action?*

When I want to up my creativity IQ, I love to have soft, loose-fitting clothing to evoke this mood! As I'm tapping away on my keyboard, I'm wearing a favorite comfy neon-pink t-shirt I slashed open at the neckline. The color and soft fabric always get my creative juices flowing.

Let's be real. How many times have you honestly stood in front of your closet and picked out an outfit with care and intention? For most of us, we just don't have time to do that every morning, and some days, the bar for our outfit selection is simply that the clothes look and smell clean. We all do the smell test, right?

However, when you get dressed in this manner, you're missing out on a golden opportunity to utilize clothing to help you create better outcomes for your day. Every day brings new challenges, and the clothes already hanging in your closet can help you master those events with more love, harmony, and confidence.

Since the majority of us don't have time to contemplate in the mornings about which outfit would be best for our individual goals for the day, I developed a simple strategy to help you do just that, even on your busiest mornings.

This fashion strategy can be implemented slowly over many days, or if you're an all-or-nothing gal like me, you can do it in one shot.

I've designed a free PDF to help you get started! Be sure to check out the link at the end of the chapter.

THE TOOL

FASHION YOUR MOOD STRATEGY

Step 1: Closet Gratitude

Now it's time to do something we rarely think of doing for our clothes: Say thank you!

Take a few deep breaths, then express gratitude for your entire wardrobe. Why? Because gratitude opens your heart and allows you to connect more deeply to the gifts your wardrobe has to offer you. Your clothes are your friends, and with this technique, a special ally!

Here are some examples that I use, which may help get you started:

- *Thank you for being in my life.*

- *Thank you for protecting my body.*

- *Thank you for bringing me joy.*

- *I'm grateful to have the ability to purchase these.*

Step 2: How do you want to feel?

Put your attention on which feelings and experiences you'd like your clothes to support you in. You can even journal about this for a few minutes.

What types of encounters or activities from your daily life would you like to feel better about? Which attitudes would you like to experience and express more deeply?

Whatever your daily needs are, there is a matching outfit in your closet!

After you determine approximately three to eight moods or vibes you'd like to express, write each one down on a different sheet of paper or Post-It note.

Here are the mood categories in my closet:

- Happy

- Serene

- Playful

- Creative

- Empowered

- Energetic

Step 3: Look, Touch, and Feel

Now that you've created a collection of moods and attitudes you want to feel, take out your garments and see what feeling each gives you. It's important to look at yourself in the mirror as you do this, as it can amplify how you feel.

Hint: With this approach, your mirror is your ally! From time to time throughout the day, look in the mirror to remind yourself and anchor the attitude and mood you want to express. You can mentally repeat, with conviction, a very brief affirmation, such as: *Lookin' good!* Or, *I got this!*

There are a few ways to do this with your clothes:

- Take out one type (tops, pants, skirts, dresses, etc.)

- Take out one color category (all whites, pinks, blues, etc.)

- Take out five to ten clothes currently hanging together (this way is best for those of you doing this process gradually over several days)

Whichever method you use, set only one group of these garments— one type, one color, or five to ten garments—on your bed so you can see them all at one time.

Now, designate different sections on your bed for each of the moods and attitudes you want to express in your life, and lay those labeled pieces of paper in each area.

Pick up each garment one at a time and hold it in your hands or against your body. Close your eyes and take a few moments to tune in to the feeling you're getting from this garment. Imagine yourself wearing it, and if it helps to try it on, please do so! That's the best way to understand how this garment can help you. Look in the mirror, even if you're just holding the garment. The mirror will help to amplify how you feel.

Do you feel more relaxed? Heightened creativity? Full of energy? More in charge? Increased confidence?

Once you've identified how this garment can help you create a mood, place it in the appropriate mood pile (confident, relaxed, creative, etc.) on your bed.

Go through this process with all the garments you have time to work with today.

You will want to repeat Step 3 continually until you've done this for all the clothes in your closet.

The very first time I did this, I had a huge pile of clothes that I realized didn't do anything for me anymore.

It's okay to let them go.

Saying thank you to the clothing that served us for some time and also saying goodbye can be part of this process, too. There are usually local homeless shelters, women's shelters, or non-profit organizations that would be grateful for your donation.

As you begin to get dressed based on your desired moods, your future clothing purchases will likely shift. When I go shopping for clothes now, I find I can quickly tune in by taking a few breaths and get a feeling for what that garment will do for me emotionally. What tone will it set for my day? Lately, I've been buying a lot of calming clothes. *Guess I need to chill out!*

Step 4: Putting it all together

Here comes the fun part.

I love making things neat and organized. Like, really love it. It's kind of my love language. When I visit my friends and family, I actually ask them if they want help reorganizing their closets, pantries, art supplies, whatever. Don't believe me? Check out my niece's lip gloss drawer.

You've already done the heavy lifting; now it's your chance to put the clothes back in a manner that will allow you to easily get dressed each morning, without much thinking. You're doing this now so you don't have to spend time thinking about coming up with an outfit that best fits the day.

This step works well if you have time to complete Step 3 for your entire closet in one shot. This may take one or a few hours, so that might not be realistic for most.

As you hang your garments back up or return them to the shelves, group them by moods. I created free downloadable closet rack dividers you can print out at home and color, label, or bedazzle for each of your moods. Grab the link to your free PDF at the end of the chapter!

When you group your clothing by your moods, you can literally transform your day.

"Change your skirt, change your mood."

~ Mindy Trisko

Now, when you look in your closet for what to wear for that day, spend a few seconds thinking about what you would like the day ahead to hold for you. What type of mood, vibe, or energy will you need to be your best? Then select an outfit from that section of the closet.

Congratulations! You've just let your heart be your personal stylist!

Now that you've created your mood-enhancing wardrobe, you're ready to meet the world with more ease and harmony. Remember to glance at the mirror from time to time to remind yourself of the tone you've set.

Mindy J. Trisko, M.A., is the owner and founder of 1030 Clothing, a women's sustainably made clothing brand with a mission of empowering women through fashion.

She graduated from Colorado State University with a B.A. in Apparel Design, quickly traded in her hiking boots for high heels, and moved to New York City, where she worked for major designers such as Calvin Klein, Betsey Johnson, and Badgely Mischka. She then returned to her hometown of Chicago, IL, where she started a tailoring business and discovered her passion for teaching.

She's been a high school fashion design and marketing teacher for over a decade, earned her Master's degree in Emancipatory Leadership, and works hard to empower and be an advocate for all students.

Being the founder of her clothing brand has been her life's dream since she first put on that black-and-white dress from her youth. Designing and sewing clothes has been Mindy's passion since she was a little girl. Learning tips and tricks from her Grandma Betty, sewing has always been her safe space where she can put on her favorite French pop playlist and jam out while designing a new asymmetrical dress. Fashion has always been the vehicle that allows her to tap into that creative flow.

If you're looking for Mindy after hours, check the sauna, local roller rink, or nearest hiking trail. Caution: If she has a matcha latte in her hand, she's in do not disturb mode. Approach with lavender or chocolate only.

Connect with Mindy:

Website: https://www.1030clothing.com

Instagram: https://www.instagram.com/1030Clothing/

Facebook: https://bit.ly/1030clothingfacebook

YouTube: https://www.youtube.com/@1030Clothing

Linktr.ee: https://linktr.ee/1030clothing

Email: info@1030clothing.com

Free PDF: https://1030clothing.com/pages/closet

REFERENCES

Bernard, Katherine. 2012. "Confidence Dressing: How Clothing Affects the Mind." Vogue. https://www.vogue.com/article/intelligent-design-how-clothing-affects-the-mind

"Enclothed Cognition." 2012. Journal of Experimental Social Psychology 48, no. 4 (July): 918-925. 10.1016.

You are a beacon of joy and love, reflecting the light from others, and illuminating the world.

It's not only through traditional talk therapy that we can voice. It encourages whole-brain engagement. Expressive art can activate multiple areas of our brain, enhancing deeper emotional processing and integration. It allows one to enjoy one's inner world with curiosity and joy while healing.

Brigette Burton

14

ART OF HEALING

CRAFTING THROUGH TRAUMA TO FREEDOM

Brigette Burton, Artistic Wellness Facilitator

MY STORY

But healing is never linear. It folds, twists, and occasionally bends, requiring me to rebuild what's broken.

Every piece of paper I folded held a memory—each cut a choice, each fold a moment reclaimed. When my hands were functioning, making artwork from the wreckage, I considered: *This is more than crafting; it is transformation.*

Amid the shadows of my childhood, crafting became my sanctuary, refuge, and saving grace. It was a place where calmness hovered, where I found freedom, not in the approval of others, but in my own creative space. Crafting was no longer an escape, but a rebellion against my past, a life that felt whole again. It was a way to create a new narrative where my hands could make something beautiful and find empowerment in each fold and cut.

CUTTING THROUGH CHAOS

The scissors' blade trembled in my grip, the soft crunch of paper slicing clean beneath the pressure. My fingers ran over the delicate edges, tracing them like the borders of the world I desperately tried piecing together. The room around me was dim, weighted with the silence of old wounds. Yet, the tiny scraps on the floor held something new: possibility!

"Go ahead! Start folding! Cut it! Shape it! Do it!" I whispered to myself.

Each moment grounded me and connected me to the present. Pressing a strip of paper with glue, I preserved delicate memories of my forgotten past—beauty! Once, my hands only knew destruction: shaking with panic, clenched in rage, curling into fists, striking the air against a world that had stripped me bare.

Now, they lifted my spirits. Piece by piece, color by color, I started crafting something unique and beautiful.

No! No! No! I was far from winning the war against my mind. In the quiet hours of creation, my mind battled softly. And here, surrounded by paper and glue, I was no longer drowning in my past. I shaped reality, shaped my future, one delicate fold at a time.

I got this! I will not give up. As I pressed the crimson paper flat against the table, the sharp scent of glue rose, and I coaxed it into a delicate curl. Petal by petal, I built each rose, each layer folding over the next, whispering stories I no longer spoke aloud. The first cut through the paper, jagged and torn at the edges, reminded me of my betrayal wounds, its shape incomplete like trust shattered beyond repair. The next round of darker petals bore the weight of my stolen innocence, the curves trembling where my hands faltered.

Still, I felt sad and alone. One minute, I felt a sense of hope; the next minute, nervousness that developed into panic attacks. I experienced severe headaches, and my heart pounded intensely, like a drummer performing heavy beats on it. Thoughts swirled in my head like a whirlpool of dirty debris.

"What's happening to me? I can't think straight. It feels like I don't belong in this cruel world. I can't take it anymore; please take me away from this Earth!" I screamed.

FROM FURY TO FREEDOM

My hands wouldn't stop shaking as I continued to fold. Between the rusted teardrops, I noticed the petals fluttering like a butterfly, as if they might disappear like the memories I tried hard to bury. Somehow, some of the petals stayed firm, like a tree clothed with scars that lingered long after the bruises faded. Nevertheless, I continued pressing forward through the pain and sadness, and as the roses grew bigger in shape and size, the meaning behind them shifted.

What once symbolized pain became proof I had made it through the fire. The layers of the petals now looked different than before. They transformed delicately as I folded each one, leaving the sharp edges smoother than before, the curves fashioned in grace with each petal standing close, weaving perfectly into the next one. The wounds closed and became something astounding—bravery where fear once stood, strength where weakness housed itself for so long, and resilience blooming from damage. With it, a poem stood alongside, each verse dressed in the language of the flower and each stanza coated with layers of my rebirth. The black rose was sorrow, the deep red, fury; the ivory rose was growth and healing, and the final in line—the golden rose—hope.

The Golden Rose

The black rose stood in sorrow, heavy and deep, a burden of loss too heavy to keep.

Ivory bloomed in hands so worn, a promise of healing, quiet and warm.

The red rose burned with fury so bright, a flame that raged, then turned to light.

Layer by layer, she shaped her fate, not just to build, but to recreate.

Until, at last, one stood alone, golden, gleaming, fully grown.

No longer stood petals pressed through pain—

But proof that she would rise again.

There was no doubt I'd risen. I felt a sense of excitement inside. I would keep fighting and creating until my soul glowed peacefully, unshattered.

As time passed, I felt different. I felt happy, calm, and confident. I felt motivated to continue crafting and wanted to share my passion with others. I came up with the idea to help bring smiles to anyone I saw with a sad look on their face. I was confident that if the paper flowers made me smile and feel happy, they would do the same for others.

I vividly recall waking up on a cold and rainy morning. Due to the gloomy weather, I dimmed the lights in the house. I got into the shower to freshen up, and a favorite song, "Over the Rainbow," played in the background, with a favorite verse ripping through my brain. As the music played, I sang with it, screaming at the top of my voice, as the hot water flowed down my face like Niagara's waterfall.

It was peaceful. This moment lifted my spirit and moved me to act on my thoughts.

A GIFT TO OTHERS

Grounded in disbelief, I felt a sense of renewal. Pressure built inside me, forcing my insides outward—like my body rejected itself, as if I was having an out-of-body experience. My brain pulsed, caught between fog and fire. Every nerve felt like it screamed without sound. At the same time, I was excited and amazed as what started as personal healing benefited others. The flowers I shaped and gifted carried stories of resilience, emotion, courage, and bravery. Those who received them felt joy, warmth, hope, and gratitude. As each held them close, their faces glowed with a smile, wide like the width and length of the ocean. Excitement took over me. I badly wanted to put my gymnastics skills to use—flip up, down, all over the place, and not even worry about where I would land.

A friend touched the petals, a reminder of her strong companionship. Others held the bouquet close, wavering back and forth with glistening eyes and grateful tears, sharing how the blooms reminded them of finding hope and faith while facing adversity. Others remarked on how the artwork profoundly impacted them and provided support levels that exceeded my expectations. Seeing the amount of others' joy brought tears to my eyes and a heart full of gratitude. I said to myself, *Thank God! I feel great! I feel alive! I am free. I can breathe. I no longer suffocated.*

Embracing the roses' transformative power took me off the path of stolen innocence onto a shared path of healing and growth, not just for me but for everyone my creations' petals touched. Now, this is a life worth living.

CRAFTING THROUGH TRAUMA

Curious about how crafting became my lifeline? Let me take you back a little, to where it all started.

Everything was black and gloomy, like a storm cloud darkening my childhood skies. It wasn't just the words—*abduction, rape, molestation,* and *abuse*—I learned so young; it was the way they invaded every corner of my world, reshaping it harshly. My thoughts' every echo became distorted, every memory shifted, and every feeling turned into a fragile, cracked mirror. Fear became my shadow, a constant companion that whispered caution into every interaction.

Hypervigilance wasn't a choice, but a survival instinct, a broad perspective through which I observed surrounding events. Trust was a fragile thing: difficult to catch, and brief. It was like trying to grab water with my hands. But even amid the turmoil, I found myself stepping into the role of peacemaker, navigating the chaos with sympathy and empathy as my compass, because I knew how it felt to be hurt and in pain at such a young age.

I wanted everyone around me to be okay. I hungered for happiness and smiles, even though I felt pain inside, like being stabbed repeatedly. I carried the weight of the world on my shoulders, trying to keep everyone from pain and sadness like I felt. I said yes when I wanted to say no to keep others smiling. Even amid my loving and satisfying others, I felt good inside. It felt good to be caring, helpful, and kind.

I learned early to read the room like a second language, coaxing calm from conflict and intervening to prevent fights and bullying even as I bore the brunt of it myself. Justice, not revenge, was the quiet wish that anchored me—a yearning so profound that it shaped the very core of who I am.

I tiptoed throughout the world during my childhood, teenage years, and early adulthood. I was an outsider looking in through a wide, self-built lens. And what I observed didn't look appealing; more so, I saw a play where actors wore masks, hiding their bruises behind forced smiles and polite conversations. I watched friendships unravel over whispered betrayal, saw anger simmer beneath kind gestures, and constantly felt the weight of unspoken truths pressing against the air like a held breath.

I'd whisper, "Brigette, you have to protect yourself. You have to keep yourself away from negative influences. You are special with many gifts and talents. Stay to yourself and keep quiet. It's okay! You have to. You can't let anyone destroy you and remove what God instilled in you."

The world's interactions were a mystery. I measured people by the tension in their shoulders, the clipped edges of their laughter, the way their eyes flickered with something unsaid. I didn't trust more than my eyes could see. Chaos was present in a familiar form; I always observed from a distance without getting too involved. The world, to me, moved at an unsteady rhythm, pulsing with conflict and fleeting tenderness, and I was unwilling to let its jagged edges pierce me. I learned to navigate it with caution.

I cultivated a mental barrier to shield myself from daily distractions and misinformation prevalent in society. I filled my brain's neurons with positive and pleasant thoughts about intricate designs on textured paper shaped into colorful flowers, patterns on canvas, vivid swirls on paper or in coloring books, transforming the images of horrific scenes into smiling faces—great things I had discovered lying dormant inside of me at the tender age of nine.

I shut out the world and let my thoughts lead me into an imaginary art museum of creativity. I was happy and peaceful living inside myself—a fun, protective place where creativity transformed my life.

Now that the stage is set with symbolism and the beauty of paper flowers, are you ready to dive in and create your transformation? Remember, when making this, it's not just about the output, but also about the impact it will have on you as you move through your journey and others who'll receive a piece of this bravery.

THE TOOL

Here's a guide with step-by-step instructions on crafting a paper rose. When creating the rose, place yourself in the experience. Listen to your feelings, trust the process, and embrace the rose's transformational power. Enjoy!

CRAFTING A PAPER ROSE: A SYMBOL OF STRENGTH AND RESILIENCE

Materials Needed:

- Colored paper. Examples: red for passion, black for sorrow, beige for resilience, gold for hope and faith—whatever symbolizes your journey to your liking.

- Scissors. Precision scissors work best for clean cutting; any scissors will work.

- Glue gun and glue sticks.

- A pencil or skewer for curling the petals into shape.

- Small rubber bands or thin bread ties to hold the rose together.

- Dark green paper for leaves, if desired.

Step-by-Step Process:

- Prepare the rose by cutting nine sheets of paper into rectangular shapes in the size of your choice.

- Fold each piece in half.

- Fold the two corners at the top into each other. Repeat this same step for the corners at the bottom.

- Place the folded paper horizontally and fold each side until it meets the crease.

- Repeat these steps for each piece of paper.

Building the Layers: Shaping the Petals

- Fold all nine pieces of paper, then divide them into three sets.

- Start one set of three by placing them inside each other to make it look like one piece. Repeat this step for the remaining sets.

- Take each set of three and place them side by side, into one stack.

- Hold them together and place a rubber band or bread tie around them.

- Bend pieces into the shape of a star.

- Take each set of three and fold back the layers into the shape of a petal. Continue until all sets are complete. Use a pencil or skewer to bend each petal into a curl.

A Paper Rose As A Gift:

- Carefully place the handmade rose in a box of your choice.

- Stuff the inside of the box with tissue paper in the color of your choice.

- Write a note and place it in the box next to the flower. Example: "This rose symbolizes your journey. It's delicate and strong, just like you. It's always unraveling in new ways. It can bring calmness after grief, a newfound purpose in your life, and new perspectives that shape us, often in ways we never anticipate. May it remind you that even in the most difficult times, you are still worthy and life is beautiful."

Your craft is a testament of strength, courage, and bravery. Let it serve as an unspoken reminder that even in the face of hardships, you are growing, unfolding, and worthy with a bright light inside. Trust the journey, embrace the transformation, and know that beauty and resilience will bloom within you.

Brigette Michelle Burton is an Artistic Wellness Facilitator, Art Therapist, Poet, and Creative Storyteller who provides safe spaces and guides individuals or groups through intermodal creative processes to promote wellbeing and personal growth. In her role, she creates supportive and secure environments where participants can express themselves, network with others, and foster their creative journey. She facilitates through art-based programs, workshops, and community projects.

Brigette focuses heavily on processes of self-expression through creative and recycled pathways, rather than skill and development. She aims to influence, inspire, and empower individuals through the arts while enhancing their mental, emotional, and physical well-being.

When Brigette relaxes from art sessions, she cooks and serves delicious dishes made with love, paints, sings, and dances with her grandchildren.

Connect With Brigette:

Website: http://kreativepathwayz.com

Facebook: https://www.facebook.com/groups/899013799051233/user/100093484495874

Instagram: https://www.instagram.com/legacyoflove5813/?_pwa=1

Email: Ladyb5111@gmail.com

Expressive artists fearlessly dive into a deep ocean of limitless possibilities. How deep are you willing to go?

Expressive arts are your living, breathing rhythm for soulfully connecting to self and all life; inviting wonder, not performance; gracefully clearing challenges, cultivating bliss; encouraging self-expression and the creative unfolding of your original magic—weaving timeless truths, inspiration, imagination and intuitive play into masterpieces of living art.

Sensei Timothy Stuetz

15

MANTRA MOMENTUM MOJO

BELIEVE IT, FAKE IT, FEEL IT, BECOME IT!

Sensei Timothy Stuetz

Stress-free BE,
Mojo ON, weakness—OFF!
Mantra flips the switch, thrive blissfully.

MY STORY

OMG! Om my God!

Talk about momentum. I envisioned another start to this chapter before sitting to write and rereading the title: "Mantra Momentum Mojo: Believe It, Fake It, Feel It, Become It!"

This could lead one to believe my story's sensationally, euphorically, even orgasmically different than originally intended.

I laugh. *Ahh, a laughter twist, too.*

Laughter—and sounds possibly emerging from what's alluded to above—could be considered mantras per standard dictionary definitions.

"A commonly repeated word or phrase, especially for motivation."

Isn't laughter motivating—a sparkling verbal expression lighting up, rejuvenating every cell?

Did you know children laugh 300 times a day?

How many times a day does laughter's incantation deep within your belly burst forth?

Fewer than 17 for most adults!

Laugh it up,
Giggles rise and ripple,
Shaking clear—trite, cheerless mind cripple.

Feel it grow,
Golden sunbeams inside,
A heart-healing, soul-bright belly tide.

Shake with joy,
Muscles strong, stretch and sing,
Endorphins dance—a bubbling wellspring!

Smile with sound,
Without a joke in sight.
Inner delight—laugh in bliss, lifelong.

TIMELESS-TIMESTAMP, 1983

Fifteen minutes into driving from Oakland to Southern California, following a weekend of chanting and meditation, time warps. I burst into belly-deep, unstoppable, raucous laughter, corked only at rest stops.

Hands and face glow red, orange, blue hues. Gawkers roll by, wide-eyed.

I don't care.

Lifetimes of stress blazing to ashes.

Seven hours laughing blissfully—a barrel of laughter forever embedded just below my navel, accessible at will. For you, too!

Feel it rise,
Tingles, thrills, fly sky high.
Laughter unwinds, what no pill can buy.

Immune glow,
Blood cells flow free in cheer.
Antibodies, health bloom, laughs no peer.

Shared delight,
Bridges, love, joy pervade,
Peace resides where sorrow once weighed.

Stress dissolves,
Laughter, like ocean roars,
Cortisol sinks, mighty spirit soars.

Sweet release,
Muscles melt their tense grip,
Tears of joy flow like streams, no guilt trip.

Are giggles and guffaws, hee-haws and laughs our first expressed magical mantras?

Laugh, you must,
Tickle, tickle within,
Life's teeter-totter—too short, must grin.

Ho, ho, ho!
Ludicrous, fear can be,
Powerful, joy is—release, you'll see.

Connected,
You soul are—always were,
Laughter your bridge—pure light, free of blur.

Yes, soul connected. Living stress-free naturally is soul easy!

You are the ultimate *Expressive Art!*

Even if feeling bereft of artistic talent, you're hardwired with built-in stress relief systems.

Did you know your voice is the greatest healing sound *for you?*

Mantra frequencies, more than words, a sound print of your soul restoring itself.

My mantra momentum began with a gasp, not a giggle—pure spontaneous shock.

MANTRA-AWAKENING, FALL 1980

No sleep for 60+ hours. I'm physically and emotionally drained. A week-long mortgage banking seminar, months in planning and execution, over.

One moment, I'm lying in bed with my beautiful partner, Jewel, then—

I'm not in my body! What the…?

Hovering in the doorway, peering through mystical mist, I sense she's about to scream. My body appears lifeless.

Gotta get back!

Instantly, I'm jettisoned in.

Spooked and shaky, in dismay and disbelief, I call Sharon, a therapist friend.

Her calm voice reassures, "I'll get out of bed, meditate, and ask Baba what to do."

Meditate? Who's Baba? Who cares? Help's on the way!

Fifteen minutes—a tiny eternity passes.

"Baba says, eat something sweet and sleep."

Sweet I can do. Sleep? Not yet—must drive Jewel to the airport.

Now, I'm more unnerved than being body-free minutes ago.

Nine months prior, I took 10mg of prescribed valium before a minor operation.

Wow, world looks so soft, way better than being drunk.

Then I popped a pain pill before bed.

Eyes closed; dream began. Rounding a winding mountain road curve with a woman passenger,

I can't control it any longer.

Eyes opened wide, beaming a ray of white light onto the ceiling. I watched our lifeless bodies pulled from the wreckage.

Since from God
We came, and back to God
We go, why not let God drive between?

Now, facing another curvy drive, woman riding shotgun, this memory vividly floods my senses, as does a *Twilight Zone* dream the next night.

Another pain pill, eyes open again, another movie plays—the glowing face of a dark-skinned, bearded man in an orange knit cap flows in and out of the wall.

Closing my befuddled eyes, treasuring a return to sleep—

No more pain pills! I'm a Certified Public Accountant. This doesn't compute!

Dream scenes real,
Visions shake core beliefs.
Out-of-bod ride, soul's warp-speed revamp.

Now dazed, sleep-deprived, death dream still alive,

Airport here I come. Cautiously!

Home at two a.m.—*Ahh, sleep!*

What the hell?

Jolted awake! Phone's ringing.

It's five a.m.! Who's calling at this ungodly hour?

Sharon: "How are you? Want to chant with me in a few hours?"

Is she serious?

"What's chanting?"

She explains.

"No! I don't sing out loud! Not even in the shower."

"Okay," she says, "how about breakfast afterward?"

A breakfast of belly butterflies, explanations, laughter, treats, and a yoga teacher recommendation—Jana, now a dearest friend.

What's yoga?

A curtain-pull on my tight and tense body, even with jogging 50 miles and 40-mile bike rides weekly.

Jana ends each class with everyone laying in shavasana listening to Baba (Swami Muktananda) chant Om Namah Shivaya.

His voice, soul-soothing—like God's heart echoing.

Three months later: "Hi Sharon. I'm ready to go chant with you."

Arriving early, I park in front of the house. Ten minutes later, calmness boils. I'm tersely told to move.

I balk. "This isn't a red curb!"

Lesson parked, ego tugged, truth inbound.

Sharon hands me a chanting book.

It's not in English!

We enter a garage-turned-plush temple.

Why are men and women sitting on opposite sides of an aisle, bowing to an empty chair?

What's this musty, alluring smell?

What's this Guru Gita? Over 180 verses!

No Om Namah Shivaya?

What the hell, some words blend into one another.

I'm surely ruining everyone's morning.

Legs hurt—never sat cross-legged so long.

Seventy-five frustrating minutes later, chanting stops. I'm plunged inward, silence supreme.

Oh my God! Every pore's vibrating. Am I levitating?

Fingers frantically clutch the thick carpeting.

I'm freaked out, body rising!

"How was that?" Sharon asks.

"I feel like a kindergartener who sat in on a twelfth-grade class!"

I play hooky for three months.

BELIEVE IT!

Yes, I now do.

But who—what—made me vibrate and levitate like that?

I start meditating daily. At first, five minutes, setting a kitchen timer. Then longer. Eventually, one hour feels like five minutes. Three hours feel like one!

I chant Om Namah Shivaya often—walking outside, between rooms; driving; cleaning; eating; and before meditation.

Not feeling it, though.

FAKE IT!

Sacred play,
Rewires you day by day,
Repetition works, feel it you will.

Om, the primordial sound, sages say. *Namah Shivaya* purifies our five elements.

- Na—Earth

- Ma—Water

- Shi—Fire

- Va—Air

- Ya—Space

Five arise,
Elements soul align,
Bod's building blocks, all creation too.

Chant with love,
Om Namah Shivaya,
Peace hums, calm ensues, mind dissolves—bliss.

Silence grows,
All echoes fade soul still,
Self reveals bright, beyond time and space.

Om you go,
Namah Shivaya flow,
Bliss blooms within and ripples outside.

FEEL IT!

Two years later, driving home from yoga, top down, wind in my hair, sun shining, warming face—ocean air, negative ion rich, rising above cliffs along Pacific Coast Highway—I'm chanting loud, free as the breeze.

Wow, I feel it! Om Namah Shivaya resounding within.

Soul-song stirs,
Mantra no more just said,
It breathes me alive, fervently fed.

Words, now notes,
Becoming what was said,
Veil between voice and vibration shred.

Mantra moves,
Becoming *Om,* I Am,
Holy vibes rewire, echo within.

BECOME IT!

Ancient Seers of India divided existence into four Yugas. We're now traversing Kali Yuga: age of distraction, restlessness, ego-centered living, and overstimulation.

"In Kali Yuga, chanting the Holy Name is the most effective path to liberation."

~ Kali Santarana Upanishad

Why so? Because Japa—silent mantra repetition—is:

- Simple, profound.

- Done anytime, anywhere.

- Mind-body-energy harmony.

- Mental noise muffler.

- Eternal Self bond.

- Kundalini dancing.

Sound body
For the Divine Being,
Mantra is—Sri Aurobindo says.

Simplest path,
Sri Ramakrishna says.
Yogananda—God's name on the breath.

The day before Baba left his body in 1981, he answered my letter—about business, of all things—adding:

"Do a lot of Japa to make your mind strong and clear."

A Siddha's guidance is a command, bearing fruit when followed.

I followed,
Curious, not yet lit.
Deaf and dumb to Japa's true power.

Nine months before that letter, the morning Sharon and I shared breakfast, she gifted me Baba's book: *I AM THAT (Hamsa)*.

Hamsa, "swan" in Sanskrit, mantra *So'Ham* or *Hamsa*—breath, soul, and supreme consciousness.

My young boy breath stops, eyes open wide in delight, on first glimpsing the pristine white grace of a swan, punctuated by its orange and black beak.

Baba says, "*Hamsa* is the highest of all spiritual techniques. It gives the direct experience of the self. If received from a Siddha Guru and practiced according to their instructions, one attains perfection—the state of a Siddha."

The primordial sound *Om* gives rise to *sa* and *ham*. From these syllables the Universe is born.

Breathe in—*ham,* breathe out—*sa.*

"Ham and sa are the source of the world," says the *Guru Gita*.

Hamsa, also known as ajapa gayatri, the unrepeated *Gayatri* mantra, is self-born. No sage invented it. It was not composed by any yogi. The Lord Himself initiates us with it in the womb.

"When the fetus in the womb is seven months old, the soul receives knowledge of its past and future."

~ Garbha Upanishad

Brahmananda said, "Become aware of the mantra *So'ham.* Fingers need not move; tongue need not sound.

Watch it; the unrepeated mantra constantly goes on within you. Twenty-one thousand, six hundred times a day—whether awake or asleep.

Contemplate it with joy, all the time."

Namdev, another great saint, said: "Just keep repeating *So'ham, So'ham* all the time, and you yourself will become God."

Hamsa **(hum-sah)** became my meditation mantra.

DESTINY-DATE, FALL 2011

Baba, appearing in form and dreams since 1981, empowers me to awaken and accelerate everyone's spiritual energy through *Hamsa* and Shaktipat, descent of Divine Grace.

Years millions,
Swans glide Earth's blue waters.
Breath whispers *Hamsa,* eternally.

Hamsa—Swan,
Living grace, mates for life.
Hamsa whispers, *I Am That,* free of strife.

Floats through time,
White wings glide, silent rhyme,
Inhale *ham,* exhale *sa*—peaceful chime.

Swan, soft sight,
Pure discernment, crystal bright.
Thoughts still, *Hamsa* shines your soul's pure light.

SEDUCTION-DREAM, SUMMER 2012

I'm sea swimming with spiritual friends, met through an energy-based community. Riptides sweep us out. I'm calm, as all vanish except the administrator and me. We wash up on a rugged mountain shore.

"Stay close," I warn, but she slips back into the waves—gone.

I cautiously follow a narrow path, winding upward. Suddenly, cosmic, iridescent ribbons of celestial colors swirl all around.

Tempted—like Christ in the wilderness—the cloaked leaders of this community I left a year earlier—offer safety, riches, a return.

Inner eye uncloaks deception.

Hamsa, Hamsa, Hamsa, declared with unwavering resolve.

POOF—never to return!

Wow! First time Hamsa's my dreamtime savior. Usually, it's Om.

Next day, a beloved friend, also from that former community, gifts me an energy attunement for my birthday three months prior. Turning the doorknob to leave, I hear:

"Wait—I almost forgot. I bought this three months before your birthday."

I so relish slowly unwrapping gifts, appreciating the paper, ribbons, love.

I'm speechless.

A tuning fork—the vibration Hamsa!

I share the dream. We smile and laugh. Grace flows.

WHITE-WATER-JAPA, 1982

Kern River, rapids rafting, snow melt-off epic.

"If you fall out," the guide warns, "go feet-first toward rocky shores."

Crash—splash—gnarly hole, icy plunge. Resurfacing:

OMG! Headfirst, lickety-split toward jagged cliffs! No raft nearby. Om Namah Shivaya. Om Namah Shivaya. Om Namah Shivaya. Om—

Suddenly, out of nowhere, a raft with oar extended.

Thank you, God!

SACRED-SYNC, LATE 1980S

Reiki Master retreat amidst tall, scented pines, along a crystal-clear, rushing river, ends. All leave. I stay.

A walk beckons. **I freeze!**

A statuesque white stallion thunders toward me. Stops. Snorts.

Mexican Standoff.

Eyes lock. I root in Tanden, below navel.

Om, Om, Om—resounds within for fifteen minutes.

Our communion test of wills ends. Another snort—he gallops off. I continue walking.

Mantras protect, invoke grace, awake and asleep, dreamtime and deep sleep.

BROTHERLY-LOVE, 1988

Standing in my grandmother's bright yellow kitchen, my brother says, "I don't believe in anything you do, but you're much nicer!"

DETONATION-DREAM, DECEMBER 2015

Mushroom cloud rises nearby.

Fallout wave heads toward hundreds I've gathered for meditation.

"Repeat *Om!*" I urge. Pure peace floods in.

TIMESTAMPS FORGOTTEN, DREAMS NOT

Tornado whirls,
Hungry lion charges.
I stand firm. *Om, Om, Om*— both reverse.

Birthday gift,
I silently ask of
Guru: *own death I want to brave.*

In dream, sink
I do, to pool bottom.
No problem, I'll just push off, rise, breathe.

Nope, dead weight!
Panic not. *I Am, Om,*
Om, Om—drown in peace, alive for keeps.

Gurumayi knew!
Underwater blast off,
Where this Pisces feels comfy, God's Grace!

GRACE-FLASH, MAY 2012

Mom and best friend in separate hospitals. Days driving back and forth.

Ray's in isolation, bacterial brain infection. I give energy sessions in full gear, wash up before and after.

Suddenly, one afternoon following hospital tours, my body aches. I lie down for a 20-minute, self-Reiki power nap. Pain builds, every cell pounding. Excruciating, beyond anything I've ever felt. Japa even arduous.

I want to die!

Om, Om, Om—mumbled hour after hour.

Around five a.m., consciousness and pain dissolve into blessed sleep for two hours.

What? Are you kidding? No pain! Om my God! Thank you, God!

OM-PIPHANY, MARCH 2020

Scrunched like a squished sardine, I'm packed with three other planeloads from Italy in the tiniest baggage claim ever seen.

Early that night, Groundhog Day. Pain beyond pain again. But this time, no death wishes.

I got this!

Om, Om, Om—echoes hour after hour.

Three a.m., sleep thankfully ensues. Awaking bright at five a.m.

Om my God! No pain! Not a trace! Thank you, God!

Om, om, om,
Om, om, om, om, om, om,
God's Roto-Rooter Pain Remover.

Hold on to
Om like super glue bonds,
Repeat *Om* often, every breath!

MANTRA-CRUCIBLE, NOVEMBER 2022

Bright afternoon sun beams through the sliders, golden sheen sparkling on the Mediterranean Sea beyond. My favorite winter lunch spot.

Ahh, soul heavenly.

Suddenly, I'm scripted into a Vietnam movie scene. A black helicopter rises over the nearest hill, whirling toward me.

I watch, caught off guard, mind not catching on—no clue I've been locked in. No clue, no time to engage energy shields.

I feel a slight twinge as it passes over.

Hmmm?

Within hours I'm bedridden, pain gradually intensifying, until more excruciating than ever.

Can't move even an inch without *scroaning,* pain flames flaring like gas poured on a fire.

Om, Om, Om—for twelve unbearable, relentless hours before blessed sleep ensues.

Again, two hours later, I awaken—blissfully pain-free.

Om, Om, Om Thank You, God!

Pain-free, but whatever hit me has taken years to clear.

Yes, there's no
Wound so severe, that a
Tidal wave of soul sound can't wash clear!

God's love can
Erase any wound deep,
Like breath Divine blows out candle flame!

Severe wounds,
Hurt deep they may, forever
Evaporate in fire of God's love!

While sleeping the next day, the special-delivery chopper returns. My beloved and several visitors watch as it circles over low, a round device attached to its underbelly.

Queasy daze felt for days, their taste and smell senses annihilated.

Life challenges,
Dream attacks, stuck, frazzled,
Who-what-wherever, *Om Shanti Om!*

Baby cries,
Child screams, friend yells, door squeaks,
Jackhammer pounds, alarm rings, bees buzz—*Om!*

Snail slides slow,
Earthworm rises through soil,
Tires roll on road, I hear *Om*—do you?

Each stanza you're reading, a modern-day mantra, aligning you to universal harmony. Teach you I can, *Tesla 3:6:9 Poetry.*

3:6:9,
Energy time Divine.
Power up, word weave, fully align.

Syllables,
Line one, 3; Line two, 6;
Line three, 9. Now, it's versify time

Tesla Tiers,
Stack lines three, story grows.
Three, six, nine stanzas—Ready, set, go!

In every line, poetic or prose, Japa prevails.

PARAMAHAMSA, SUPREME SWAN, REALIZE YOUR CROWNING GLORY

Hamsa, Om,
Japa, Japa, Japa
Potent potion for modern madness.

I don't chant or mantra repeat anymore to get somewhere.

Waves of mantra rise and fall as breath, as heartbeat, as knowing beyond the known. Not as sound, nor as belief!

Presence, pulse of grace, restoring what's real.

There's nothing left to hold, do, or fix.

Matters not
How you arrived here now,
Say God's name with each breath. *Be here now!*

Be here now,
Do you want to know how?
In each moment before you, *do bow!*

Stress-free *be,*
Anchor, on mantra's ship.
Soul simple, closer than thy tongue tip!

Soul-u-tions,
Sacred mantras repeat.
Use, ascend, *Om*—Ignore, suffer, *Ouch!*

Waking, dream,
Deep sleep awareness states,
Observe, live in Turiya state 24/7.

Round the clock,
Rejoice in Turiya.
Life's eternal quest achieved—you're h*O*me!

Not body,
Nor what it does. Not mind,
Nor what it thinks. Not highs or lows—*no!*

Pure land of
Consciousness, you so are!
Universe, sparkles inside you—*yes!*

Be peace, love,
Bliss, but not ensnared.
Beyond these and all, you truly *be!*

My story,
Yet untold, seeing you
Actualize your *crowning glory.*

THE TOOL

Om, Om, Om,
Silently echo *Om,*
Walking, sitting, standing—*everything!*

Engage will,
Feel, believe, *I Am Om.*
Japa your way h*O*me, becoming *Om.*

Hamsa too,
Mantra Mojo Supreme.
"You yourself will become God"—Namdev.

Sit still, watch.
Breathe in—*hum,* breathe out—*sah.*
Meet, merge, be with the One breathing you.

Free 1:1 Kundalini Enhancement Session: https://www.timothystuetz.com/crowning-glory

"My life story's proof—ignite, actualize your crowning glory, I can!"

Sensei Timothy, The Magical & Mystical Fairy Tale Wizard & Poet is a visionary educator, celebrated for writing 260+ children's stories—100+ more than Hans Christian Andersen.

For 44+ years, he's used fairy tales, meditation, Reiki, qigong, yoga, and everything between, empowering thousands to achieve their full potential.

A Book Excellence Award Winner and Amazon #1 Bestselling Author, he weaves myth and mystery, fantasy and reality, poetry and proven developmental principles to boost creativity, vitality, bliss, brilliance, and wire everyone for success.

He's created:

- *BE: Blissfully Empowered:* a 1:1, 12-month personalized transformation, 24/7 support.

- *Bliss Weaving Community Circle:* 4 x 90-minute group sessions, monthly.

- Sacred Sciences Alchemy Academy—turning teens into *Certified Personal & Business Black Belts*—and a similar *Adult Academy.*

- *Tesla 3:6:9—Poetic Power Tyme* and *Personal Empowerment Poems.*

- The Magical Miracle of You—children's and family self-development program.

A Science of Mind Minister and Retired CPA, he's developed programs for the State of California and private foundations.

Embracing people at birth, death, through challenges colossal and tiny, his life—a constant stream of unfolding miracles:

- Seeing crystalline white light as the screen on which God's many faces play.

- Enjoying a focused, patient, serene mind.

- Feeling life's Universal energy pulsating throughout his body, strong and flexible, pain and medication free.

- Blissfully full of laughter, sparked spontaneously within—no outer "fuel" necessary.

- Immersed in harmonic inner music and the sound of silence from which all sounds emerge.

- Free of fear, addictions, anger, depression, and such.

His offerings are created with God's Grace, shaped by 74+ years of life experiences, including the wonders of being a father.

Connect with Sensei Timothy:

Website: https://www.timothystuetz.com

Email: timothy@timothystuetz.com

Linktr.ee: https://linktr.ee/timothystuetz.com

Through the expressive arts, healing was made possible for me.

Expressive arts provide a platform for people to enjoy the moment when they are connected to their uniqueness. The expressive arts open individuals to their inner therapy. These exercises allow you to focus on things that add value to life.

Norman Gordon

16

THE AMAZING LIFE I ALMOST TOOK

HOW TO TRANSFORM FROM SUICIDAL TO PASSION AND PURPOSE

Norman Gordon, Life Coach, Poet, Creative Writer

"The road to excellence is not always beautiful, yet the end always brings beauty."

- Norman Gordon

MY STORY

"Norman, don't kill yourself!" my eight-year-old sister painfully cried.

At ten years old, I'd grown tired of being abused and decided to end my life. I took a rope from the back of our house, tied one end around my neck, and the other to the limb of a mango tree. My mom beat me a lot. My little sister, based on the close relationship we share, usually cries for me. After a beating that attracted pain and embarrassment, out of frustration, I sped to the back of the house. My sister, who cried incessantly while I was being beaten, followed me. I said to her, "I am going to kill myself." To my knowledge, there was a piece of rope under the house cellar. When I took it up, my sibling, fresh on the heels of weeping for me, cried out. "Norman, don't kill yourself!" I proceeded with the attempt; however, when I felt the pain in my sister's trembling voice, I wondered what to do.

The love for my sister and how she pleaded with me forced me to pause. Her screams made me nervous. When I felt her hand pulling my shirt, I was frozen to the point where the attempted suicide was fully stopped. As compared to putting the rope around my neck, untying was difficult. At that moment, I was in pain, my heart throbbed rapidly, and I felt weak. The rope had the most uncomfortable feeling. It felt thicker, and I had difficulty pulling it from around my neck. After a few attempts, it was loosened. Tearfully, we walked back to the front of the house. That ended a moment that wasn't just for my pain, but the collective.

A TASTE OF FREEDOM

That Friday night, I packed a weekend bag and left the house. At about 8:30 pm, I boarded a bus to an anonymous location. I gave the conductor the name of a community I had heard of. On that trip, I felt relieved. After traveling for over an hour, the conductor shouted, "Who is going to Prospect?" I replied, "Me."

At about 10 pm, I was greeted by a seemingly sparsely populated community. Upon arriving at the first house, which was about a minute away from the bus stop, I knocked on the gate. After several attempts, a woman accompanied by two children came to the door. I said, "Goodnight." She asked, "Who are you here to see?" I replied, "Aunt Monica." She responded, "No Monica lives in this area." I was lost for words. She invited me in, and I met her daughter and son. The woman asked what my occasion was, and I told her that my mom beat me, and I came to stay with my aunt. She asked where I was from and my parents' names. After a brief conversation, supper was served. It was late, so she offered me accommodation for the night, then told me to board the bus in the morning and return home. That moment gave me comfort. I felt loved, accepted, appreciated, listened to, and celebrated. The healthy family spirit made me cry. The joy I felt inside was enough to take the pain away.

I returned to my home the following day when my mom and siblings were gone to church.

CREATIVE SURVIVAL

It was a childhood on a richly tilled farm that looked idyllic at a glance but contained a dark underbelly of abuse.

Intimacy spiraled among the trees on our farm, limiting breathing space for leaves and roots bent on living wild. The intricacies of harvesting inspired mixed feelings. With multiple bearings in existence, sometimes, the hand caught the opposite of what the eyes saw. Bruised fruits had to be eaten immediately to avoid spoiling.

Being exposed to variety, abundance, and succulence was a favorite pastime of mine. Apart from mosquitoes, centipedes, millipedes, chickens, and bugs, a herd of cattle enriched life on a year-round, fertile farm in the Cromwell Land community of St. Mary Parish, Jamaica. A nearby clean river with a waterfall served as our main source of water.

Many essential resources were unavailable, so creativity lent itself to survival. This tedious situation got more painful on visits to the outside world. Amid the dimness, going out to associate with others, seeing street lighting, looking at the jovial nature on the outside, vehicles going by, modern houses, and children having fun gave me hope that one day I would be living in an area with such experiences.

Mama and Daddy put our domesticated chickens, lush, green leafy vegetables, eggs, milk from the cows, and ground provisions to good use.

There were times when all I had in my beautifully brewed tea was the combination of cane juice and a tea plant—an unforgettable aroma indeed. Another standout was the fresh, flavorful coconut milk used in various dishes. The natural flow of crystalline oil moistened the soul instantaneously.

Daddy, a hardworking farmer, tilled the soil to perfection. His level of dedication made the Earth conducive to plant growth and development.

Mama's face was the enemy of a smile, but she did her best to make the home comfortable. Clothing was a rare commodity; still, she kept us and our garments clean.

My sisters and I shared a healthy relationship. We weren't always happy, but our childlike aura provided fun. Our joyful spirits experienced an increase whenever we visited family members, friends, school, and church.

It was excruciatingly painful to watch Mama struggle downhill to do the laundry by the river and then uphill, carrying containers of wet clothing on her head and in her hands. Sometimes, my siblings and I accompanied her. Amidst the intrusion of mosquitoes and flies and my mother's protective utterances, like "be careful of rocks, stray animals, and falling tree limbs," we enjoyed the adventure.

Our house was made of soft, termite-prone timber braced by bamboo wattle coated with pages from old magazines and newspapers. Sheets of galvanized zinc covered the exterior. Wear and tear were inevitable, based partly on the fact that the dwelling was a hatchery for insects. This warranted regular repair work—an entertaining, yet scary experience.

I was too young to get involved in repairs, so I watched Mama and Daddy while flying and crawling insects swarmed. Upon completion, we enjoyed a sheen more immaculate than before, especially when my mother buffed the wooden floor with a beautifully designed brush made from coconut husk glazed with a special kind of polish, usually red. As I watched my mom put the finishing touches on the floor, my imagination led me to the next repair day.

Daddy, Mama, my two sisters, and I lived in a one-bedroom dwelling. The search for answers to how we all slept in one bed is still not over. Perhaps it's because we were small children.

The absence of a secure kitchen and the use of a wood fire for preparing meals didn't stop us from being fed. However, when the logs were soaked with rainwater, lengthy and painful delays followed. When Mama or Daddy attempted to make a fire and keep it ablaze under such harsh conditions, we felt sorrow. We composed sweet little songs, eagerly waiting to be served. Each succulent meal brought smiles and an abrupt end to our singing.

Lonely life in the dark valley was a long walk from street lighting and public buildings. Our main sources of light were stars, colorfully clad fireflies, kerosene torches, and table lamps. There was no comfortable bathing or toilet system. Television sets and other electrical gadgets were out of reach. Every opportunity to leave home was a joyous endeavor. My school life as an eager learner benefitted from this.

FINDING MY COMMUNITY

Attending church on Saturdays was a getaway for us. Mama religiously took my siblings and me with her. My visits were infrequent, as clothing was limited. Getting to see other children and outdoor attractions increased my interest in the church. On days when I didn't attend, I spent most of my time crying, singing, talking to myself, or eating. After about seven hours by myself, my favorite people's return mended my broken heart.

These Saturday night reunions had my mother making supper while my sisters shared their experiences at church. There was also enough time to create playful moments. We went to bed relatively early, since it was pitch black by 7:00 p.m. at the latest, and we had no other form of entertainment. Rest was much needed, yet daybreak seemed to have been the order of the night. We slept, waiting for joy to appear in the morning.

School was another leg of life's path. The first was called basic school, as it provided the foundational aspect of education. Due to my outgoing nature, adjusting to this era was manageable. I always looked forward to the next day with great expectation.

The transition from home to school was a significant turning point in my life. Being open to education on a broader scale gave me an understanding of the importance of the use of knowledge. The opportunity to join the local library at age six allowed me to think wisely and express myself better. I became so hooked to interesting dialogues in books to the point where I started to write my own stories and create inner dialogues. This exciting aspect of life connected me to my creativity.

On the opposite side of childhood joy and a thriving farm were Mama's struggling countenance and continuous tears in response to Daddy's constant abuse. Mama suffered the most because she had to bear her pain in addition to ours. The reasons for Dad's unacceptable behaviors were unknown to me.

There was hardly a day of peace at home, stemming from Daddy's manipulative ways. Even when he went out, the atmosphere was bland.

Nights, like days, were equally interrupted by Daddy's frighteningly loud tone, shocking expletives, and crippling body blows to a woman of worth. It was painful watching Mama being battered and bruised. One heartbreaking incident came when I was four years old.

My younger sister and I were in the backyard playing. Suddenly, an unusual commotion sounded from inside the house. In a most degrading way, Daddy had Mama pinned to a wall between two pairs of chair legs. I stood behind him, crying incessantly and helplessly, while he violently punched, slapped, and kicked her. Mama wept, trying to hold her ripped clothing together.

Eventually, Mama grew tired of the chaotic situation. One afternoon, she hurriedly made an exit through the corridors of the home with a huge uncomfortably packed metal bath wobbling at top of her head. I tearfully watched my sisters as they struggled to catch up with my mom, with my younger sister's voice repeating, "Mama."

For a moment, I stood confused. The huge container Mama had on her head was used for laundry. I first thought she was going to the river; however, she made the left turn that led to the main road (the opposite direction of the river). A clear sign she was leaving the home environment, this time, not to wash clothing. I ran to Daddy, who sat speechless and shyly said to him, "Daddy, may I go with Mama?" He said, "Yes." I hastily ran to join my mom and sisters.

SURVIVING ABUSE

After a sad, quiet, 12-minute journey, we were introduced to a room at my maternal grandparents' packed, three-bedroom dwelling. I felt like a lost stranger until my cousins and neighbors jovially greeted me.

Although life away from remoteness brought me comfort, being away from Daddy was the opposite.

Unemployment, limited access to food, little support from Daddy, and returning to an unfavorable environment contributed to Mama's frequently angry voice, wrinkled face, and teary eyes. Despite her refusing assistance, kind souls in the home gave us food.

Harder times came, evident in our about six-mile walk to and from elementary school without money or food, worn clothing, emotional breakdowns, and physical depletion.

Mama's fearfully boisterous tone and violent nature were foreign to me. She abruptly transformed into the kind of person who needed no evidence to give me deafening slaps to the face, thunderous thumps, and bruising body strikes. To her, the smallest things that made her uncomfortable didn't deserve a warning, but a beating.

Her actions attracted laughter from cousins, who found it entertaining to falsely accuse us of doing things we didn't even imagine. Being out in public was slightly different from home; there were more aggressive thumps and slaps. For no apparent reason, I attracted more violation, to the point where one day after a beating, I stared into her eyes, then boldly asked, "Why didn't you kill me at birth?" She didn't respond.

After numerous complaints to Daddy, expecting a change in Mama, she didn't. I also thought my dad would take me to live with him, but he didn't. To me, peace wasn't forthcoming. I felt alone to the point where I said to myself, "No one loves or cares for me."

My thoughts grew violently wild when I remembered two of the most embarrassing clobberings and slaps in the face. The excruciating lashes were done in the presence of many family members, and the slaps were in the busy town center and at church.

Little Norman got to the point where he expressed his frustration through anger and crying. He used safety pins, sewing needles, and cutting tools to inflict wounds on himself. Trees around me were used for punching. My crying areas were behind doors, under the bed, and behind trees.

I decided to leave a life that involved more pain than joy after a cousin mischievously made a false report about me to Mama. Prior to this cruel beating, Mama's outrage told me what she was about. Her preferred act was to firmly grip my shirt by the collar and brutally grab me.

An era that relished the phrase, "Children should be seen and not heard," offered me no opportunity to express my innocence. The usual pleas from surrounding adults to exercise leniency arose, but Mama was more about an uncontrollable, bitter ego. A neighbor who was at the house sensed Mother's intention. She said, "Don't beat him, give him a chance." Mama ignored that plea.

The decision not to take my life opened me to my sister's love. Being on the bus brought flashbacks. I asked myself the question, "If I died, what would happen?" I stared through the window in the darkness and remembered seeing nothing when the rope was around my neck. The beauty inside the lit bus and the home I went to made me happy.

REWRITING MY LIFE

Through my story, my life coaching career has taken a path of transformation. Some clients had similar encounters, and because of that, they experienced positive changes. My heart for people led me on this path. I know that if my life could be redeemed, others' could be.

Life on the other side of the attempt is beautiful. There were moments when I reflected on my life and cried tears of joy. The new Norman that was discovered through creative expressions received a love likened to what a good parent exudes. That era of newness was the true definition of a purposeful life. My focus was on a version of myself I enjoyed being around.

That paradigm shift is an adventure I decided to take my clients on. The wealthy life exposes one to a path for everyone. These people I commit myself to deserve to live happily. Through my life coaching exercises, clients have met professional, personal, financial, and relationship goals. I aim to touch hearts through verbalization and literature. Norman is available to meet the world with a message of transformation through self-help books and life coaching sessions that are tailor-made to meet its needs.

My application of limited contact without malice opened me to discovering so many interesting things about myself. Isolation was a healthy endeavor that allowed me to richly pour into my being, so I could give freedom to a potential person who was worthy of being seen and celebrated.

THE TOOL

Now that you have a heartfelt connection with my story, let me open you to my turnaround. Below is a set of workable tools that allowed me to be where I am now.

READ AND WRITE

Being an avid reader since I was six, books gave my ten-year-old self the drive to explore words on another level. My creative side came out when I started to write enlightening love notes to myself. I wrote positive descriptions of my peripheral and internal aspects, which helped me start to feel good about who I became.

WRITE POETRY

Another expressive art I explored was poetry writing. Those poems were about things around me and the wonderful traits I possessed. One magical thing about my work was that whenever I put it on paper, there was an opportunity to bring joy into the life of a broken child.

For me, producing these materials wasn't about perfecting the arts, but consistently showing up as a reminder that I am worthy of expressing myself. I deserve to be seen and celebrated.

ENGAGE IN POSITIVE SELF-TALK

Positive self-talk played an important role in my writing. Making myself the center of attention gave me a starring role. In focusing on my being, I created a platform of honor. Seeing myself through the most colorful character-building epithets was something I prided myself on doing.

SPEND TIME IN NATURE

Embracing nature and its operations stimulated my literary growth. Nature helped me unwind and opened me to a flow of ideas. Watching how insects reacted to plants and how vegetation communicated inspired beauty within me.

After a nature encounter, I used my writing pad to reflect. Describing moments with the trees and their uniqueness became prose to acknowledge myself.

CREATE FEEL-GOOD-ABOUT-YOURSELF MOMENTS

Creating feeling-good-about-myself moments wasn't always easy. Emotions must be allowed to flow to connect with truth. Flashback scenes brought tears, anger, frustration, bitterness, fear, and low self-worth. However, these were also tools for transformation.

My passion for what I do was immensely tailored by shifting my focus from what hurt me to developing a pattern that elevated my self-esteem to a level where I could congratulate myself for being worthy of growth. My esteemed reader, I truly believe in you, and I know that you have the capacity to feed your worthy souls with the abundance you deserve.

Norman Gordon is a father, certified life coach, life partner to his beautiful Abby, son, uncle, mentor, speaker, poet, writer, and nature lover.

He grew up in the cool farming community of Cromwell Land in St. Mary Parish, Jamaica, where he did his best to navigate profound poverty.

As a child, Norman struggled to balance family situations, school, hunger, and uncomfortable living conditions. However, the mindset to aim high set him apart. After starting grade school at age six, his love for reading pushed him to become a member of his local library.

The avid reader in Norman opened his mind to a broader picture of life. He developed writing and speaking skills as a result, and by age nine, he was teaching children's lessons at church. Inspiration from a host of authors glued him to the arts of spoken words, writing, listening, emotional intelligence, reasoning, and critical thinking.

Norman's passion for literacy led him to many classrooms as a volunteer literacy teacher, where he always achieved his goals for his students.

Connect with Norman:

Amazon: https://www.amazon.com/author/morninggratitude

Clubhouse: https://www.clubhouse.com/@coachnorman

Facebook: https://www.facebook.com/share/1BjDjPQauL/

Instagram: https://www.instagram.com/thepoetryman9

TikTok: https://www.tiktok.com/@the_poetry_man

YouTube:
https://www.youtube.com/@normangordonthepoetry-man9465

Email: islandthoughtsng@gmail.com

Expressive arts are a gateway to self-discovery, healing, and liberation. We reconnect with our authentic selves through movement, sound, and visual expression, transforming inner wisdom into creative energy. It's not about technique—it's about feeling, freedom, connection, and the raw power of expression. Dance, paint, write: let your soul speak!

Bonnie Sheldon

17

FREE TO MOVE, FREE TO BE

SOUL IN MOTION: THE POWER OF DANCE

Bonnie Sheldon, EFT Master Trainer, CMA

MY STORY

My hand fumbles for the bathroom door, shoving it open, my breath caught in my throat. I barely make it before the tears come. The lock clicks into place behind me. Safe. Hidden.

And then—I crumble.

The sobs come fast and sharp, pressing into my ribs as I slide down against the cold tile wall. Every day, the same thing. Endless hallways. Indifferent faces. The weight of being invisible, untethered in a place where everyone else seems to belong.

No one to sit with. No one notices.

High school isn't supposed to be like this.

I imagined something different—laughter at lunch tables, the easy rhythm of friendship, a sense of belonging so effortless I wouldn't have to think about it.

But instead, it feels like the walls are closing in.

Like I'm drowning.

And no one even sees.

Yet, through the chaos inside me, my body remembers—my dance!

DANCE IS ALCHEMY

I rush to class after school.

"Alright, everyone." My teacher claps her hands, her voice steady, grounding. "Close your eyes if you want. Let go. Move like the music is inside you."

I hesitate, my body still carrying the weight of the week—the looks in the hallway, the expectations pressing in, the feeling of not enough. But here, in this room, everything feels different.

I inhale. Exhale. Then I move.

A step forward. A turn, sharp but controlled. My arms lift as if reaching for something unseen beyond me. And with each motion, the day, the thoughts, the strain, the layers of exhaustion begin to dissolve.

It's happening now—my body shedding stress, tension, and stagnant energy, breaking through the heaviness in my chest.

Movement takes over. Blood flows, muscles awaken, my nervous system finds balance.

This is what it feels like to be at home in myself. I am here—fully alive, fully grounded, completely me.

This experience isn't just movement—it's presence, alignment. Layers peeling away, maybe down to my very soul.

Dance is alchemy!

Each motion unravels what was stuck, replacing it with breath, momentum, the undeniable pulse of vitality.

I feel my body awakening, my spirit stretching beyond thought.

No thought? I wonder. And then I know: *Movement is my language, my truth.*

Right now, I am free.

"Yes!" My teacher's voice rings out, but I barely hear her. I am deep in the rhythm of release, immersed in the language of motion—a conversation between body and spirit, bypassing logic and speaking directly to something deeper.

My inner being is alive.

Stagnation dissolves into momentum. Energy ignites, sensation expands. Every leap carries me higher, untethered, beyond the limitations I felt moments ago.

By the end, I stand still, breath slowing, mind quiet in a way it rarely is.

"That," my teacher says gently, "is dancing the truth." My spirit soars. *Movement is my gateway to joy.*

Movement has always been my refuge. Rhythm carries me through time; dance is the one language that feels entirely my own. In college, dance becomes home. Late nights in the studio, raw movement, and endless rehearsals transform me, not just as a dancer, but as a person and artist.

And then, New York. The city's pulse shapes my movements, my creativity, and my storytelling through motion. Choreography transcends mere steps—it embodies meaning, exploration, and a conversation between dancer and audience.

Dance gives me something real—a way to understand myself, to move through emotion, to feel deeply alive. The understanding is so profound, I feel the pull to teach.

I can't keep this to myself. I have to pass it forward.

It's not just about teaching steps or refining technique. It's about helping people discover the freedom already waiting in their bodies.

I see it in them—that moment when they find the rhythm. When breath aligns with motion. When awareness settles in, their body's wisdom speaks, and movement becomes something more.

That's when I know—this isn't just sharing. It's a calling.

A calling that soon leads me to a school unlike any I've taught in before—a place with no dance, no movement.

The students are as varied as their stories—troubled youths navigating inner battles. Genius-level minds who don't quite fit into traditional education. Neighborhood children on scholarship, finding their way in a space designed to welcome them all.

The school's philosophy centers on the belief that there's good in every person, that every child has something unique within them, something worth nurturing.

And yet, they've never had dance.

Until now.

EXCITEMENT RIPPLES

The program stretches through the year, and the change unfolds quietly, almost imperceptibly. Teachers notice it first.

Students are calmer in class—less disruptive, more focused. And then, the measurable proof arrives: Reading scores go way, way up. "Something about the mind/body connection," we all say.

The movement isn't just giving them a break—it's resetting them, helping them process, focus, breathe.

By spring, the dedicated students prepare for their recital. But that isn't enough. I want something for everyone, a way for each child to experience their creative expression and share it.

It starts as an idea, a simple thought: *What if every child creates a dance?* Not just the select few who sign up for improv and choreography, not just those who move gracefully in studios outside of school. Every child. Every body.

It isn't about performance, precision, or even rhythm. It's about intentional movement—about letting each student express their way of being in motion.

And so, Dance Day is born.

At first, they aren't sure. Some resist, arms folded tightly, watching others step into movement with skepticism. Some laugh, uncertain of what it means to create a "dance" without the safety of rules or structure.

In each class, students are given a simple challenge: Make a dance. They spent the year learning to improvise. They have the tools.

Any movement they want—something they can repeat, something uniquely theirs. Thirty seconds, or more if they choose.

As word spreads, excitement ripples through the school. Groups begin forming—pairs, clusters of friends—gathering early to rehearse their ideas. Some arrive before sunrise, waiting at the door for me to unlock the studio, their eagerness too bright to be contained. By 6:45, movement fills the space—experimentation, whispered counts, bursts of laughter as they refine their creations.

The school has never seen anything like this before.

Not everyone meets the idea with ease. For some, stepping into movement feels like stepping into the unknown. Others hesitate, their feet rooted to the floor, the weight of expectation pressing in. It was freeing when movement was just exploration, just play. Now, with the certainty that their work will be seen by others, doubt creeps in.

Little Danny stands in the corner of the studio while his classmates start, small hands gripping the edge of his sweatshirt. He avoided movement all year, behind quiet nods, behind the walls of uncertainty. But today, there's nowhere left to hide.

I walk up to him, crouching slightly to meet his eyes.

"You don't have to do anything big," I say gently. "Just one movement. One step. One motion that feels right for you. Then the next. You could even run."

Danny hesitates, his fingers tightening around his sleeve.

And then, he lifts his arms—not high, not gracefully, just a small motion, tentative but real. A beginning.

"That's it," I whisper. "You're starting your dance."

SOMETHING DEEPLY THEIR OWN

The school hallways usually buzz with the rhythm of routine—lockers slamming, whispered conversations, the hurried footsteps of students moving between classes. But when Dance Day arrives, something else pulses beneath the surface. Anticipation crackles in the air—an electric mix of excitement, nerves, and the quiet thrill of something entirely new unfolding.

Movement. Everywhere.

The school becomes a stage, not just for performance, but for sharing creativity and happiness. Classes are suspended so students can witness each other's creations, their friendships unfolding in movement. Teachers and students alike move with a kind of radiance—not just performing, but revealing something true, something deeply their own.

"I came to see my Susie, but I couldn't leave."

A mother stands near the doorway, hands clasped, eyes wide with quiet wonder.

"I thought I'd watch her for a few minutes, but then..." She shakes her head, as if searching for words. "I don't know. Something about this—it's different."

Around her, other parents murmur in agreement, lingering in the spell of movement, of something rare and beautiful unfolding before them.

In the classrooms, even the teachers craft their dances.

Mr. Pederson from math, always deliberate in his movements, orchestrates an intricate finger dance, his hands weaving through the air with unexpected elegance. A ballet of fingertips.

Mrs. Bloomfield, our English teacher, slowly steps around her room, shifting her arms with quiet precision as if mapping the air through movement alone.

Dance unfolds in unexpected places. Dance fills every available space.

At each floor, the elevator doors slide open to reveal eagerly awaiting crowds, faces lighting up as bursts of movement spill into view. Dancers twist, their weight shifting effortlessly, feet gliding across the ground in pulsing rhythms. Some dip low before springing upward, their momentum propelling them into fluid sequences. Cheers and claps ring out as spins, footwork, and sweeping gestures transform each elevator landing into a stage. The doors close, with applause growing at each stop—every performance a joyful, anticipated spectacle.

"What's happening?" a teacher murmurs, watching students stretch into sweeping gestures on the playground roof, circling each other, feet shifting, bodies rushing through the space, expanding into pure motion. Their steps echo into the open air, as if reaching beyond the limits of the building itself.

The foyer becomes center stage. At once, a beautiful movement unfolds. "Come on!" a student urges, spinning forward, energy contagious. Bold leaps follow, laughter tangles into footfalls, and hesitation melts into joy.

"I've never done this before," a teacher admits in the auditorium, shifting uncertainly.

"Just start your moves," a student encourages, stepping forward to begin her piece. "There's no wrong way."

And so they do—students and teachers alike, letting movement take over, untested and uniquely theirs.

The headmistress stands quietly at the back of the large gymnasium, watching as movement fills the space.

She whispers, "Something has settled into these walls. A change so subtle yet undeniable."

Looking around, seeing her school with new eyes, she says, "This isn't just movement. It's access to themselves, to one another, to an essential part that's always lived inside, waiting to be discovered."

I nod, feeling it too.

"For the first time," she continues, "every student, every teacher, every body in this school is dancing. Hesitant or bold, playful or profound, they are discovering something new."

Her voice is steady, but there's wonder in it.

"A way of knowing themselves beyond words. A way of seeing each other beyond roles or assumptions."

She pauses, taking it all in—the joy, the expression, the freedom unfolding before her eyes.

"Dance has opened a door," she says, "and none of us will ever move through the world quite the same way again."

THE TOOL

FINDING YOUR DANCE: A GUIDE

SECTION 1: GET MOVING— LEARNING SIMPLE DANCE STEPS

Dancing is for everyone. It's not about getting it "right"—it's about discovering movement that feels natural. If you've never danced before, begin with structured steps. Start with music you enjoy, something that makes you want to move. Rhythm is your foundation.

Beginner-Friendly Dance Styles

If you're looking for simple ways to get moving, try these accessible techniques:

1. Zumba

2. Basic Salsa and Merengue

3. Hip-Hop Grooves

4. Ballroom Basics (Foxtrot and Waltz)

5. Jazz or Contemporary Foundations

Each of these introduces different movement qualities—some quick, some sustained, some rhythmic, some flowing. The key is letting go of perfection and trusting your body's natural ability to respond to music. Easy, basic classes can be found on YouTube.

SECTION 2: FREE DANCE— EXPLORING SPACE, EMOTION, AND EXPRESSION

Once you've gained some comfort with structured movement, it's time to break free and let your body lead. Play music that resonates with you—a favorite song, a nostalgic melody, electronic music, or an energizing drumbeat. Let go of any pressure to "look good" or "do it right." Dance is instinctual. Your body already knows how to move—you just need to listen.

How to Get Started with Free Dance:

1. **Start with breath and stillness.** Before moving, stand or sit, feeling the sound and any beat. Allow the music to flow through you. Notice where your body naturally wants to sway or pulse.

2. **Begin with small movements.** Shift your weight from foot to foot. Add a little sway. Let your arms follow effortlessly. The goal is to move in a way that feels comfortable and easy for you.

3. **Experiment with motion.** Circles, stretches, sways, or steps— whatever feels natural, lean into it. Let the rhythm dictate your movement rather than overthinking.

4. **Use emotion as a guide.** If the music feels joyful, let your movements bounce. If it feels reflective, allow for slower, flowing motions. Dance is not just about movement—it's about feeling.

Free dance encourages self-awareness, confidence, and playfulness—without labels or limits. The beauty is in letting go and trusting that your body was built to move.

USING SPACE TO UNLOCK MOVEMENT

In dance, space is a playground, allowing you to explore movement in different ways. Consider:

- **Levels.** Move high (reaching, jumping), mid-range (swaying, walking), or low (bending, crouching, moving on the floor).

- **Size.** Take small, contained steps or stretch outward, expanding into the room.

- **Pathways.** Move in straight lines, curves, circles, diagonals—let movement travel instead of staying in one place.

- **Stillness.** Sometimes, pausing in space is just as powerful as motion. Use breath, weight shifts, and tension to emphasize contrast.

LABAN'S EIGHT EFFORTS: A PATHWAY TO EMBODIED EXPRESSION

Rudolf Laban revolutionized movement theory. His system of contrasts enhances awareness, revealing how movement expresses mood, energy, and unlocks natural expression.

1. Quickness vs. Sustainment. Play with speed—sharp, energetic motions versus slow, elongated gestures. A playful bounce versus a long, stretching reach.

2. Direct vs. Indirect Motion. Move with clarity and precision (direct) or allow movements to evolve fluidly (indirect). Example: A powerful arm extension versus a soft, spiraling motion.

3. Bound vs. Free Flow. Bound movement isn't restrictive; it's controlled and intentional, embodying strength or containment. Free flow, in contrast, is effortless and expansive, letting movement feel unstructured.

4. Strong vs. Light Weight. Weight influences the intensity of movement; strong movements feel grounded, forceful, or intentional, while light movements are airy, delicate, and lifted. Think of a firm stomp versus a gentle, floating step, or a weighted press versus an effortless glide.

DANCING THROUGH EMOTION—MOVEMENT AS RELEASE

Not all dance is about joy. Sometimes, movement is how we process sadness, anxiety, or grief. We "dance it out."

- If emotions feel heavy, allow slow, weighted movements—pressing the feet firmly into the ground, rolling the shoulders, bending forward, stretching long.

- If you feel overwhelmed, embrace repetitive gestures—swaying side to side, shaking out the hands, circling the arms to clear space.

- If sadness sits deeply, let it unfold in free-flowing motions—soft, open, expressive movements that let energy move outward.

- If frustration or restlessness needs an outlet, try sharp, dynamic actions—stomping, pulsing, punching through space to release tension.

Dance doesn't have to be pretty. It just needs to be honest. Movement lets emotions shift, transform, and leave the body.

LET YOUR BODY TAKE OVER

Once you start moving, trust that your body knows what it needs, and choose music accordingly:

- If the music feels joyful, let your movements bounce and expand.

- If the song is grounded, lean into weighty steps and slower shifts.

- If it's energetic, let yourself lose control for a moment—jump, shake, let momentum take over.

Most importantly, dance like nobody's watching. No form. No choreography. Just movement, connection, and release. You will find the joy!

Bonnie Sheldon is a distinguished embodiment coach, somatics specialist, and lifelong dancer dedicated to the transformative power of movement. Beginning dance at age four, her journey led her to choreography and performance in NYC, while also teaching students from Montessori children to Broadway stars. As an adjunct professor at Juilliard, she guided dancers in improvisation and choreography.

She was an early contributor to the field of dance therapy, working on the psychiatric unit at Bellevue Hospital/NY Health and Hospital Systems and teaching in Hunter College's groundbreaking program.

Bonnie earned the coveted Certified Movement Analyst (CMA) designation at the Laban/Bartenieff Institute of Movement Studies, where she had the privilege of studying with somatics pioneer Irmgard Bartenieff during her final year of teaching. This expertise deepened her understanding of movement's profound role in healing and expression.

Her work has extended into Sacred Dance, choreographing and performing in services at Riverside Church and the Cathedral of St. John the Divine in NYC.

Beyond dance, Bonnie is a Certified Accredited Master EFT Trainer, mentoring aspiring practitioners and established coaches seeking certification. She is also a Certified Accredited Mindfulness-Based Cognitive Therapy Practitioner. She has worked with over 9,000 clients, integrating somatic awareness with cognitive techniques that empower individuals to reframe patterns, regulate emotions, and achieve self-mastery.

Renowned for her transformative capacity to aid individuals in overcoming diverse challenges, she has contributed to the Wounded Warrior Project, helping veterans with PTSD, and developed programs assisting women with issues related to divorce, exercise aversion, and body image, among others.

She champions an embodied fitness approach that merges physical movement with deep sensory and cognitive awareness, helping individuals transcend chronic stress, release trauma, and reclaim emotional freedom.

Connect with Bonnie:

Website: https://www.bonniesheldon.com

Email: bonnie@bonniesheldon.com

LinkedIn: https://www.linkedin.com/in/bonnie-sheldon-aa38b01b0/

Facebook: https://www.facebook.com/MindBodyIntegrationWithBonnie/

Instagram: https://www.instagram.com/bonnie.sheldon/

Your body wants to speak without words.
How can you help it move and express itself?

Creativity is the heart's expression made manifest in the physical realm as an extension of its desire to emotionally connect feeling and form. There are no limits to how we achieve this; there are no limits to how we can express and heal through the arts.

Megan Edge

18

THE HEART'S JOURNEY TO HEALING AND WHOLENESS

FROM CHRONIC PAIN TO SELF-LOVE

Megan Edge, Master Healer

MY STORY

How does she know? How does Anaïs Nin know precisely how I feel, before I even know? All these years, I've asked why: Why am I in such pain? Why does my body hurt, ache, feel numb, and tight—all the time?

I stand in front of a rack of greeting cards in a local metaphysical shop. The shop is full of customers browsing the shelves and seeking answers to solve their problems in a world of crystals, oracle cards, candles, and incense.

I'm drawn to a card with a painted rose just beginning to open. I like the pink hues and the delicate brush strokes. I open the card and read the quote inside as the sound of conversations, the tinkle of the shop door as it opens, and the noise from the street all cease. My world becomes these words:

"And the day came when the risk to remain tight in a bud was more painful than the risk it took to blossom."

A thunderclap of recognition fills my body from head to toe. It's as if my life flashes before my eyes, and everything I held onto so tightly floods to the surface of my awareness. Doctor after doctor, specialists for my back pain, mobility issues, digestive upset, brain fog, and what I call Old Lady Syndrome. I feel like the unhealthiest 90-year-old woman, yet I'm only 36.

I realize I'm holding my breath. I give myself a shake, breathe deeply, and suddenly burst into tears.

How much time, effort, and energy do I spend each day holding it all together? I wear my "happy face" 24/7, holding so tightly to the illusion that I can change my circumstances by standing perfectly still and doing nothing more than all the things I've already done.

The words, "to remain tight in a bud was more painful," open a deep yearning I'm not aware I have—to live my life on purpose and follow my dreams—my dreams, not anyone else's. My chronic pain shows up all over my body, desperately trying to get my attention. In this moment, I know my healing will only happen when I embrace my soul's purpose.

In this moment, I know healing is possible, and it's my birthright!

REMOVING MY BLINDERS

I dry my tears and take a deep breath. I feel lighter and inspired. I head to the counter to buy the card.

"This card, the quote in it, just changed my life," I say to the store clerk, smiling.

She smiles back at me. "Of course it did. That's what happens in this store. The budding rose symbolizes the healing to come, and Anaïs Nin's words will always remind you to fully bloom."

Walking home, I notice how bright everything looks. It has been such a long time since I saw the beautiful color of the trees and flowers, as I've focused on my constant physical pain. I know what's different now. I understand now that my emotional pain is what's holding my physical pain in my body.

I can't wait to get home and share this epiphany with my husband. I always take care of his emotional needs, but it's time for things to change!

Later that evening, after I make dinner, clean the kitchen, and put our daughters to bed, I'm ready to relax and tell him about my day and newfound understanding. I can't wait to show him my greeting card and read the quote together. I know he will be as moved as I am.

It turns out I'm wrong.

"I don't see any reason to change anything about our lives," he tells me. "Leave the past in the past. Why do you need to rehash everything?"

That's rich, coming from the man who only lives in the past and is afraid of planning for the future. This, coming from the man who has looked on Facebook for all the women he has crushed on or had an emotional affair with over the years of our marriage, and reconnected with them to sort out his feelings for them!

He sees the look on my face. He realizes I'm serious and backpedals.

"I promise to be a better husband. I'll help more around the house and stop leaving my dirty socks on the floor. I'll look after the girls when I get home so that you can have a break. I'll do anything you need me to do. Just promise me one thing: Don't change so much that you realize you don't need me. Just don't leave me."

This isn't the first time I've heard this mantra of promises. I must have absorbed Anaïs Nin's words into my very cells, because I feel an unsettling emotion—I think it's distrust. I realize my husband's promises have an emptiness to them. There's a pattern. He says the words but fails to follow up with lasting actions. His love comes with the condition that I don't question his motives or behaviors.

This is it, I think to myself. *This is the moment his control of me begins to slip because I can see through his manipulations. I can see what he's so afraid of.*

It takes me a few days to fully process this new awareness and the emotions I've kept at bay for so long. I look more deeply into what's happening within and around me. I acknowledge the chaos, dysfunction, feelings of being unsafe, and struggles I've been unwilling to admit exist in my marriage.

I look at my life honestly and openly and allow the feelings I pushed aside to surface. I let myself feel, want, and believe I deserve something different. I deserve to be treated with respect, taken seriously, and loved unconditionally.

I see the possibility of the healing I seek, of living life with purpose and evolution, of living without pain.

I slowly remove my blinders, and my carefully constructed world unfurls and unravels.

GETTING UNSTUCK

I see red flags within my marriage trying to get my attention: my husband's emotional affairs, his addiction to spending our money on his collections, and his controlling and manipulative behaviors.

How have I allowed these behaviors to persist, and more importantly, why? How have I unwillingly or willingly participated? How is it possible that I find myself in an emotionally and financially abusive marriage? This must be the emotional source of my physical pain.

We're stuck in outdated ways of relating and being with each other. We developed unhealthy patterns of intimacy, and our relationship with our debt and money is out of control. We face bankruptcy.

I see what I haven't wanted to see: My husband seeks comfort and validation from other women while I shut down, holding so much pain in my body that some days, I can't move. We retreat further into ourselves and away from one another. I distract myself with his needs and have little energy left for anyone else, least of all myself.

I sit with all this, unsure how to move forward. Even though I know my constant physical pain originates from my emotional pain, I don't have a road map for how to release any of it.

I need a wake-up call, some event I can't ignore, something that pulls the rug right out from underneath me!

It's Saturday morning, and we're going to the air show. I'm getting the girls ready, packing snacks, tying shoes, and zipping up jackets. He's waiting in the car—in the passenger seat, as he prefers me to drive. I keep forgetting things, running back into the house, becoming increasingly flustered and exasperated.

"We're going to be late, and we won't find parking," he calls out as I head back to the house for sun hats.

I'm aware! I yell back in my mind. I don't say anything, however. What would be the point? He's always right, after all.

Traffic is heavy. My older daughter is asking for her crackers.

"Wait until I can stop, honey."

Why isn't he handing them to her? Honestly, I do everything! Where did I put those crackers?

In my distraction, I don't realize the car in front of me has slammed on its brakes. Holy shit! I miss hitting the back of his vehicle by inches as I, too, slam on my brakes. I turn in my seat to look at my girls.

"Is everyone alright?"

Crackers are all over the floor, and both girls stare back at me with wide eyes. Before I can say anything else, I'm thrown against my seat so hard I see stars.

What just happened?!

The police officer tells me the car hit us from behind at a "significant" speed. The airbag deployed. The driver is an elderly man who, while apologizing profusely, admits he shouldn't be driving because he recently had a stroke.

"I tried to put my foot on the brake, but it slipped, and I hit the accelerator instead. I'm so sorry!"

I realize I'm in shock as I become aware of a new and unfamiliar pain in my neck, head, and shoulders.

Whiplash. Concussion. Dazed. My girls and my husband are okay. I'm the only one with injuries.

Is this my wake-up call?

It isn't, but it does change everything. The dynamic in our home shifts as we all struggle to adapt to the fact that I'm no longer Wonder Woman. I can't pick up my girls from school or run and play with them. I tire easily and have little patience for things that once seemed manageable. I'm in new and constant physical pain.

MY WAKEUP CALL

It's a few weeks after the accident, and my husband comes home from work, grinning.

"You'll never guess who poked me on Facebook!"

I go through the list of our high school friends but come up empty-handed, and a little exasperated. I have three pots on the stove, a two-year-old wearing nothing but the Cheerios she's just dumped all over the floor and herself, and my neck is killing me.

Read the room! I want to shout at him.

"Here, I'll show you," he says as he opens his Facebook page. At my husband's insistence, I don't have a Facebook account. "You don't have the time," he says. "All our friends are the same anyway. You don't need your own."

Oh my god! That's my first boyfriend from high school! How on Earth?

My heart drops into my stomach when I see the photo of him with his wife.

That should have been me.

Wait! What? Where did that come from? I'm perfectly happy in my marriage. I intend to spend the rest of my life with my husband, grow old with him, and live happily ever after.

Don't I? Aren't we going to save our marriage, together?

I don't want this. This can't be happening. I don't need this!

"You should message him." I hear the words, but don't understand what he means.

"Whatever for?"

"To clear away any lingering feelings you still have for him. It will be good for both of us if you do, like how good it's been for me to reconnect with my past crushes."

But there are no lingering feelings. I loved him once, but that was long ago. I'm not holding a torch for him; of this I'm very aware—at least not for the boy he was then.

The man he is now? I don't know yet.

I realize my husband is still talking to me. I smell the now-overcooked broccoli and realize my daughter is no longer in the kitchen. I follow the trail of Cheerios into the living room to find her. I need a distraction. I can't deal with this right now!

It's midnight, and the house is asleep—except for me. I quietly get out of bed and head to the kitchen. I open the family computer. My husband has left his Facebook page open. "Just in case you change your mind," he told me.

I look at my old boyfriend's profile, feeling deliciously daring and equally terrified.

I feel an unmistakable pull of energy, vast and insistent.

So, this is my wake-up call—the one thing I cannot ignore, make sense of, or dismiss. Now what?

Now what, indeed! With nothing to lose, I ask the Universe:

Show me a sign! A sign so obvious I can't miss it. A sign so that I will know I'm following my heart above all other voices and making my choices from a place of integrity and love!

MY HEART'S JOURNEY

The next morning, I take my girls to school and head to the beach for some contemplation time, hoping to calm my heart's erratic beating when I see my first sign: a heart-shaped rock at my feet!

From then on, I see hearts everywhere, especially when doubt, regret, or pain overwhelms me about the choices I know I must make. Hearts come into my consciousness: in the rocks at the beach, in driftwood, and on the sides of buildings—powerful signs I'm following my heart. When I try to go back emotionally to old ways of being, I'm inundated with hearts. They shout at me to continue moving forward.

In the quiet of the night, my family sleeps. I lie awake on the sofa, where I am most nights now. Several months have passed since my husband insisted I reconnect with my old love. This connection has opened something deep inside me, and there is no going back. I'm learning that when I say yes to myself, my pain diminishes; when I say no, it flares again.

Can we heal this rift, fix all the broken pieces, and stay together, even for our daughters?

The answer is no. There is too much pain and hurt between us. Yet, we continue to try, with weekends away and long, exhausting conversations deep into the night. It is agonizing and painful. I look at our beautiful daughters and wonder what will come of this. I'm in anguish, desperate not to hurt them or him while feeling such a pull to follow my heart, even knowing the path ahead is full of the unknown.

Still, I see hearts everywhere. I take photos of them on my phone and look at them to remind myself I'm following my heart. Beyond finding heart shapes in nature, I seek guidance through oracle and Tarot cards, rune stones, meditation, and metaphysical studies.

These divination tools become lifelines, offering insight when our words fail. When our communication breaks down, we pull oracle cards and leave them for each other to find—silent messages placed where we can both see them. His messages speak of holding on and fear of change; mine talk about freedom and new beginnings.

These exchanges remind me how powerful divination tools are for finding clarity and grounding. From this practice, I created oracle cards using my nature photographs to offer my clients meaningful, heart-led readings.

I'd love to share with you the simple steps I use to prepare for an oracle card reading. These steps help me find peace and direction. These are the moments to pause, listen, and trust the guidance from within.

THE TOOL

ORACLE CARD GUIDANCE

THE POWER OF THE PRACTICE

1. Sacred Space:

Creating a special or sacred space is the first step in any oracle card reading. Light a candle, burn incense, or play soft music. These simple actions help transform your environment into a sacred and intentional space. These elements deepen your connection and create a sense of peace, helping you receive clear messages.

2. Setting Your Intentions:

Close your eyes and take a moment to set your intention. Ask Spirit to guide this reading for your highest good, inviting clarity and openness. This intentional moment helps align you with the energy of the reading, ensuring you are open to receiving what you need.

3. Drawing Your Cards:

With your question or situation in mind, begin to shuffle the cards. As you shuffle, let your thoughts quiet and let the cards fall naturally into your hands. Trust the first card that presents itself—it holds the message you need.

4. Your Cards Messages:

When you draw your cards, take time to reflect on their meanings. If you're familiar with the deck, the messages may be clear. If not, you can refer to the guidebook for deeper insight. Trust what comes up for you in your aha moments.

5. Concluding the Reading:

When you receive the messages you need, take a few quiet moments to reflect on the reading. Let the wisdom settle into your heart and mind. This is the time to be gentle with yourself and honor the messages that come through.

You may feel clear, calm, or energized. Whatever you're experiencing, take a deep breath and acknowledge the journey you've just completed. You invited Spirit into your space, trusted the process, and received the insight you needed.

Carry the peace and understanding of the reading with you as you move through your day, knowing the messages will continue to guide you. Trust the insights will unfold in their own time, and you can return to this sacred space whenever you need further clarity or guidance.

This is the power of the practice. Creating space, setting intention, and receiving divine insight strengthen your connection with your intuition and higher self. You completed the reading with intention and care, leaving your space filled with peace and wisdom, ready to support you as you move forward.

Megan Edge is a Master Healer, Educator, and author dedicated to helping others unlock their full potential for healing and transformation. She is the creator of *The Heart's Journey: Healing Hearts Oracle Cards and Guidebook, Falling into Being Human: An Introduction to Intuitive Healing,* and two professional certification programs: The Confident Healer® and the Intuitive Energy Massage Practitioners Certification®. Her innovative work blends Intuitive Counselling, Energy Healing, Aromatherapy, and Plant Medicine into a unique approach she calls Mind, Body, and Soul Healing®.

Megan's work empowers individuals to heal emotional wounds, release limiting beliefs, and step into their most vibrant, joyful selves. She's passionate about providing practical tools and heartfelt support for lasting personal transformation.

Growing up in a foraging family, Megan developed a deep love of nature and a lifelong connection to the healing power of the land. Today, she teaches ethical wild harvesting and shares her knowledge of plant medicine, encouraging others to reconnect with nature's wisdom.

Megan lives in Victoria, Canada, with her husband, two daughters, and their Labradoodle, Frankie. When she's not supporting others on their healing journeys, she can often be found foraging local beaches, digging for clams, harvesting seaweed, or in the forests, searching for wild mushrooms and the gifts of the wild.

Connect with Megan:

Website: https://meganedge.ca/

http://www.beyondthegardengate.ca/

LinkedIn: https://www.linkedin.com/in/meganedge/

Facebook: https://www.facebook.com/megan.edge.779

https://www.facebook.com/beyondthegardengatebotanicals/

https://www.facebook.com/meganedgehealing/

Instagram: https://www.instagram.com/megan_edge11/

https://www.instagram.com/beyond.thegarden.gate/

YouTube: https://www.youtube.com/@MeganEdgeHealing

The creative force lies within you each day,
waiting for you to embrace magic,
spark love, and ignite it into form.

Expressive art inspires you to allow your awareness to expand inside your body. Your innate abilities can align with natural flow, nurture your sensitivity and give expression to what's alive in you. Constricted energy unfolds naturally into coherent resonance inherent in creative flow from the inside out.

Grace Rosen

19

TRANSMUTE REPRESSED RAGE INTO CREATIVE POWER

MOVING FROM SEETHING SILENCE TO CALM, OPEN STILLNESS

Grace Rosen, M.C., M.Ed.

MY STORY

Four decades ago, a violent act, triggered by years of demeaning and screaming, blew my family apart. My stepmom called on a Sunday evening. "Something terrible, just terrible, has happened. Your dad is flying to you in a few days. You need to take an undetermined amount of time off from teaching."

"What happened, Ellie? You can't tell me this much and not the rest."

"All I can say is it involves your brother and your mother. Your dad wants to be the one to tell you."

When we hung up, to alleviate the stress around what I'd say to my principal, I opened the fridge and poured a full glass of chardonnay from the box. Turning on the bath water, I found some lavender oil and lit some candles. Stress lingered along the edges of my mind as I tried to relax my rapidly beating heart.

Somebody must be dead for Dad to fly out to meet me. My mind went to the worst-case scenarios: *Danny killed himself? Mother? They hurt each other?*

Stress compounded when the principal silently raised his bushy eyebrows when I told him there had been a family tragedy and I needed my class covered for an indefinite amount of time.

When Dad arrived, we walked to the car. He hung his head in despair.

"Just tell me, what happened?"

He barely managed to say, "Why don't you guess?"

"Danny killed himself?"

"No, worse."

What could be worse than that? They killed each other?

Dad finally said, "Your Mother is dead. Your brother killed her. She's been dead for several days. Your sister will meet us at the funeral parlor this afternoon."

We rushed to plan the funeral; my sister already had Mother's clothes ready.

Angry words flew out of my mouth. "We're not going to have an open casket. She's been gone for days now; what's the point?"

During the funeral, Dad, Toni, and I sat in the side room next to the pulpit where the minister said, "We reap what we sow." I'm certain he said more than that, but that's all my agitated mind heard. *He's blaming Mother for her own death.*

I leaned close to Toni's ear. "I can't listen to this any longer, I feel like I'm going to explode," I whispered.

She nodded toward the exit.

Somehow, I stood up and walked outdoors to a tree near the building.

Built-up stress exploded into, "Fuck you!" as I punched my fist into the sturdy oak's bark. I opened my hand against the trusty tree, my knuckles stinging and bleeding as I leaned against it and attempted to calm down before my family came out to join me.

My sister and I stayed up that evening talking. We both wondered why our brother didn't just leave home like we did when life with Mother felt intolerable.

Grief left an emptiness in its wake, a deep cavern of layers, of letting go of life as I knew it. The stress of restrained rage felt like a sharp pain in my left chest. Within my heart grew a wound knot of emotion I couldn't seem to free myself from.

At 30, my mother's death became the catalyst for an intense emotional, mental, and spiritual quest to discover how this could have happened in our family.

MY SPIRITUAL JOURNEY BEGINS IN EARNEST

After completing my teaching position in Omaha, I moved to Arizona to begin a new life chapter. I began my spiritual search for forgiveness and relief from the suffering I carried inside of me. I was accepted into a sixty-hour master's-level counseling program at ASU in Tempe, Arizona.

Walking from my little ivy-covered brick cottage to Changing Hands Bookstore was part of my daily ritual. Downstairs was a vast used section of books. I gravitated to the bench between the shelves labeled Psychology and Spirituality.

The Tao te Ching by Lao Tzu drew me like a magnet. I read the koans repeatedly. Contemplation helped me absorb a deeper inner resolve to hold two opposing ways of being simultaneously. For the first time, I felt there was a way forward, a middle ground between opposites, a way to weave the *yang* or assertive approach and the *yin* or receptive approach into my life.

As a tortoise, I transitioned from just reading about various current healing modalities to having the courage to explore some of them. Motivated by the knot in my heart, needing to release more layers of grief, I met a faculty member who offered counseling on campus.

After our first session, he said, "I notice you have a reason for everything." He encouraged a Gestalt therapy group. I attended several times but felt too frozen inside, afraid of losing emotional control, held back, and decided to see a Gestalt therapist privately.

What I found most helpful was the *empty chair* where I dialogued with disowned parts of myself, learning about projection through the mirroring process and how we project onto the perceived "other" what we reject in ourselves.

One morning, my therapist commented, "It's feeling heavy in here. Would you be willing to leave your entire family here and go for a walk with me along the canal?"

Feeling light as a feather for the first time in a long time, joy bubbled up inside of me. Leaving everyone in the room empowered me to set boundaries. I could control what I chose to place in the foreground or in the background of my attention. This was the beginning of me not feeling overwhelmed or a victim of family circumstances. The gestalt of my life began to unfold.

EMBODIED ART THERAPY

During my first art therapy circle, I sat in inertia in front of a five-pound bag of red clay; I couldn't make anything. I tore it into tiny pieces. A deep urge rose inside to cut it with a sharp knife. Throwing fists of clay onto a wooden board, I loved the sound as it thudded onto the floor. My arms connected more with my chest, I began to relax in the back of my heart, my belly and guts softened as I slammed the clay, landing like cow piles repeatedly for several months. My body opened, and I felt ready to pick up a paintbrush. I painted black and red chaotic scribbles for a long time, then the strokes became more like waves of grass moving like water. Then lavender and black. My Gestalt therapist asked me to frame several of the ones I brought to him during a session.

TAI CHI DANCING INTO GENTLE STRENGTH

I joined a movement class called tai chi on the lawn area next to the clinic.

The tai chi teacher's face looked pure, soft, and open. She radiated her presence, especially when she smiled. Centered, grounded, she exuded a flexible strength I longed for deep inside of me.

She clarified she was offering yin style, a more open, receptive, free-flow way of moving which felt like swimming in the chi. I loved to swim!

The moment I kicked off my sandals and wiggled the grass between my toes, this practice of moving with the chi became my happy place and solace. I felt the chi from the Earth moving up through the palms of my feet, like a bubbling spring.

Playing with this invisible ball of chi between my palms, I felt instantly connected with nature and all of creation. When I synchronized my breath with the slow movements the teacher modeled, I could feel a current of pure energy flow around and through me.

We moved like water. Some of the form movements felt easy and natural to me. Our teacher assured the form would reveal itself to us. My body became a reed of bamboo, an instrument of energy flowing from the sky to the earth and back up from the earth to the sky.

I expanded this fluid dance at home and began to be aware of how this level of chi movement was helping me find my inner balance between pushing *(yang flow)* and releasing, allowing which opened me up to receive more energy flow with nature *(yin flow)*. Combined with breathing, this conscious, slow movement empowered me to embody a place that lives beyond conflict, duality, and separation.

A seemingly bottomless pit of tears began to arise in a natural ebb and flow. Allowing myself to feel into the knotted tension in the left side of my heart, I sobbed, wailed, and no matter how intense the emotion felt, there was always a subsiding and a deepening into silence.

BREATHWORK AND CREATIVE EXPRESSION: FOUNDATIONS OF MY HEALING JOURNEY

My intuition and body awareness expanded with circular breathing. This gave me more courage to channel my grief in creative ways through Gestalt therapy, expressive art, and tai chi.

I discovered the power of connected breathing in a series of ten sessions. During my first rebirth, I lived in a heavenly realm prior to being born into this lifetime. We were all called back, and I didn't want to return unless I could be with the Divine Mother. *I release feeling lost in the void.* Rebirthing freed me from feeling abandoned or a failure. I *am free to begin again and live.*

I experienced being multidimensional (in this reality and the past at the same time) during a holotropic breathwork weekend and had a powerful emotional release of a past life as an African woman tortured and killed by a ceremonial fire. I had an intense pain in my left hip that the facilitator pressed on, and primal fear, rage, and horror released through my voice.

AFRICAN DANCING WHILE EXPANDING MY CONSCIOUSNESS

During the first summer of my three-year master studies, I attended my first talks with Krishnamurti while sitting on grass under a grove of live oak trees in Ojai, where I met several African friends. Afterward, I joined them for dancing and drumming and felt transported to the same prior lifetime.

The following summer, I heard Krishnamurti speak for the last time. Tears welled up after everyone left the grove. I cried for a long time, knowing this was his last time here. I requested on the inner plane, *let me know when you pass.*

I returned home in an expanded state of awareness—no thoughts— that lasted for two weeks. During tai chi in my back garden the following spring, a little bird landed on the branch nearby, confirming Krishnamurti had passed.

MY JOURNEY FROM UNDERSTANDING TO FORGIVING

Several years after my mother's passing, I began to have significant dreams and prophetic insights. My mother communicated with me in dreams for about six months. In my dreams, she called me on the phone, "I need to speak with your brother." Each time, I replied, "He's not here, Mom, call him."

Then, while sleeping on the rooftop where I lived, I heard her voice calling my name in real time—and it was not a dream.

The following night, she woke me and was present in my room when she telepathically gave me a message to deliver to my brother:

Can he forgive me for pushing him too far?

Tell him I want him to have a happy life.

I visited my brother in the halfway house close to his twenty-first birthday, and we went for an outdoor picnic at a lake where swans swam.

I asked him if Mom ever came to him in dreams, and he nodded. I shared that she'd come to me as well, requesting that I ask him, "Can you find it in your heart to forgive me?"—owning her part in her death and asking for his forgiveness.

I held him as he cried in my arms. As his sobbing subsided, a pair of swans soared into the sky above us.

Through this epiphany between my brother, mother, and me, I forgave my brother and opened my heart to begin the journey of forgiveness for Mother and myself.

UNWINDING MY INNER RAGE WOUND CONTINUES

One day during the third year of my graduate program, in a family therapy class, my teacher was leading us through a somatic regression, and suddenly, all I could see was red. Looking through the eyes of my toddler self, I desired a toy on the floor outside of my crib. Determined to get it,

I climbed out of the crib and took my first steps, feeling full of joy! My mother saw me standing; walking to me, she stepped in poop, which fell out of my diaper. Enraged, she grabbed the diaper off me and rubbed my face in it.

Later, I was lying on my bed when confusion flooded through me. Rather than resisting, I relaxed and allowed the feelings to arise. Freer to feel rage, sorrow, and resentment, a gentle strength and trust grew, expanding my ability to transmute deeper density.

WRITING BECOMES MY HEALING MEDICINE

I began to write, knowing intuitively it was my next step to heal and integrate what had happened. I began writing at 50, the same age as my mother when she died; my only son was 17, the same age as my brother when he killed her.

While I wrote extensively about our family trauma, it took me 20 more years to finally write the phrase: *My brother killed my mother, and I have forgiven them both.*

I found a transformative writing class and began writing diligently. This group was instrumental for me to go deeper to find empathy for family members and myself. To be able to read aloud without breaking into uncontrollable tears, be heard, and listen to other women read their stories was liberating and empowering.

Writing in Mother's voice helped me gain more insight into our family shadows. She came to me as a muse, shared her childhood wounds, and expressed her abuse and pain to me. I recorded what she telepathically communicated to me in her voice. Slowly, I began to forgive her for the painful punishments I believed could never be forgiven. I slowed down my life to feel, empathize, and heal via writing in my own developing voice about my challenging childhood wounding with beauty, love, and tenderness.

NATURE AS MY GUIDE, MUSE, AND SOLACE

I've found that being intimate with nature is what truly feeds and nourishes me. Going to the ocean reminds me to be more present in daily tasks. I forget to contract into busy-ness, remembering to enjoy the beauty all around me.

Mother Nature's love lives in cooing doves outside my bedroom window, a caressing breeze, ebbing ocean tides washing my feet, screeching eagles, and soaring red-tailed hawks reassure me I'm in the right place, right on time. Love prevails in deep stillness, with wafting aromas of lilacs, pine trees, and sage. It's from this inner devotion that I've lived a beautiful life.

I know from personal experience the vitality of immersing myself in nature. Remaining naturally open and receptive is the most powerful medicine to nurture an experience of being a part of everything, and everything being a part of me.

You, too, can choose to live in love each moment. You can begin to trust your intuition and cultivate your senses inward. Allow emotions to move through you as energy in motion. Embrace your wholeness and feel your feelings, no matter how intense or stressful they may appear. As you raise your frequency, by relaxing more deeply into your body, you can naturally rise above the stressful fray around you.

THE TOOL

YOU ARE YOUR OWN BEST MEDICINE

MAKE YOUR MEDICINE YOUR OWN

It's not an exercise, practice, or technique that heals. It's time now to stop imitating or copying some image of what you believe might fix or heal you. There's nothing to be fixed; there is nothing wrong with you.

What's most important is your connection to your bioelectrical current, sparking creation, nature's source, not a practice or ritual. You have the power to heal yourself.

Trust what flows through you. It's important to claim your body's ability to heal. Your human body's innate intelligence is its self-healing ability.

You can sit, relax in silence, and receive in stillness, natural healing energy—for nature and you are one.

Give yourself quiet time, devoted to being with what arises to be felt.

Acknowledge your authentic voice and feel the truth of what's coming up for clearing, since purification is a natural human process.

Laughing, singing, or spontaneous sounding eases the body by expanding its cells' frequency. Your voice's vibration creates more space throughout your body, widening your capacity to absorb more pure love.

Allow yourself to pause, to shift your energy consciously by taking your power back from tech screens, distractions, and frequencies keeping you disconnected from your authentic self, nature, and your self-healing abilities.

You have the power of intuition not to be persuaded or imitate an image, object, or mental construct. Your power lies in your belly, an inner compass fed by the spark of creation that nourishes the fullness of your energetic forcefield.

Where you feel wounded needs to be unwound. Stress patterns need space and time to heal through an unwinding process. It's up to you to choose your next steps.

Identity is fluid; we're not our wounds, shadows, or challenging emotions. We are what lives and thrives beyond all these illusions, images, and conditioning programs created for us to forget who we truly are.

Grace Rosen holds master's degrees in counseling and education. She's a certified rebirther, sensual shaman, shen qi relaxation practitioner, and tong ren healer. The creator of *Grace's Peace Oasis* and *Pure Energy Integration,* Grace is an artist, caregiver, counselor, hot springs devotee, ocean dipper, Gene Keys guide, *Unleash Your Inner Genius* salon facilitator, peace activist, published poet, and a Substack publisher of *Embody Your Truth* and *Dancing with the Divine Dimensional Self.*

Grace loves all cultures, people, and travel. She climbed the pyramids of Mexico, explored Europe, Scotland, and the United Kingdom. Grace counseled children with expressive arts while living on two native lands of Arizona: Navajo and Hopi. She recently explored light language in Leysin, Switzerland. Grace has lived in seven states, Kansas, Missouri, Nebraska, Arizona, California, and Maine. She resides in Northwest Washington and loves exploring Vancouver Island, BC.

She offers private consults, creative collaborations, and group sessions to people interested in clearing their minds, calming their hearts, or integrating aspects of themselves they have forgotten or lost. Her passion is to inspire innate creativity and joy.

Grace guides you to deeper ease in your body to reveal how to transmute stress into vitality. She encourages intuitive and gifted women to regenerate or rejuvenate their bodies through their inner bioelectrical current. Her compassionate, deeply relaxing approach empowers you to experience your divine nature more fully through energetic alignment, which she introduces in person and online.

Grace's genius lies in her ability to inspire you to feel your beauty and wholeness just as you are. She holds a loving presence for you to release energy constrictions; her voice guides you safely through deeper emotional clearing with breath, sound, movement, and stillness.

Connect with Grace:

Website: https://gracespeaceoasis.com/contact/

Substack: https://gracespeaceoasis.substack.com/

https://dimensionalself.substack.com/

Substack Link:
https://gracespeaceoasis.substack.com/publish/post/163309361/

You are a creative force, with limitless, positive possibilities through the expressive arts.

When you engage in creativity, you awaken a powerful inner channel that unlocks your true potential, inviting unexpected blessings, profound insights, and opportunities beyond your wildest dreams to flow effortlessly into your life.

Anna Pereira

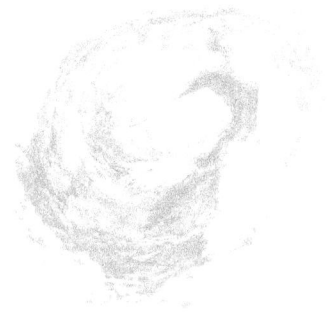

20

DIAMONDS AND SAWDUST

CREATIVE EXPRESSION FOR JOY AND MANIFESTING

Anna Pereira, CEO and Founder of The Wellness Universe

MY STORY

Okay. I'm a manifester. When I want something, I usually get it. I put in the action, patience, and everything needed to manifest what I seek.

I first realized this a few years ago upon revisiting what I did to attract the man and life of my dreams. I wrote about how I manifested my husband in *The Wellness Universe Guide to Complete Self-Care, 25 Tools for Happiness* book introduction. It's a great story and proof we can manifest our desires, and if we're careful, we can be blessed with even better results than we can possibly imagine.

For the last several years, I built a community of support for the world to find help, healing, and health. I know in my heart of hearts, we need each other to heal from suffering. Once we're aware we need to take responsibility and steps toward healing and transformation.

I'm not only passionate about wanting the world to be healed because I believe a happy, healthy, healed human leads to world peace; I'm equally passionate about community. A place where like-hearted wellness leaders and folks making the world a better place find each other. We're a peer and support network of wellbeing leaders for the world to tap into, connect with, and find what helps them to heal. This best describes the unique utopia known as The Wellness Universe.

This vision came to me in 2013, as if God spoke directly to me:

There needs to be a place where people who change the world come, collaborate, co-create, and can be found, and you're the one to build it.

I heard this in my head and my heart. Not too big of an undertaking, ya think?

Well, I followed the instructions in 2014, and The Wellness Universe was seeded and launched online in late January 2015.

OPENING THE PORTAL TO MANIFESTING MY DREAMS

Manifesting doesn't just happen because you dream of something big. You can't be an iconic singer just because you want to. You need to have the talent, get out there and perform, make the right connections, and learn a little about the business.

There are some conditions beyond the practical that the quantum, energetic, or spiritual realms help us with—if we're doing the work in those areas to help us manifest our dreams.

My theory, from observation and experience, is when you engage in self-love and self-care, you have better chances of manifesting your dreams. Feeding your soul feeds your joy, which raises your vibration, helps you heal, and allows the Universe to bring you what you desire and are ready for.

Recently, I was inspired to clear out and clean my home office in Portugal.

Drowning in day-to-day work was toxic enough. My space was making it more burdensome.

I can't do anything in here anymore!

My cats claimed my office; half the space was a spare bedroom, leftover clothes to iron, and a mishmash of other items. I classified it as a "level one hoarder room." The décor was never my own. I never claimed the energy.

Embarking upon the metamorphosis of this space to make it completely mine thrust me into what would have made a great makeover reality show episode. I don't have "before" photos, because the "before" was just too horrendous to revisit and be reminded of.

As I began feeding my soul with the transformation of my space, I realized I had opened the portal to manifesting. *If I manifested this, what can I do next?*

DOES SCIENCE SUPPORT CREATIVITY AS A PORTAL?

I turned to one of my dear, trusted, and respected friends, Jennifer Whitacre Gardner, who works as a trauma specialist and is described as one who straddles the line between science and "woo-woo."

"Jennifer, I'm trying to connect the dots between being creative and feeling good, which leads to manifesting the life of your dreams. My head is so full of thoughts and feelings around this. When we're joyful, we can allow dreams to come true, but can you give me a more 'sciency' way to explain this?"

"I know there's science between play being the antidote to anger, and play and creativity are related. However, scientific evidence behind creativity is a little harder to nail down. Creativity is not something you do. It's the result you get when you allow your inner passions to emerge and merge."

I marinated on that for a moment. *Very interesting.* I found what she added fascinating!

"As you know, I do parts work with Internal Family Systems, so a lot of times it's like doing couples therapy as you're working with different parts within that have conflicts. A lot of those conflicts come from adult, mature parts who are overriding young, childlike parts who want to be creative. That creativity gets overridden with protocol-driven, systemic practices that come with work-life, for example. It can be a lifeless, colorless life, droning on day by day, because we can't put our passions and creative pursuits into action.

"When we explore our different parts and the different creative passions within those parts, and allow them to not only emerge but merge, emotion is behind that (such as passion). And if there is no emotion, then it really isn't creative. When we're exploring and being in the action of our creativity, our head, heart, and gut are most aligned. And when we can get to that alignment, then yes, we'll manifest the life of our dreams."

Nailed it!

HITTING BOTTOM AND NEEDING SELF-CARE

As soon as I heard Jennifer "science-splain" what I was feeling, it validated me.

I shared all this because it's an ever-evolving process bringing to life my passion project, The Wellness Universe.

Lots of experimentation. Lots of funding. Lots of time. Lots of heart. Lots of putting my own self-care and needs in the backseat.

"I'm mentally, emotionally, and spiritually eroded," I shared. "I can't keep going like this." The leadership I embody and show up with daily comes with a cost.

I worked on rebuilding my entire life investment for several years, feeling accountable for it not becoming all I expected, seeing where I needed fine-tuning, and finding a sustainable way for The Wellness Universe to make the world a better place.

It took sitting down, reevaluating, redesigning, and reinvesting while I ran on a treadmill I couldn't escape. It all became overwhelming and seemingly impossible.

So much reflection. So much mustering up emotional fortitude.

I'm taking care of myself. I'm going to take a hiatus after SoulTreat.

That never happened.

For a business owner, if you are one, there's no vacation. There is no space for me to rest in my schedule. But I knew I was going to shatter into a million pieces if I didn't take a break.

On the heels of acceptance; on the heels of finally saying, *You have to put yourself and your self-care first, Anna;* and finally, after emotionally releasing guilt and aligning with my team that I would, in fact, be taking a break after our last book launch, *25 Tools for Goddesses,* I was ready.

Then my team fell ill.

No rest for the wicked! The break never came.

Then I got COVID-19.

It was a long month of stress and contemplation. My team came first, and their health was the most important thing. I was so stressed, pulled in a hundred directions and still struggling.

What am I doing with my business?

I needed self-care more than ever.

CREATIVELY REBUILDING MY LIFE

One of the ways I experience joy and submerge myself into self-care and self-love is by working with my hands, heart, and head. Being creative is where I heal and feel my purpose.

I feel like a child again. I have the power to make and do anything I want. I create. The process brings me joy, a sense of accomplishment, and the knowledge I created something only I could make, the way I made it, exactly how I want it to be, from my imagination.

Typically, I will make jewelry, soaps, or custom dye, paint, and print t-shirts and other garments. But this time, since I was under renovation with my office, I was inspired to grab a hammer and build.

I entered my garage, claimed it as my new workspace to channel my joy, grabbed a hammer and wood, and went to work, without much more thought. I didn't take off my jewelry, file my nails, or prepare. I made sure I had sneakers on rather than flip-flops to protect my feet, and took action.

DIAMONDS ON, SURROUNDED BY SAWDUST

Diamonds on, surrounded by sawdust.

I was in heaven.

As I fed my soul, the Universe was my witness. I was in motion with my own self-care, feeding and nurturing my inner child, and everything I advocated for, healing myself, and the portal for manifesting opened.

In the end, I combined my talents. I designed and built custom-created and beautifully adorned storage boxes painted in colors inspired by the ocean and sun on the coast of Portimao and Madeira, Portugal.

For the aesthetic handle, I took leather lacing from storage from jewelry making, copper wiring, and an array of crystals, beads, and gemstones to adorn them, giving a Bohemian look. They're as much décor as they are functional. I can seriously have an orgasm over something that is both aesthetically pleasing and functional!

The process brought me back to life! I was rejuvenated and felt like I reconnected with a part of me I sadly ignored and put in the backseat for far too long.

The result: Not only did I feed my soul; so many new possibilities came in left and right that found me manifesting opportunities and dreams (as I said earlier) beyond what I could imagine.

I hope that my real-life experience and outcomes inspire you! Now, here is my tool.

THE TOOL

So many experts have their own recipes for manifesting. For example, the one I shared in my *25 Tools for Happiness* book is a detailed description based on my personal beliefs that delivered a life-awaited dream.

My self-care tool for opening the channel to manifesting is the way we open the portal to achieve our dreams. It consists of four steps:

1. Believe in the Universe

2. Do it for love and joy

3. Open the portal to manifest blessings

4. Love the inner child

Step One: Believe in the Universe

Based on my beliefs, the Universe will plug up a hole, and we must allow the space for this. If I keep filling a hole—mine was with work, and putting everyone before me and my self-care all the time—it stops my superhighway from manifesting.

In my experience, manifesting is a balance between doing the work, practicing self-love, setting our intention, believing the Universe to have our best interest at heart, and allowing it to take place.

The Universe could only see me doing what I do day in and day out. My routine demonstrated to the Universe, "Well, she must like what she's doing because she keeps doing it."

Although I asked for specific things to manifest in my life, was I making room and showing the Universe I desired differently?

Also, was I showing the Universe I would take care of the blessings I sought and love my life experiences if it rewarded me with what I wanted? Was that the message I was sending?

Step Two: Do It For Love And Joy

Behind the person, place, or thing we want is the desire for what we believe will fill us up so we can experience joy, happiness, fulfillment, pleasure, accomplishment, and live in the highest vibration for ourselves.

Doing something creative allows us to express what's inside of us. We can all do something that brings us joy. We don't have to be great at it. You can be terrible at something, but it doesn't matter because you're doing it for you and your inner child, not for anyone else.

The reward lies in that.

That is when manifesting happens.

Serve yourself from a place of love and joy without expectation. Do what you do for the sheer joy of doing it.

An apple tree blossoms, gives apples, and repeats the cycle. It does what it does.

Step Three: Open The Portal To Manifest Blessings

Life is about love, creation, and transformation. It's about diversity and experiences. When we play in that energy, get completely lost, and enjoy life, we allow a portal and clear channel to open to opportunities and events.

I encourage you to open the portal to allow blessings to manifest by immersing yourself in something creative, fun, fulfilling, playful, or relaxing.

Turn to creativity and expression of your inner self and serve your heart, mind, body, and soul with creative expression. Here are some ideas:

- Paint

- Dance

- Sing

- Sculpt

- Build

- Color

- Write

- Play music

- Reupholster furniture

- Upcycle old pieces

- Craft with your kids or grandkids

- Knit or crochet

- Sew

- Make jewelry

- Bake and decorate cookies

- Tie-dye old shirts—it's always in fashion!

These are just a few suggestions, and the bonus is many of these ideas, once created, can be shared and given as gifts.

Step Four: Love The Inner Child

Do something you really enjoyed as a child! Revisiting a childhood activity is so healing.

My inner child found such great joy in building my boxes. It reminded me of when I was a child; my grandmother gave me a block of wood, a hammer, and two or three substantial nails. I would drive nails into and remove them from a piece of wood for hours. Not only was it fun for me, it was also a skill builder.

May you find your own way to express yourself and find joy through creativity, self-expression, and play. May it lead to manifesting your dreams beyond your expectations.

Please reach out to me at the link below to find out more about The Wellness Universe and how I can help you creatively manifest your dreams.

This chapter was first published in 2022 in *Inspired Living: Superpowers for Health, Love, and Business,* by Carolyn McGee, Brave Healer Productions. It has been edited and reformatted to fit this book.

Anna Pereira is the CEO of The Wellness Universe and Wellness Universe Corporate, where she creates wellness events, programs, and projects. She's also the founder of Wellness for All, a donation-based wellness initiative. As a leader of a woman-owned business, Anna believes happy, healthy, and healed individuals are the key to achieving global peace.

An inspirational mentor and connector, Anna has guided thousands of wellness business owners in sharing their transformational resources with those seeking well-being. Now, she's expanding her focus to help organizations improve through a focus on company culture and employee wellness. Her dedication to this mission is reflected in over 150 written recommendations on her LinkedIn profile, highlighting her impact on those she's worked with.

Anna's personal life is equally rich. She splits her time between Portugal and New Jersey, USA, where she was born. She lives with her husband, Hugo Varela, a sports expert, and their beloved pets, a dog, two cats, and a highly talkative African Gray parrot. Maintaining close relationships with her loved ones is her top priority, and she finds balance through creative pursuits, time in nature, and the beach.

Dedicated to her calling, Anna is a conduit for change, committed to leaving a legacy of health, happiness, and well-being in the world. With a collaborative spirit and a passion for intentional action, Anna continues to inspire and lead others toward a brighter future.

Connect with Anna:

Website:
https://www.thewellnessuniverse.com/world-changers/annapereira/

We all have a heart, meaning we all have art living inside. Without expressing it, we block our flow of love and life-force energy and feel depression because we push down what is designed to bring us peace. The healthiest habit and greatest gift you can give yourself and the world is expressing your heART.

Katie Bruzzone

21

TURNING WOUNDS INTO WISDOM

SOUL-MAP TO MEET YOUR MAGIC

Katie Bruzzone, M.S., Leadership Coach, Innovation Consultant

MY STORY

IF I WERE A ZOO

Since my fingers were strong enough to hold a pen, my notebook has been my refuge for expressing the wild weather of my world. Blank pages give me a cocoon to express my pain and find the treasure in it.

I wrote every day growing up. I also drew, danced, painted, played basketball, sculpted, sang, ran, read books, hit baseballs, threw footballs, baked, cooked, gardened, and explored nature. Love was my best friend, and so were animals.

A pack of wolves, three elephants, two bears, and a rhinoceros raised me. Two older brothers and six boy cousins, the wolf pack, ignited my tenacious spark through sports and learning to defend myself. My mom and grandmothers, the elephants, tuned me to listen to the wind with my heart through art. My grandfathers, the bears, kept me singing and thinking strategically about community and entrepreneurship.

My dad, the rhinoceros, kept me disciplined, mastering the technical details of everything with creative code names.

"Hippity Hop" is my code name, and a reminder that a good jump stop is the key to keeping control and balance.

"Lil Rat" is my nickname, a reminder that "God is in the details" and the sacred is everywhere in the mundane.

Mary Kathryn is my real name, and a reminder to love deeply, fully, and with unwavering belief.

My animal friends' creative intelligence made me overflow with love. In first grade, I declared, "If I could give a present to the world, I would give love."

My purpose is still the same, but now it's fueled by an unshakeable faith from an arduous journey that invited me into the heart of darkness and the divine. It has more gravity because love was tested, challenged, and ripped away. Luckily, my zoo prepared me for what was to come.

THE BEAST

When I was 13, my life shattered into a million pieces.

I didn't know it then, but my life ended as I knew it, and I began my hero's journey into the underworld. I was thrown into the lands of loss, blind to the ways of the beast, but luckily, love was with me. These barren lands led me to some very dark places with beastly defenders.

I met ghouls and ghosts, demons and dark forces that taunted me until I learned their secret: They protect an insurmountable amount of pain. A pain so excruciating it's impossible to understand. A pain that feels so big, they'd do anything to protect against it and deny it, so it doesn't have to be felt again.

The roars ripple. The howls haunt. I can hear the phantom cries echo inside.

I know how to translate pain and fear now, but I didn't then. What I did know was how to become like my zoo and the superheroes I saw on TV.

I learned how to channel their strength and sensitivity. I let their wisdom awaken mine.

The thick skin of the rhino helped protect me when words became weapons. The big feet of the elephant helped me hear when the beast was hunting to hurt. The hibernating bear helped me find refuge in my bed under the covers and draw what I saw on the dark, cold cave walls.

BEAST TRAINING

We learn to follow what we see rather than listen to the unseen. But the unseen is the driving force behind everything we experience.

The beast had a strong hold on the soul of someone I love dearly. Darkness was suddenly all I could see. The destruction of drug addiction and the chaotic chain reaction it has on a system hijacked me and activated my stress response.

I can feel it now. The terror. The shaking. The replay of everything that wasn't good enough. The freeze. The voices calling me names and blaming me for everything I did wrong. The shame. And then the tears start to flow like rivers down my cheeks.

Draw it out. Don't let the beast hijack your heart any longer.

Ah, yes, hello soul. Where was I?

I began to learn the ways of the beast: trickery, confusion, manipulation, distraction, violence, and guilt. The beast does everything it can to confuse your heart and harden it, to plant seeds of fear in your soul's soil, trying to make you believe you're wrong, broken, lost, damaged, flawed beyond repair, that you're beyond redemption and forgiveness, and that you deserve the pain you feel.

Lies. All lies.

The beast tries to weigh you down and anchor you to shame that feels impossible to climb out of. Its strategy is to disconnect you from the heart so you act from the void rather than virtue, from the wound rather than wisdom.

The beast keeps you focused on fear and fault, so you become addicted to it. And it works, until you wake up and choose another way.

WALK BY FAITH, NOT BY SIGHT

I spoke to God every day and night. I prayed for my family and friends and every other soul suffering and lost. I asked God to tell me why it happened and what I could do to help make it stop.

God spoke softly, but not always swiftly. I learned that sitting in silence is part of the journey to the place of peace within.

Don't worry, sweetheart. I know it hurts. It's the fracture you chose to mend. The blocks you chose to break through. The areas of weakness in the system that you chose to repair. The pressure and stress you chose to experience so you can learn how to train and tame the beast. It will all make sense. These are the lands of loss you chose to explore so you could lace lessons of love into them.

I lost myself in my journal and wrote what I heard from God.

I called on Hippity Hop to lead me down rabbit holes that led me to studying neuroscience, psychology, consciousness, and quantum physics, so I could understand holistic health and our inner nature because a wiggle inside told me to.

I hugged my dogs and ran up the hill when the screaming and fighting got bad.

I chased the beast down the street to prevent him from hurting people I love.

I wrote the beast notes to tell him he's loved.

I'd cry, shake, and snuggle my stuffed animals as I stuffed everything I couldn't process inside my body and pages.

A CALL TO RETURN TO LOVE

I had seven concussions by the time I was 16. Luckily, my wolf pack instilled in me the ability to move with pain, and my elephants led me to water the seeds in the darkest parts of me.

I had a headache and word-recollection problems for over a year. It compounded my stress exponentially, leaving my brain seething in pain or completely blank like a black hole. But I kept drawing the dark out onto the white pages before me.

Keep your heart on the lesson in love. Lean into the learning. You can do this.

What if I can't? What if I never heal? What if my words don't come back? What if I get dementia? What if it gets worse?

The what-ifs plagued me, but the chaos in my environment kept me busy problem-solving and playing defense against the dark.

The training paid off. I felt the light cracking through the belly of the beast. Hippity Hop reminded me that when I stop, move without fear, and return to balance, new neurons and networks in my brain and body come alive.

Remember what God told you. Everything happens for a reason. Trust. Have unwavering faith. It all comes back around. You studied the brain, and now you're putting it to practice. Whenever the chaos comes, it's a call to return to love.

BREAKDOWN TO BREAKTHROUGH

I always wondered how long I could keep going or when it might come crashing down. I lived in survival mode for over a decade, silently battling depression, anxiety, PTSD, and insomnia. Each battle, the beast removed a brick from the foundation of my tower. My nervous system was a game of Jenga nearing collapse.

Just like the bricks, I crashed to the floor.

I remember knowing that if I didn't wake up before the light ran out, I'd die. I remember seeing God and my team of angels. I remember hearing my intuition whisper loud and clear, telling me our bodies aren't designed to harbor this stress.

I remember the absolute peace I felt for the first time and saying, "I'm not ready to leave this Earth yet."

I remember waking up and knowing everything was going to be different.

DIGGING FOR GOLD

Waking up from a near-death experience flips your world upside down. I felt numb and scared, buried under piles of bricks, rubble, and ruins. All I could remember about my life was the pain and darkness. But my angels and zoo reminded me there were love and good memories there, too.

I was determined to dig in and find it. So I headed home full throttle in my gold SUV from San Francisco and started digging.

I started in my room under my bed. Then to the closet. Then to the garage. Then under my brother's bed. I gathered everything I could find from my childhood.

"Mom, where's all my old schoolwork?"

"I saved it in a few boxes. I think it's in the tiny closet in the game room."

Jackpot.

I found it all—the journals, essays, paintings, notes, and homework from my younger days. My whole life was scattered on the floor right before my eyes.

Then it found me. My soul calling me out of the cold and into my center.

"In the center of me lies my powerful soul.
In the voice of the singer, the strong chorus breathes.
In the heart of my dogs sits a playful note.
In the flow of the wind, the mighty wolf runs.
In the soul of the bear, there's power and might.
In the soft leap of the dancer, she floats like a swan.

In the chirp of the bird, its soul flows.
In the center of the world, all this lies beneath."

I wrote that poem when I was seven, and I didn't know then that those words would be the light that saved my life and led me home.

How did I know that when I was seven? When did I forget? I couldn't write that poem now. I don't know what my soul feels like. What is my soul?

Can I get back to that place? I have to try.

I didn't know where this adventure would lead me, but I knew I needed to answer the call for Lil Rat and every child.

THE MAGIC

The call was clear: share your story and follow your dreams. I packed up my life and moved to New York to get my Master's in Strategic Design and Management to refine my craft, innovate, and inspire systems change.

While there, I started studying epigenetics and the technology of our DNA. I learned our DNA has two jobs: to listen and respond. So I started feeding mine different words, weaving my way back to my soul and out of the web of wounds I was stuck in for so long.

I started creating a language with the help of Lil Rat, which gave me the freedom to speak rather than stuff.

I started watching all my favorite childhood movies, so I could decipher the symbols my soul uses to communicate.

That's when magic started to happen. The world, my drawings, and writing became a treasure map leading me to the art of my heart.

"Yes, you're seeing it!" Lil Rat whispered. "Keep going!"

So, we studied how animals move, their environments, how they listen and what sounds they hear, body language, adaptations, prey and predators, and how all that connects to the adversity we face as humans and our beastly behavior.

We studied nature, migrations, rhythms of the elements, cycles of plants and trees, seasons, moon phases, sun and stars, storms, and natural disasters.

Day in and day out, Lil Rat and I studied. I listened to her and wrote down words, patterns, connections, structures, and systems I could share to help people express their pain through a language their inner child, subconscious, and spirit could feel and understand.

THE WIND WHISPERS

Exponential growth lives in our pain if we courageously turn toward it. Remember, seeds take root in the darkness, so dig in.

Our soul leaves clues everywhere—people, places, books, synchronicities, symbols—to guide you home to your heart. The beast tries to make you believe those clues are crazy, but they are your call to courage and adventure. Those clues come whispering in the wind like a balm to your wounds.

In our suffering, we seek. In our suffering, the soul speaks.

I returned to what I knew to find what I lost: Lil Rat, Hippity Hop, Mary Kathryn, and my zoo.

I turned inwards and went back to basics. I mapped my way out of the mess and back into the magic of love, page by page, to draw out the fear.

PERSONAL MASTERY

We gather here today because fear needs to step back. The pain served its purpose. We learned its tricks: distract, create divide, hit us where it hurts, taunt us, wear us down. It's time to take back the wheel and unfurl our creative genius. We have something the beast doesn't: the ability to unite in love, the trust to join in a power that upholds good, the mastery to tune into the flow of creation, and the infinite potential of light and life.

We all have a heart, which means we all have art living inside. Each adversity and adventure you experience in love and loss is here to guide you to what only you can create, but it requires getting quiet and honest with your pain. Past adversity ignites now, and how we engage with that fire determines whether we burn bright or out.

There are things only you can say, ways of weaving words that will only whisper from your lips, woven with your lands of loss, love, learning, and unlearning.

Personal mastery is a sacred responsibility and a magic wand. Use your time and tone wisely and precisely.

Become as pure and innocent as Lil Rat before she got hurt, because we all deserve to heal, hope, and live the life of our dreams. No matter how deep the pain may be, love can find you wherever you are. You just have to remember one thing: turn on the light.

After all these years, I learned something essential: What happened isn't the point. Who you become through it is.

We're made for these times. We are peacemakers, dreamers, soulful singers, harmonizers, healers, explorers, adventurers, teachers, scientists, catalysts, builders, innovators, and most of all, we're Jung ("Young") at Heart. We're made to create cathedrals from ruins. We're made to awaken our divine design and sacred timeline. There's nothing to fear. Remember, when pain pokes and prods, it's just **p**ast **a**dversity **i**gniting **n**ow. Trust it's visiting because you can weave love where it was lost and find the gold in the soil of your soul. Put your hand on your heart and call on your unshakable faith.

It all starts here and now. With this breath, you begin. Welcome home—time for your first Beast Training. Grab your pen and paper. Let's water your dreams together.

THE TOOL

HOW TO SOUL-MAP

Soul-mapping is like drawing a map of your heart, thoughts, and story without knowing where you're going. It helps you unwind wounds, discover hidden patterns, and connect with wisdom inside you.

Start with a feeling or theme.

In the center of a page, write something that feels alive—maybe a dream, word, challenge, emotion, or phrase. Circle it.

Let your seat of unconditional love speak.

From there, draw lines outward like branches. Write a thought, memory, image, or body sensation on each line that feels connected. Don't judge or overthink—just follow the flow.

Surprise yourself.

As new ideas come, draw smaller stems. Surrender to flow. You might remember a moment from childhood, a song lyric, a book, or a symbol. Trust it all.

Pause and contemplate.

When you feel ready, stop and look at your soul-map. What stands out? What connects? What's asking for your attention?

Close with care.

Write one word or sentence that feels like a message from your soul. Return to this map often and remember it's here to guide you home.

If you want support on your discovery and mastery journey, please contact me at the link below to receive a discounted product or schedule a free 30-minute session.

Katie Bruzzone is a leadership coach, innovation consultant, inspirational speaker, facilitator, artist, and writer on a mission to unleash creative genius and develop the Jung ("Young") at Heart. She offers products and services that build confidence, creativity, and mastery in all ages.

A student of life and weaver of worlds, Katie is devoted to reviving an unwavering spirit that cultivates holistic health and a passion for learning. Her specialty is finding inspired and effective ways to implement innovative strategies that help individuals, families, and organizations grow and excel. Katie is a former collegiate athlete, a graduate of the Haas School of Business at UC Berkeley, and a Master of Science in Strategic Design and Management from Parsons School of Design.

Connect with Katie:

Contact: https://www.katiebruzzone.com/book-online

Website: http://katiebruzzone.com

Email: bruzzonekatie@gmail.com

Instagram: https://www.instagram.com/katiebruzzone/

LinkedIn: https://www.linkedin.com/in/katie-bruzzone/

Expressive arts holds the power to move, touch, and inspire; as a collaborative creative art, I say yes to that!

Ingrid R. Tyson

22

TIME AND PLACE APPROPRIATE

CREATING SACRED SPACE

Ingrid R. Tyson, MFT, DD

MY STORY

"Daddy, why is the cover of this book blank?"

My father was a Prince Hall Grand Master Mason, and he changed the subject.

"Daddy, every Saturday at the youth chapter, we do the 'line of march,' and I want to know why and what it means."

Looking away, he asked me to get his paper, and never responded to my inquiry.

My dad was a sweet and compassionate man, yet he was stern about not talking about his experience as a Mason or helping me understand mine.

THE LINE OF MARCH

As an adolescent, I was involved with the youth chapter, and there was a children's chapter. Even though there were things I did not understand, what I did understand was awesome. While in youth court, the adults encouraged us to use our sacred time and space to strengthen our talents, be it writing plays or poetry, reciting prose, orating a speech, performing a song or dance, playing an instrument, taking part in spelling, mathematical competitions, and the like. As it turned out, twice a year, we would go to the Grand Chapter and participate in the line of march competition, as well as the other activities mentioned.

Nevertheless, I wish I did get to experience the children's chapter to get my questions answered:

Why do we have to cut corners perfectly?

What is the reason we march around chairs?

How is this going to enrich my spiritual growth?

Who created the competition for the line of march?

"Wouldn't it be easier to go to church on Sundays like other families do, Daddy?"

RECOVERY - NO MORE LIES

Much later in life, I learned how to keep things simple. And what a huge price I paid to learn about serenity and simplicity. I've been sane and sober for 35 years, and the journey has been incredible.

The 12-step recovery programs have a clear outline, and a global community is committed to carrying the message of hope. Wellness happens in 12-step recovery programs, and we're as sick as our secrets. Recovery is sacred, not secret. At one point, I was so fed up with fairytales, and I no longer wanted to live a life of lies.

"Will someone please give one honest answer to any one of my questions?!"

My life feels like one big lie after another!

No truth about my birth?

No tooth fairy?

No Easter bunny?

No Santa Claus?

No cowboys and Indians?

No leprechauns or four-leaf clovers?

No Cupid shooting love arrows?

No witches flying on brooms?

No gold trim on the Golden Gate Bridge?

No such thing as race?!

MY PRINCE HALL MASONIC FAMILY

One of many family secrets is my being adopted when I was two months old. My Catholic birth mother stipulated to my Catholic adoptive mother that I was to be Catholic. Everyone signed the agreement, sealed the adoption, and delivered the baby. My adopted mother broke the deal, and the adoption remained secret for eleven years. I suppose it was easier for them to be more authentic as Masonic parents since my dad was Baptist, and my mom was Catholic.

One of the few things my parents agreed on was the Prince Hall Masonic family as a significant staple and pivotal part of how my story began. The deception of my conception is another chapter altogether, from sacred secrets to scandalous ones! The sound of silence can sometimes be shameful, and sometimes very holy.

What is this, the mob? And why are we turning the other cheek?!

Is there significance in what we're listening for, or what we're listening with?

The three little monkeys were right to hear no evil, see no evil, speak no evil.

"I guess some things are better left unsaid or ignored, huh, Daddy?"

To his credit, my dad was a veteran of two war conflicts and suffered hearing loss. *Is this one of those Saturday mornings when he turned down his hearing aid?*

After I learned of my adoption, Mom and I argued, and Dad turned down his hearing aid. So sick with toxic secrets, they needed the sacred, and we all needed holy space.

LONGING FOR MY HOLY SPACE

"Did the paper boy deliver the paper yet? Please bring me my paper, Ingrid-Renee!"

It was a typical Saturday morning in my house during my adolescent years. Two Saturday mornings out of the month, after chores and breakfast, we went to the Masonic Hall. Grown-ups were upstairs. Youth were downstairs to honor our sacred space and time.

Other sacred times and spaces with my parents were with relatives during holidays and celebrations of birth, weddings, or specific family achievements.

Sometimes, we traveled across the state. Other times, we traveled across the country to share time and make sacred spaces with family. Me, the paper map, my toy poodle Fife in the back, Mom and Dad in front, the journey itself sacred.

SACRED SPACE WITH MY DAUGHTERS

After returning from the destruction of alcoholism and while parenting my daughters as a single, sane, and sober mother, I had opportunities to create sacred space with them, and they were so adorable and always excited.

Eagerly searching for items to bring to the altar, one daughter would lead the prayer, and the other would blow out the candle. They each took turns using the sharing stick to say the poem, sing the song, share their feelings, or express their needs, one and the other, until the timer rang and our time ended.

One of my most precious memories of creating sacred space with my daughters happened on a windy, cold, foggy Saturday afternoon. My eldest daughter, Jessica, had chubby cheeks that jiggled like Jello when she talked, and she asked, "Mommy, can I please be first to hold the sharing stone and sing my song today?"

My youngest daughter, Tiffany, was a delight, always skipping and hopping to the next task. When her big sister requested to be with the sharing stone first, she said, "I will give it to her, Mommy, 'cause I want to put the candle and the crystals on the altar table mat today. Okay, Mommy, okay?"

I made hot chocolate and popcorn to enjoy this gloomy Saturday afternoon. Their sweet smiles and bright, beautiful brown eyes warmed my heart that foggy day.

These days we all live in this technocratic society. We enjoy few family trips, couples' nights, community gatherings, and I think we would all agree that corporations need more personal development days. It sometimes takes a tragedy to stop and be present with one another. The invitation here is a tool to set aside time and space to be present with reverence and respect, which can only happen when we intend and attend to it.

There are many opportunities for making our meetings meaningful: breakfast, lunch, or dinner; change of season; moon phases; cycles of the stars; honoring ages and stages; or developmental accomplishment. Restructuring traditions can be launch pads into precious portals of connection. Creating the place and space for intentional connection is essential in building teams or dreams.

MY SUPPORTIVE COMMUNITY

My inability to handle the secrets and lies of life sent me on an alcoholic black-out bender that took my sanity, mind, body, and spirit to the brink of a soul sickness that has no cure. Finding a G.O.D. (good orderly direction) to solve all my problems, from drinking to thinking, became my life goal.

As a person in recovery, discovering that feelings are not facts, I appreciate the structure of 12-step programs.

The encouragement and support have been second to none. My daughters were toddlers when I became sane and sober. It was the rigor of academia and the recovery from alcoholism that allowed an opportunity for my motherhood to develop and my community contribution to flourish.

CEREMONIES AND CELEBRATIONS

There were always ceremonies, ritual celebrations, and rites of passage arranged for my daughters, enabling their growth as secular society's challenges increased.

As a single parent, it was a comfort of recovery in having access to a spiritual way of living and I openly shared with my daughters and others. As the years rushed by and my girls got older, sharing sacred time and creating space were essential, especially since our lives were so busy.

Sometimes I ran on four calendars for all our life tasks, together and apart. My daughters enjoyed creating sacred spaces with altars as they selected or made items symbolic of the five elements, signs, and digits for the four seasons and four directions.

These things changed over the years depending on their ages and stages regarding their feelings, needs, values, goals, and the development they were experiencing. At the very least, one daughter lit an incense and candle; another daughter placed a stone, plant, and flower on the altar. The occasion may have been a special time of the equinox, solstice, full moon, or new moon.

A new school year, homecoming and birthdays, winter ball, Kwanzaa, and Xmas; spring dance, Easter dinner, and graduations; first menses, first love; driver's license, cheerleading competition, student government events, community gathers, and many other family traditions, personal, professional, social services, and civic duties began and ended in the sacred space at the altar or sacred place mat for the occasion.

PRECIOUS MEMORIES

I miss the times we spent together creating sacred space over the years.

I feel so happy when they share their fond memories with their friends.

I hope my grandsons have more opportunities to create sacred spaces together.

Who knows what joy or sadness they will bring and take from the altar?

My family is lucky to have a spiritual warrior like me, if I must say so myself!

You have just read about my family and our precious memories of creating a sacred space. Now it is your turn. Below is the tool I have used with my family and other families to bring celebration, support, honor, and community.

THE TOOL

My tool is a sacred place mat. A designated family or community member will put it on any flat surface to use as a treasure map, an altar, a circle centerpiece, a meditation mat, and a place mat. Create the shape of a circle for a clock or square to spin, and when standing, call in the four directions: north, south, east, and west. The process can also be done through writing or by drawing signs and symbols if seated.

Materials

Materials needed to create the foundation, according to maturity:

1. Paper plates

2. Construction paper

3. Small cardboard box

4. Colored pencil

5. A coin

Symbols and Signs

Symbols and signs to consider, create, or collect, according to maturity:

1. Sun, moon, star, and four seasons

2. Five elements

3. Four directions

4. Feelings, needs, values, and goals

An Invitation

This tool invites you to create an opportunity for quality time. Given our busy lives, it's important to distinguish quality from quantity. The following steps are simple when at least an hour is set aside to include the materials and supplies as well.

The greatest advantage of this tool is its usefulness in various group settings, whether in family groups, spiritual groups, parents, couples, or professional groups. It's a nice addition to weekly family meetings, foster families, or reunions. In couples' counseling sessions and with parenting group classes, all will receive help from this simple, expressive art tool. It can be helpful for diverse groups in spiritual communities, in corporations for personnel, and in personal development practices.

Here are a few suggested steps to start implementing this tool to create a sacred space.

Step 1. Keep a journal or calendar for participants to sign and commit to show up.

Step 2. Choose one or two monthly days to gather and create a sacred space.

Step 3. Decide the time of day and one or two hours to start and complete the process.

Step 4. Select someone who will lead the process and take notes in the journal.

Step 5. Decide if a meal or music will happen, and who will handle those parts.

You have all the tools to create a sacred space. Remember, I'm a phone call away when it's all said and done. I'll be ready, willing, and available to share my experience, strength, and hope—as well as my greatest ideas for sharing sacred time and creating sacred space, making altars or sacred place mats so you and your family can have memories to cherish, as did mine. Please reach out to me through the contact links below.

Reverend Dr. Ingrid-Renee Tyson is a holistic life coach with a Master of Arts degree in Marriage and Family Therapy, emphasizing holistic health principles while practicing Transpersonal, Archetypal, and Somatic Psychology.

She holds a Doctorate of Divinity in Spiritual Counseling and is an adult educator in the field of Behavioral Health and Holistic Science, working as a group facilitator. She is also a certified holistic health counselor and certified sexual assault counselor, with a focus on mental wellness, addiction recovery, healing trauma, and family violence treatment.

Reverend Dr. Ingrid-Rene is the founder and lead practitioner of Tyson Holistic Health. She offers holistic healing presentations for psychotherapists, clergy, educators, various institutions, individuals, couples, and families. Through education, coaching, counseling, and group facilitation, she uses somatic healing movement and performance arts. Upon request, she provides family wellness retreats, workshops, and seminars.

Her mission centers on transformative growth from pathological patterns to a mythological perspective. Ingrid's poetic expression of her experience, strength, and hope is employed as a teaching tool to cultivate conscious conversations.

Reverend Renee's approach to restoring health as an expressive art and holistic healing tool includes practical guidance for all to engage in daily living to regenerate creativity and access resources for well-being in the body temple and body of affairs.

Experience and Education

Certified Provider - Family Violence Unit, Monterey County Probation Unit
Chaplain, Holistic Health Services, Teacher - Unity of Monterey Bay
Licensed NIA Teacher - NIA International Headquarters, Portland, OR

Doctor of Divinity - Spiritual Counseling, Holistic Life Coaching, UMS
Master of Arts - Counseling Psychology, Holistic Studies, JFKU
Bachelor of Arts - Social Psychology, Community Studies, UCSC
Certificate Programs - Holistic Health Counseling, Crisis Intervention
Certificate Programs - Grief Counseling, Sexual Assault Counseling
Certificate Programs - Adult Vocational Education, Metro Ed., San Jose, CA
Certificate Programs - Chemical Dependency Counseling, UCSC
Adjunct Faculty - Chapman (Brandman) University, Monterey, CA
Advanced Certification - Substance Abuse Counseling, Villanova, PA

Connect with Ingrid:

Website: https://www.tysonholistichealth.org

LinkedIn: https://www.linkedin.com/in/ingrid-renee-tyson/

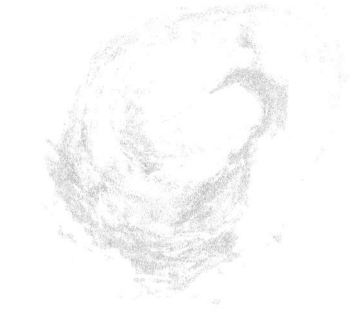

Afterword

YOUR STEPS TO SUCCESS

Jean Voice Dart, CATP, Expressive Arts Therapist

YOUR STEPS TO SUCCESS

You might be instinctively drawn to this book, skimming the pages and wondering, *What can this book offer me?*

Unlike research studies or educational narratives, *Expressive Arts: The Ultimate Creative Guide to Transforming Stress* is a fresh, collaborative collection of documented life-shifting experiences and practical solutions. You'll find stress-relief stories, effective strategies, and step-by-step creative techniques that deeply resonate.

After you read a few stories, your life may begin to change. These experts provide powerful plans to transform stress and help you achieve your dreams. You are the maker and shaker, a dynamic, manifesting force, ready to change your life.

Each chapter features real-life stories by expert artists, creators, creative writers, wellness professionals, coaches, healers, performers, therapists, counselors, and teachers who inspire and motivate others to change their lives.

LIFE-SHIFTING STORIES AND TOOLS

For centuries, people have found storytelling a persuasive, dynamic tool for bringing about change and healing. It has always been a powerful creative force for uplifting and shifting. Our ancestors gathered around the fire, sharing real-life experiences to impart truth, wisdom, and spiritual guidance to those struggling with daily challenges. They didn't search the internet for solutions; they told stories, passing wisdom from one generation to another and later preserving them in books.

Like my parents' banquet of creative activities, the collaborative co-authors provide a feast of expressive arts exercises to explore. But you're not here to overindulge—you thoughtfully scan the table of contents, pick what nourishes you, set aside what isn't useful now, and savor the techniques that satisfy you today. Later, you return, selecting new tools when you need fresh nourishment and support.

So, what do you hunger for now?

DISCOVERING YOUR NEXT STEP

The best place to start is to listen to your heart. Ask yourself, *What do I need to change? How do I feel? Where should I begin?*

It's a good time to tap into your magnificence and remember your passion and purpose in life. Then, scan your physical body, mind, and emotions, and write down a few goals or steps.

You might spend some time writing your goals for the year, month, or day. You can gently review the book, flip through the pages to see which chapters you feel most drawn to, and then list the chapters that boost your ability to achieve your goals.

Most of us know that goals don't get accomplished without a plan.

Scheduling daily creative time to practice these physical, mental, emotional, and spiritual expressive arts techniques raises the probability that you will succeed. One helpful idea is to set alarms, reminders, or notifications through phone or computer apps for essential alone time.

Old-fashioned visual cues are great for memory. A whiteboard, bulletin board, or calendar stands out on a wall. For some, physically writing on a calendar or daily journal is more potent than a digital reminder. Adding drawings or stickers makes goal-setting more effective. A sticky note on your refrigerator, mirror, or front door ensures daily visibility.

MAKING A DIFFERENCE

You were born to accomplish something uniquely yours. When you embrace your life's purpose, you align with your highest vision and ideals—this is why you're here. You are making a difference.

Each day, you can imagine yourself gaining momentum and creating positive shifts to uplift yourself and those around you. The expressive arts tools in this book will help you navigate challenges, transform negativity into creative flow, and step into your true potential. Please let your imagination soar as you envision yourself serving, inspiring, and uplifting others.

Always remember—you are a beacon of light, guiding those who seek your gifts of truth, wisdom, and love.

TEN STEPS TO SUCCESS

I invite you to try these ten steps to success in transforming stress:

1. Close your eyes, breathe, and trust in your abilities.

2. Express gratitude for the creative process.

3. Gently scan the book, flipping through the pages.

4. Ask for inner guidance and divine wisdom to select the tips, tools, and techniques best designed for you.

5. Choose one achievable goal and "next best step" for your mission or purpose.

6. Imagine this goal already accomplished, and use your senses to see, taste, hear, touch, and smell it.

7. Please select one or more of the chapter techniques that align best with achieving and maintaining this goal and incorporate them into your daily routine.

8. Imagine yourself uplifting your loved ones, local community, and the world by taking steps to achieve your goal.

9. Bring courage, love, and gratitude into your heart as you step closer to achieving your goal. Then share that love with others.

10. Set and reset your daily, weekly, and monthly goals, and applaud yourself when you succeed.

CHOOSING A PARTNER

Success is rarely a solo journey. The right partner can make all the difference in marriage, business, or wellness. Coaches, therapists, doctors, and teachers offer unbiased support, helping us step forward toward our goals.

The specialists in this book care deeply about your well-being. Why? When someone experiences devastating life experiences and overcomes obstacles to reach their destiny, they receive inexplicable joy and an intense hunger to give back through service. Each step forward deepens their desire to serve, making their success their mission.

If you're struggling, you don't need to face it alone. Many of these expressive arts experts have walked similar paths, healed, and moved forward. A master teacher, practitioner, or coach helps others stay on track, offering expertise and understanding. When you need support, reach out—they'll be delighted to hear from you.

A FAVOR FROM YOU

The making of this book involves the collaborative efforts of many generous, talented, kindhearted, and hardworking souls. If you discover something of value, please write a positive review on Amazon and share the book with a friend. Thank you.

Naturally, not every story will resonate with every reader—that's not the goal. Each creative expert brings a unique journey and valuable tools. However, a few chapters may deeply connect with you. If so, consider mentioning the authors you enjoyed in your review. Your encouragement will uplift them and help others discover safe, practical methods for relieving stress.

GIFTS FOR YOU

The co-authors and I have special gifts for you in each chapter to help you creatively de-stress, express, and find success. When you do that, you awaken the world to the transformative power of the arts. Your courage inspires others to believe, receive, and achieve. Thank you for believing in yourself and shining your light. You are a gift to the world.

Jean Voice Dart, MS, CATP, RMT, Expressive Arts Therapist

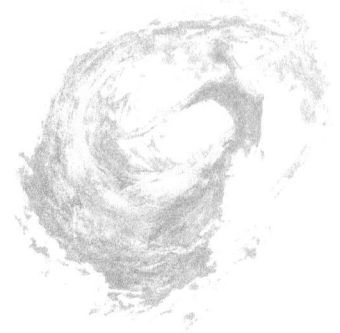

Acknowledgements

I am profoundly grateful to God, the Holy Spirit, and my spiritual guides who watch over me, gently whispering words of comfort and encouragement, guiding each step toward fulfilling this vision. Through them, all is well.

To my grandmother, mother, father, and two sisters—thank you for giving me a childhood brimming with joy and opportunities for creative flow. The music, storytelling, drawing, craft making, dancing, and imaginative play you nurtured are treasures that warm my heart daily. Your love and creativity planted the seeds of this venture.

To my brilliant and talented co-authors—this book exists because of your willingness to say yes to my passion, purpose, and vision for this collaborative endeavor. Your hard work, compassionate efforts, and vulnerability in sharing life-shifting experiences with the expressive arts have made this project extraordinary. Your contributions are a source of inspiration and motivation for anyone seeking stress relief through creativity. I will always carry you as cherished partners on this journey.

To my husband, son, and daughter-in-law—thank you for your boundless patience and unwavering love. Thank you for understanding and supporting me while I participated in this project. A special thank you to my granddaughter, Amelia, and my sweet dog, Pumpkin, whose smiles and joy reminded me to step away, breathe deeply, laugh, love, and live. You all sustain me in ways I will forever treasure.

To Laura Di Franco, Kelly vdH Kaschula, and the dedicated team at Brave Healer Productions—your wisdom, guidance, and support were invaluable in bringing this book to life.

To Anna Pereira, CEO and Founder of the Wellness Universe, and her core team—thank you for inspiring, encouraging, and walking alongside me through this venture.

To our talented artist and designer of the book cover, Davide De Angelis —thank you for your inspirational work. You truly captured the essence and transformative power of the expressive arts.

To you, dear reader—thank you for investing in yourself and embracing the healing power of the expressive arts. I applaud you for your courage in following your dreams. Thank you for your positive reviews, support, and kind words. You are making a lasting difference in this world.

And lastly, to the expressive arts creators and performers across the globe—you are the heartbeat of transformation, uplifting consciousness through the power of imagination. This book is a tribute to your compassionate commitment to making the creative and performing arts accessible worldwide. You are the healers and dreamers who inspire us all.